Issues in Macroeconomics

Issues in Macroeconomics

RONALD SHONE

Martin Robertson

First published in 1984 by
Martin Robertson & Company Ltd.,
108 Cowley Road, Oxford OX4 1JF.

British Library Cataloguing in Publication Data

Shone, R. (Ronald)
Issues in macroeconomics
1. Macroeconomics
I. Title
339 HB172.5

ISBN 0-85520-535-0
0-85520-536-9 Pbk

Typesetting by Communitype, Wigston, Leicester
Printed in Great Britain by
T. J. Press Ltd., Padstow

Contents

Preface

Many changes have been taking place in macroeconomics, with respect to both theory and policy. The teaching of it is both exciting and frustrating. One unfortunate development has been the emphasis on the mechanics of the subject. Students can construct *IS–LM* diagrams and shift these curves, along with many others; but give them an *issue* to discuss and they fail to see how to apply these techniques. It is not sufficient to give students a tool kit: they must be given guidance on how the tools can be used. One way to do this is to take specific and important issues and see how economists have attempted to answer them. This is the approach taken in this book.

Each chapter takes a central question and attempts to answer it. Although many alternative views are given, it goes without saying that the author's views will predominate. For this I make no apology. Economic issues are entrenched in values, opinions – and possibly delusions. What matters is that these are made explicit. Although the issues are diverse and full answers are beyond the competence of a single writer (certainly this one), it was still felt that some degree of consistency in applying economic theory could be ascertained by readers if the book were written by a single author.

The emphasis throughout is on applying economic reasoning to answer relevant and pressing problems that face the British economy. To do this it is necessary to deal with theory, description and to some extent recent history. As soon as one tries to make economic theory 'relevant', it is necessary to use it in discussing a particular economy at a point in time in its history. Throughout I have concentrated on the British economy in the period since 1945. This is simply because I know this country and period best. But there is another important point. Much of the discussion on macroeconomic issues has come from the United States. Important as much of this is, there is a great gap in the literature. American economists almost always treat the discussion in terms of a closed economy. Britain is *not* a closed economy. Throughout the post-war period the balance of payments, or more recently the exchange rate, has played a most significant role in many of the macroeconomic issues facing the UK. With the exception of chapter 6, I do not deal explicitly with the exchange rate or the balance of payments as an issue (largely through lack of space), but these aspects enter almost all the discussions throughout the book.

There are no definitive answers in this book. One of the purposes in writing it has been to illustrate to readers that there are no 'right' answers; that much depends on the model used, on one's basic beliefs, on the institutional arrangements which operate, and many other things. Teachers of economics know this very well but somehow it gets lost, and students persist in believing that economics is going to supply the 'right' answer to any particular issue. The techniques and tools which economists use are very precise, and it may be this which gives students the impression that when they apply them the application will involve this same precision. But no. Application too is a technique, and it is this which students lack. Applying economic theory cannot be taught like the *IS–LM* model: it can be taught largely by demonstration. And so this book is offered as one person's demonstration of the application of macroeconomic theory.

PART I

The Problems

CHAPTER 1

What are Britain's economic problems?

Britain has a number of problems which are serious enough to be called the 'British sickness' or the 'British disease'. But the analogy is misleading, because it implies that there is only one disease and only one cause. It is very important from the outset to realise that Britain's problems – and there *is* more than one problem – must first be found. Even this first step in methodology is not so easy. As we shall see shortly, many problems have been attributed to the UK economy, such as inflation, overmanning, too little investment, etc., but there is not complete agreement on what they are. Even if we agree with the list, there is certainly no agreement on the ranking from the most important to the least important. But does it matter that we cannot rank the problems? It does, because it is important to seek solutions to the important problems first. Even if we admit that the problems may be interrelated, it is still necessary that, whatever solution or solutions we devise, the important as well as the less important problems are solved. A person with a gangrenous leg and a cold requires the gangrene to be treated with some urgency. What use will it be if the doctors spend all their time worrying about his cold and ignore the fact that he has gangrene? If we recognise, therefore, as we must, that not all problems are equally serious, then it is important that economists direct their attention and efforts in proportion to the importance of the problems.

Let us suppose we have established a particular important problem, say inflation. Then the next step is to find its cause or causes. Here the illness analogy is useful. A cure cannot always be found (except by accident) without knowing the cause of the ailment. But it is important that we recognise that there is invariably more than one cause to any given problem. Inflation does not have just one cause. If it did then its cure would be that much easier. But it has many causes, each quite distinct – and yet at times occurring together and interacting. Even the way we define a problem can limit what we consider to be the cause of such a problem. In the case of overmanning, for instance, there could be a confusion with underproduction.[1] We must be clear about what we mean. The symptoms may appear to be the same but the cures are likely to be very different. Let us, then, state this point in the form of a proposition:

The cause of a problem can depend upon how we define it.

This equally applies to any possible solution we may consider.[2]

Suppose we have defined the problem and found its cause(s). Our next task is to find a solution. The solution may not depend on the cause. (I may be able to cure a cold by taking aspirin, regardless of why I caught a cold.) But in economics, we invariably find that the solution to a problem depends very much on what we believe the cause of that problem to be. If we believe that inflation is caused by excessive growth in the money supply, then monetary growth must be controlled; if we believe inflation is due to excessive wage demands, then these must be curbed. If we believe that excessive growth of the non-marketable sector which is not matched by reduced consumption in the marketable sector is the essential cause of Britain's inflation, low investment and balance of payments difficulties, then this structural shift must be reversed. We have then a second important proposition:

The solution to an economic problem invariably depends upon what causes it – and there may be more than one cause of any specific problem.

Having established the causes of a problem, then to each cause we can find one or more solutions. Each of these solutions involves instruments and targets. In the case of inflation (a target), we may wish to control the growth of the money supply (an instrument). Having established as clearly as possible such instruments and targets, we must be clear as to which institutions, if any, are involved in the policy solution. In the illustration of inflation just given, the Bank of England is the institution involved in controlling the growth of the money supply. One problem is that it is not always the case that an institution is involved in the mechanism necessary for a solution. If the cause of inflation is excessive wage demands, then what institution can be called upon to curb them? Or if inflation is caused by excessive growth of the non-market sector not matched by reduced consumption in the market sector, then what institution can reverse this trend?[3]

At this point a number of issues are involved which are interdependent:

(1) Can a margin of error be placed on various instruments (e.g., a range for the growth of £M3)?

(2) Are objectives related? Are instruments related? Are there enough instruments to achieve multiple objectives?

(3) What kind of model should be used to analyse the problem? (Or, even, should a formal econometric model be used?)[4]

(4) How long does the solution take?

(5) Can the government in fact solve the problem? In other words, is it within the government's sphere of influence?

(6) Is the solution politically acceptable?

Although not an exhaustive list, it does indicate the way an economist would consider the issues. The sequence of events is illustrated in Figure 1.1

Four further general points are worth making before we get down to specific problems. First, it is important to know whether the problem is a long-run problem, such as the decline of staple industries, or a short-run problem, such as reduced profits arising from an appreciating pound. Second, it is important to know whether a problem is new to the post-war period and common to all OECD countries. Third, even if common, why is the magnitude greater for the UK than other OECD countries? Fourth, is the problem new but specific to Britain?[5] There has been a tendency in discussing the 'British sickness' to lump these questions together. Solutions are better sought when the problems are defined more specifically, and these four distinctions can help to specify the problems more precisely, and hence can help in analysing any possible solutions.

Having considered how to look at the problems, in the next section we shall attempt to list and classify them. This will show the great diversity of opinion as to what Britain's economic problems are. In the third section we shall attempt to distinguish the fundamental economic problems from the many others listed. In the final two sections we shall take up the issue of the government's role and that of the market mechanism in solving Britain's problems. Basically we are asking the question, 'Should the government (or even, can the government) take responsibility for the solution to certain problems?' From this discussion it emerges that solutions are not independent of political affiliations.

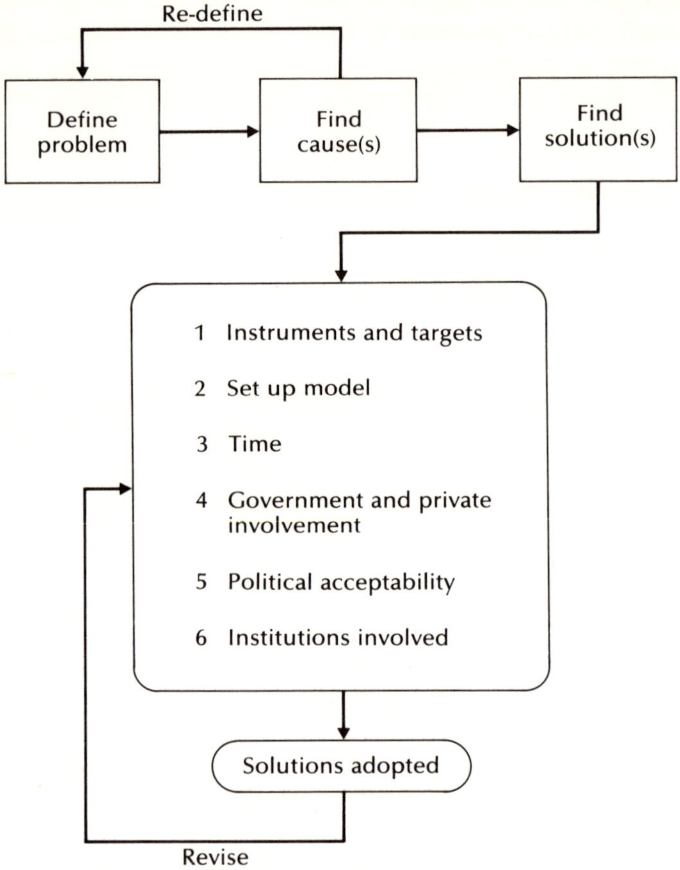

Figure 1.1 A way of thinking about economic problems

1.2 Categorising the Problems

The number of problems attributed to the UK economy is quite large. They include slow economic growth, a domestic and world recession, declining profit margins, balance of payments deficits, inflation, too high a set of wage demands, overmanning, uncompetitiveness, a declining marketable sector, too little investment, rising trade union power, etc. The list goes on and on. There is a danger here of confusing the symptoms for the disease. (The problem may be measles but the symptom is the spots.) We shall clarify this further in the next section when we discuss the fundamental issues. For the moment we simply wish to list all the problems which have been made concerning Britain's poor economic performance.

The information is contained in Table 1.1. The problems themselves are listed under four headings:

(1) Aggregate demand

(2) Aggregate supply

(3) Aggregate demand and supply

(4) Other

This seems a useful division because it allows us to consider the possible failings of demand management (see chapter 10) and why some economists have turned to supply-side economics (see chapter 11). Each problem is then considered under four headings:

(1) Time (short-run)

(2) Time (long-run)

(3) New to all OECD countries

(4) New but particular to the UK

Like all classifications, some problems can arise under more than one heading, but the table is a convenient starting point.

What is immediately apparent from the table is that many of the problems occur on the supply side of the market. This would suggest that traditional demand policies will not be very effective *for these problems.* There is in this statement a basic methodological point. If a problem is a demand- (supply-) side one, then a demand (supply) policy is called for its correction. It is the same as reasoning that if you have a domestic (international) distortion, then the appropriate policy is a domestic (trade) one and not vice versa.[6] Table 1.1 also indicates, however, that a number of the problems arise from both demand and supply sources. Following the line of reasoning just mentioned, this would suggest that a demand (supply) policy alone will not be the most effective approach *for these problems;* they must be approached from both sides. This is a most important point. Politicians have a tendency to use just *one* means of tackling a problem, e.g., either incomes policy for inflation, or else controlling the money supply for inflation. These 'solutions' are either not effective or are doomed to failure because they deal with only part of the problem.

Table 1.1 Britain's economic problems

Problems	Short run	Long run	New, all OECD	New, just UK
Aggregate demand				
Low investment		*	*(S)	
Fiscal policy		*		
Monetary policy	*	*		
Balance of payments constraint	*	*		
High marginal propensity to import	*	*	*(S)	
Aggregate supply				
Low output		*	*	
In/out of EEC		*		
Overmanning		*	*(S)	
Relative pay differentials		*		
Trade union power		*		
Low and declining profits	*		*(S)	
Taxation		*		
Low productivity		*	*(S)	
Aggregate demand and supply				
Uncompetitive	*	*		
Public/private mix		*		
NSO	*	*		*
Inflation		*	*(S)	
Rising import penetration		*	*(S)	
Unemployment: young	*	*	*(S)	
old	*	*		*
Bankruptcies	*	*	*(S)	
Declining real output	*	*	*	
Rise in 'black economy'		*	*(S)	
OPEC price rises	*		*	
Other				
Declining industrial base		*	*(S)	
Lag structure	*	*	*	
Lack of market clearing		*		
Increased uncertainty	*			
Reduced confidence	*	*		
Breakdown of Bretton Woods system		*	*	

Note: (S) denotes more severe in the UK than in other OECD countries.

Another feature shown by Table 1.1 is that many of the problems are long-term and are shared by most OECD countries – but they are more severe in Britain. This would suggest that Britain is slow to adapt to changing world conditions.

1.3 The Fundamental Issues

The previous section listed a number of problems faced by the UK economy. There is, however, a confusion of cause and effect: of illness and symptom. At present unemployment, for instance, is over 3 million. Is this a problem or merely a consequence of the government's fight to reduce inflation? If the latter, the presumption is that in the long run the unemployment rate will settle down at its natural level. If, however, this natural level is high, then *this* is the problem because it means a permanent high level of long-term unemployed. If, on the other hand, the natural level is sufficiently low, then there is no long-term problem. The only problem is that of *adjustment.* To take another example, bankruptcies at one level are a problem. Table 1.2 shows the generally rising incidence of failure (i.e., the number of insolvencies to the total number of companies registered). Is this, however, a consequence of falling world demand or is it due to some fundamental weakness in the economy? Falling world demand must give rise to adjustment problems, as must the production and selling of North Sea oil. In this section we wish to direct our attention to the separation between adjustment problems and other more fundamental problems.

Table 1.2 UK bankruptcies, 1970-81

Year	Incidence of failure	Year	Incidence of failure
1970	0.75	1976	1.06
1971	0.71	1977	0.99
1972	0.61	1978	0.58
1973	0.50	1979	0.69
1974	0.65	1980	1.00
1975	0.95	1981	1.19

Source: Midland Bank Review (Spring 1982)

Investment is crucial for growth, productivity and, ultimately, employment. Is Britain's problem a lack of private investment? In the first place, this is basically a component of aggregate demand. Second, it plays a crucial role in Keynesian demand management. Third, it is not simply a question of interest sensitivity: it is also linked to the institutional framework of the economy – most especially to the source of venture capital[7] and the extent to which the commercial banks and other financial institutions are involved in supplying finance for industry. Fourth, investment in industry is closely associated with company profits (since a major source of investment funds is undistributed profits). Does this mean that low profits are the cause of low investment?[8] If so, the problem is low profits, with low investment simply a symptom. Or, as S. R. Sargent (1979) argues, is declining profitability the result of lower real capital costs? Fifth, investment is influenced by government policies – especially the 'stop-go' variety.

There are two components to investment: first, the amount and second, the type (i.e., investment in what?). It can be argued that Britain has had too low a level of investment and/or investment in the wrong sectors. The latter problem is difficult to prove; but ask the question, 'What should Britain invest in?' and then ask, 'What has Britain invested in?'

High inflation has been cited as the cause of many ills of the British economy. This has meant a loss of competitiveness on world markets and a fall in real wealth. (The costs of inflation are dealt with more fully in chapter 3.) As we argue in chapter 3, it is not anticipated inflation which is a problem but rather *unanticipated* inflation. Both the Conservative and Labour Parties see inflation as a major problem. Any attempt to reduce it, however, will itself create *adjustment problems*. For example, the present high unemployment rate, falling output and bankruptcies could be attributed in part to the particular policy that has been adopted to fight inflation. These are adjustment problems. Once inflation is down and the unemployment is at its natural level, then output and competitiveness will be maintained; profit margins will rise and so too will investment. All these, so the argument goes, will be achieved in the long run. (The period of time is, however, not specified.) The Labour Party's solution to inflation will itself create adjustment problems, but of a different variety – largely in the form of price controls. But whatever these problems are, they too are supposed to disappear once inflation is brought down to an acceptable level and adjustment is no longer necessary. There is one difference, however. The Conservative Party's solution is largely market-determined and as such can be maintained so long as there are no shocks to the system. The Labour solution, however, is a *desired* position and as such will almost certainly require constant adjustment to maintain it. *There is in this case a permanent adjustment problem.* The question remains whether the free market solution, with its long run problems, is a 'better' one than the artificially maintained solution with its long-run problems.

There is no doubt that unemployment is somehow related to inflation – exactly how is not fully understood. There is, however, a fundamental difference of political opinion as to whether high unemployment will be tolerated in the short run (no party will accept high unemployment in the long run). This political difference leads to a different perspective on short-term unemployment. If inflation is treated as the major priority, then short-term unemployment is regarded as part of the adjustment process. If, however, full or near-full employment is treated as the major objective, then short-term unemployment is a problem *per se.* Where it is considered an adjustment problem, generally nothing is done about it, because any attempt to do so will simply hinder the adjustment process. Only if it is considered a problem in itself is something generally done. Of course, it is not as simple as that. The adjustment process can be short or long by design. The point is that if unemployment is recognised as an adjustment cost, the question is over what period the cost should be spread, which is quite different from the decision of whether or not to reduce it.

Is Britain uncompetitive in world markets, and if so why? Let us take it as accepted that Britain *is* uncompetitive. The reason why is a fundamental problem. Like many problems, it almost certainly has many reasons and not just one. A higher rate of inflation at home relative to our trading partners is undoubtedly one reason. But others involve higher unit labour costs, poor after-sales service, poor advertising, an incorrect product mix, and too diversified a geographical distribution and not enough specialisation – either by product or market.[9] Others put the blame on an over-valued pound. This keeps export prices higher and import prices lower than they otherwise would be. Whether the value of the exchange rate is a cause or a consequence of other policies is a difficult question to answer. For instance, it has been argued that North Sea oil led to a high exchange rate and a fall in the output of the non-oil sector; while a counter-argument is that the exchange rate was high because of government monetary policy.[10] What can be said is that if the exchange rate is kept artificially high then this will lower Britain's competitive position in world markets.

Notice here the importance of distinguishing symptoms from the illness. Suppose the exchange rate is kept artificially high – for whatever reason. A consequence of this is high import penetration. The problem of high import penetration, although a problem, is in this illustration a symptom of an over-valued pound. The same is true if we observe bankruptcies in export industries and import-competing industries.

However, the same consequences follow if the reason for Britain's uncompetitive position is relatively higher unit labour costs. Policies directed at the symptoms and not the causes will not succeed in eliminating the problem.

One final fundamental problem arises from the fact that Britain was the first country to industrialise and, furthermore, was not devastated during either of the two world wars. The industries Britain has now are basically those she acquired during her hey-day. The structure of British industry, the structure of the financial system and the relationship between them have little changed. One major change, for better or worse, has been the rise of trade unionism. This is the major structural difference between the late 19th century and the present. More significantly, perhaps, is that it began very early in Britain and has taken on a different shape than in other countries. The problems of inflation, unemployment and lack of competitiveness cannot be isolated from the structure of the economy in which these occur. The essential question is whether the structure has or has not contributed to these other problems, i.e., whether the structure of Britain has been a contributory factor in its decline. This is not unusual in history. Something can be a country's strength at the outset, but if it does not adapt it later becomes the country's weakness. The same can be said of its attitudes; e.g., in Germany, says Dahrendorf (1982), people live to work while in Britain they work to live.

This issue over structure is directly relevant to the problem of unemployment. As Britain is slow to adjust to the new technology and the 'information revolution', so there is a rise in long-term unemployment (see chapter 2). No matter how much aggregate demand is raised, this long-term structural unemployment requires a change in the structure of the economy. But who carries out such changes, even assuming they can be identified? Is it the government or is it the free market mechanism?

1.4 Government Involvement in the Solutions

The title of this section arises from a pronouncement of Margaret Thatcher's government that it is not the government's job to create full employment: it merely creates the *climate* for growth and increased employment – no more and no less. It does believe, however, that government should and can bring down the rate of inflation. Prior to the Thatcher government it was considered a government's responsibility to maintain full employment. The basic point here is that the government can choose its objectives: the 'should' is purely a political question. Whether a government *can* achieve its stated objective(s) is more a question of economics than of politics.

There is no such thing as *no* government involvement; it is a question of *how much* involvement and in what way. It is here that political ideologies enter – and enter they must. The issue of whether to subsidise a particular industry or to impose import controls on synthetic carpets cannot be divorced from the basic philosophy lying behind subsidies and import controls. Whether to nationalise or denationalise is also a question of political ideology. Economics can indicate (tentatively) the implications of each: but finally it is a question of politics. This does not mean that the economist simply ignores these normative issues; it means only that the normative and positive issues are kept clearly distinguished in the arguments.

It is certainly the case that post-war economies have been governed along Keynesian demand management lines. This approach gives a 'natural' leaning towards greater government involvement in the economy. Whether this is more towards planning or is simply a way of increasing the efficiency of the market mechanism is a moot point. But what we can highlight here is the fact that past involvement by governments in the UK economy has been very much on the side of aggregate demand. The supply side has had very little *purposeful* influence. Supply has undoubtedly been influenced – by taxation especially – but this has been *ad hoc* and more for raising taxes than for creating a desired position for over-all aggregate supply.

These remarks raise the question not so much of government involvement *per se,* but of whether the involvement has been misplaced. This can be made clear by posing the following question: 'Can all of Britain's problems be solved by means of manipulating *only* aggregate demand?' When put this way the answer is clearly 'No'. But an analysis of post-war UK policy would suggest that no alternative route has been sought. It could be argued that this was because the economic paradigm of the day supported only demand management and that it was not until the inflation of the 1970s that the weakness of the paradigm became obvious.

Like many crises, there is a danger of going to the other extreme, and in the present context this would be the implementation of solely supply-side policies. Consider the following list of policies (see Midland Bank, 1977):

(1) Reduce government involvement in wage fixing

(2) Amend legal position on trade unions

(3) Increase denationalisation

(4) No support for 'lame ducks'

(5) Enterprises to reap rewards of success

(6) Abolish many administrative controls

(7) Reduce real government expenditure.

With the exception of the last, all these involve supply-side policies – the last involves both aggregate demand and aggregate supply. This is basically the approach of Margaret Thatcher's government. But such policies are both long-term and slow to operate. They will likely have limited success – just as demand management policies had limited success. The success will be in those areas where the problems arise solely on the supply side. Demand-side problems, or problems arising from the interaction of aggregate demand and aggregate supply, will not be solved from such an approach. This swing of the pendulum arises from false reasoning: 'look at demand management: it has failed, so let us abandon it!' Just as demand management cannot solve supply-side problems, so supply management cannot solve demand-side problems – and neither can solve those arising from both demand and supply. The solution of Britain's problems requires a package which has four components:

(1) Policies to deal with demand-side problems

(2) Policies to deal with supply-side problems

(3) Policies to deal with demand and supply-side problems

(4) Policies to change the economic structure.

1.5 Can a Free Market Mechanism Solve Britain's Problems?

Both in the United States and in Britain there was in the late 1970s a swing over to the view that the market mechanism should be left to get on with its job of efficiently allocating economic resources. Although associated with monetarism, it must be realised that this is an ideological premise: unregulated markets are 'better' than regulated markets. In Britain this has led to three kinds of policies:

(1) What appears a no-industry policy but is basically a policy of withdrawing constraints, withdrawing subsidies, denationalising and abolishing controls

(2) A withdrawal of government involvement, where possible, from the wage bargaining process (although it cannot withdraw from wage settlements in the public sector)

(3) A curb on trade union power and a possible reduction in unemployment benefits.

In essence, it has led to a reduction of government regulation of the market and to allowing the market mechanism to work efficiently and without constraint. This is the *climate* which the Conservative Party refers to.

A point constantly made throughout this book is that free unregulated markets create *equilibrium* solutions and not necessarily *desired* solutions. This confusion abounds in macroeconomic policy discussion. It is most clearly illustrated in the foreign exchange market. Consistent with other policies, the Conservative government has had a (fairly freely) floating exchange rate since 1979. In early 1983 the dollar/pound rate fell dramatically and put in jeopardy the government's primary objective of reducing inflation. Two points arise from this. First, if you believe in free market forces then you must allow the market rate to find its own level – whether this means a rise or a fall in the rate. Objecting to the fall is strictly having a desired rate and not letting free market forces operate. Second, the same government argued that Britain 'should pay its way in world trade', which basically means a zero balance on the *current account* of the balance of payments (i.e., the value of imports of goods and services equal to the value of exports of goods and services). But a free market exchange rate brings into balance the current *plus* capital account – at least theoretically. It is most unlikely that an equilibrium exchange rate which brings about a balance on current *and* capital account coincidentally is the rate which balances only the current account. The confusion here is that the government is not being clear on what the objective is. Is it to eliminate a balance of payments constraint on domestic policy-making? In that case a freely floating exchange rate is called for. Or is it 'to pay our way'? In that case a desired exchange rate must be established which results in a balance on current account.

One other implicit assumption about free markets which is crucial, both theoretically and practically, is the assumption that markets clear quickly. This involves two features: (1) markets actually clear, and (2) the clearing is achieved quickly. (One other assumption which is implicit rather than explicit is that the equilibrium is unique.) For instance, the presumption that in the long run the natural rate of unemployment can be achieved at zero rate of inflation assumes that the labour market clears. Once this is realised, it is clear that policies to reduce trade union power and to increase the efficiency of job search are policies to speed up the process of clearing in the labour market. Similarly, the withdrawal of controls, constraints and subsidies are all consistent with the aim of speeding up the clearing of markets.[11] This policy is consistent with other objectives. If, however, it leads to bankruptcies and unemployment then these must be treated as adjustment costs. On the other hand, the *free market equilibrium* outcome cannot be objected to if the logic is to be consistent. The major problem, therefore, arises from the fact that the equilibrium solution may not be a desirable solution. Once this is accepted and a decision is made to move the economy to a *desirable equilibrium,* then the debate is on the degree of government involvement, which we discussed briefly in the previous section.

Another difficulty for Britain attempting such a free market solution in isolation is that it could come under great trade pressure. If, for example, other countries subsidised their home industries, then this would lower their prices on world markets and give them an 'unfair' competitive advantage. All this would do is lower the (say) dollar/pound exchange rate still further. Will this be a solution to Britain's problems? Free trade is a first-best solution for the world only if *all* countries participate. We live in a second-best world, and it is not clear that freeing *some* markets will lead to an increase in welfare.

The final issue in the debate over free markets is that it could lead to some industries being smaller than is considered appropriate for security, e.g. agriculture, shipping and steel. The point here is that there have always been some reasons for government intervention. But where do we draw the line? The line is purely arbitrary and is based on objectives; political as well as economic. It indicates, if nothing else, that there can be no general rule, no general principle which can be followed in all markets. But suppose we have two opposite general principles – which we shall label A and Z. Suppose we choose A but arrive at state E by *ad hoc* changes in the general principle A. Now consider having general principle Z and arriving at state T by *ad hoc* changes in the general principle Z. In comparing states E and T we are in theory choosing to apply general principles A or Z. The free market mechanism can be thought of as principle A, while state control can be thought of as principle Z. The final choice, however, is political. The solution to Britain's problems depends on whether we are in state E or state T. Once the state is known, the solutions are largely economic – but no less difficult to solve.

Questions

1. Why are the economic problems of the UK economy ranked differently? Does it matter that different people rank the problems differently?

2. Does the cause of a problem always depend upon how we define it? Give an economic example where the cause does (does not) depend on how it is defined.

3. Make two lists of Britain's economic problems. Let one list contain all problems with only (or very largely) a *single* cause and the other those problems where there is more than one cause. Is this categorisation useful?

4. Is the theory of economic policy which relates instruments to fixed targets a useful way of analysing Britain's economic problems?

5. Is the problem of unemployment an issue the government should concern itself with? That is, should it set a level of unemployment which it considers desirable and set in motion policies when the level rises above this rate?

6. If it is appropriate to analyse Britain's economic problems by means of a large econometric model, then why not scrap all but the Treasury model – for at least then the same model will be consistent across discussion? (On the large UK econometric models see Cuthbertson, 1979 and Chrystal, 1979.)

7. If Britain's problems are very supply-dominated, then why have governments persisted in demand management policies?

8. Distinguish between an *adjustment* problem and a *fundamental* problem. Why does this categorisation differ depending on the political party in power?

9. Present two alternative arguments, one to show how investment is a cause of Britain's low growth and another to show how it is a consequence of low growth. Which do you favour and why?

10. Why is it important to distinguish between equilibrium positions and desired positions? Does this distinction have any bearing on problems which are adjustment problems only?

11. Turn to the tables on import penetration in the *Monthly Digest of Statistics* and account for the high import penetration Britain is experiencing in a number of industries. Is this a contributory cause of unemployment or a consequence of Britain's poor competitive position?

12. Discuss the importance of the assumption that markets clear quickly in analysing Britain's economic problems and their solutions.

13. Would the theory of second best support the view that Britain's

liberalisation of trade and capital flows, which is not followed by other countries, can only be harmful to the the UK?

14. Criticise the assertion that 'since only money matters we should not be concerned about reduced productivity, increased market power, monopolies and import penetration.'
15. What is divestment? Given the type of problems outlined in this chapter, would you expect divestment to increase over the next ten years? (On divestment see Chiplin and Wright, 1980.)
16. A fundamental problem for the UK is its inability 'to grow at more than one-half the rate of the Western world without the growth of imports exceeding the growth of exports' (Thirlwall, 1978). Do you agree?
17. 'Why has the contraction in manufacturing relative to other sectors of the economy been so widespread and prolonged?' (See Midland Bank, 1982.)
18. Was North Sea oil production a cause of a high exchange rate and a fall in non-oil production, so giving rise to the 1980-82 slump?
19. Do you agree with the proposition that 'the exchange rate ... is the most powerful mechanism available to the British government for influencing the competitive position of manufacturing industry' (CLARE Group, Midland Bank, 1982).
20. Was the rise in UK manufacturing productivity in 1981 during the downturn of the business cycle indicative of a change in the lag between employment and output? (See the series of articles in August 1982 issue of the *National Institute Economic Review.*)

Notes

1. Overmanning would suggest a reduction of the labour force employed, while underproduction would suggest raising output per employee. On the use of these concepts see Pratten (1977) and Shone (1981, Section A6.5).
2. Where a problem is based on a statistical series, suich as unemployment or the consumer price index, it is possible that the 'problem' is dependent upon the base year for which the series is compiled. The problem of base year(s) is not confined to a particular series. In the analysis by Taylor (1978), on the causes of Britain's recession in the 1970s, he takes the years 1963-74 as a *base period,* i.e., the average experience over these years.

3. This was especially stressed by Meade in his Nobel Prize lecture, (Meade, 1978).
4. More recent work on model building would suggest that it is not necessarily the model which gives different answers to questions, but the way expectations are formulated in the respective models. In other words, one of the most crucial features of any model is the assumption about the way in which agents in the economy form their expectations, (see Griffiths and Wood, 1981, Introduction). It is not clear, however, whether it is the formation of expectations or the assumption as to whether markets clear quickly.
5. A distinction stressed by the CLARE group: see Midland Bank (1977).
6. See Bhagwati and Ramaswami (1963).
7. On the changing pattern of venture capital along US lines, see Bank of England (1982b).
8. Not only low investment but also possibly a cause of deterioration in non-price areas, such as design and performance, because of reduced incentives to innovate: see OECD Economic Survey, (1980) and Panic (1975).
9. See Connell (1980).
10. In support of the former, especially with respect to the real exchange rate impact, see Bond and Knobl (1982); and for the latter view see Midland Bank (1982).
11. On other aspects of the market mechanism see Hahn (1982) and Sen (1983). The first, in particular, raises reservations about blinding belief in the invisible hand as a solution to UK problems.

PART II

Unemployment and inflation

CHAPTER 2

What are the causes of, and cures for, unemployment?

Unemployment has presently reached unprecedented levels. Comparisons with the inter-war period are not uncommon, and although we shall not here concern ourselves with that period, the comparison does highlight the magnitude of the problem.[1]

Unemployment, like inflation, is riddled with confusions of terminology, measurement difficulties, a plethora of theories (none of which is satisfactory) and no concrete solutions. This area of economics shows how the issues of the day dominate the development of economic theory. Since the White Paper of 1944, all governments, with the exception of the present Conservative government, under the leadership of Margaret Thatcher, have taken responsibility to achieve full employment. For most of the post-war period they were successful in their stated objective. Because of this economists gave very little attention to the theory of unemployment. The Keynesian theory, outlined in the *General Theory* (Keynes, 1936) and developed and put into practice in the post-war period, seemed adequate. But as the 1970s progressed it was clear that the existing theories were totally inadequate. They simply could not explain the growing levels of unemployment – more especially, they could not explain the presence of *both* unemployment and inflation. This *stagflation*, as it became known, simply did not arise in the standard macroeconomic theories. There was high inflation and low unemployment, or low inflation and high unemployment (the Phillips trade-off, as we shall outline in the next chapter) – but not both. Furthermore, the standard theories were dominated by demand-side economics, and as such the labour market was relegated almost to oblivion, or at least to a very minor role. But any attempt to explain unemployment, especially at the macroeconomic level, must have a suitable theory of the labour market. The move to 'supply-side economics' at the very least turns attention to this neglected aspect. But it is important that both sides be constantly kept in mind. A theory which deals only with the demand side cannot be a full explanation; but the same is true of a theory which considers only the supply side. Both must enter the analysis. It is the case that, when using the analysis to explain historical events, demand (or supply) may be the overriding reason at the time; but this does not mean that the same is true for all time and in all countries.

One other aspect must be kept in mind when considering unemployment. One reason that is often put forward for the growing level of unemployment in the UK is the power of the trade unions. But if a theory is constructed without taking account of this institutional arrangement, then it cannot be used to answer questions about trade unions being a possible cause of unemployment. This is a vital conceptual point that is worth stressing. If a theory is set up which, by assumption, excludes x, then by construction it cannot analyse the effect of x on any of the variables in the model. Here we see an immediate difficulty about model construction: how do you model trade union power? Not only trade union power, but also other institutional arrangements, such as collective bargaining, cannot be easily modelled. We come to the obvious point that the labour market is not like the market for a manufactured good. It is quite unique and incorporates norms that society either has come to accept (rightly or wrongly) or wishes to change. When we deal with the labour market, economic, political and sociological (not to mention psychological) aspects all play a role. Although it is difficult to know what the balance is, to consider the issue as only (or exclusively) economic is to mislead.

As we have just pointed out, repeated governments in the post-war period accepted responsibility for unemployment and clearly believed that they could alleviate (and hence create) unemployment. In the inter-war period it was believed that unemployment was a result of the individuals themselves, and as such was out of the hands of the government. A similar (although not identical) view is held by the present Conservative government. They believe that full employment is not a gift that governments can bestow: it should be neither promised nor provided. These totally opposing viewpoints are not economic. What can be looked at from an economic point of view is the implications of each.

From these introductory comments it should be clear that the issue of unemployment is not a simple one. We can do no more in this chapter than lay out a framework within which to discuss the issues. We begin, therefore, with a section on the meaning of 'unemployment'. There seems little point in analysing statistics if we are not clear what interpretation should be given to them. With the aid of the discussion in the first section, we turn in section 2.2 to the statistics. This will enable us to highlight, at least from the point of view of the compiled statistics, what and where some problems appear to be – if we take numbers as our main measuring rod. In section 2.3 we consider some of the traditional explanations for unemployment; and in section 2.4 we consider the more recent search theories. In the final section we consider some of the possible ways to alleviate unemployment in the light of the analysis presented in the first four sections.

2.1 The Meaning of 'Unemployment'

The term 'unemployment' has many adjectives attached to it; including involuntary, demand-deficient, seasonal, structural, frictional, cyclical, long-term, short-term, and many others. In addition, the term 'natural rate of unemployment' was introduced into the literature by Milton Friedman. Some of these terms are simply ways to categorise unemployment; some are measurable; while others are non-observable.

One of the major distinctions is that between voluntary and involuntary unemployment. In considering this distinction we shall abstract from the issue of inflation by assuming that it is zero. (We shall return later to the difficulties a positive rate of inflation has on various definitions.) The distinction can be appreciated with the help of Figure 2.1. The demand for labour is a function of the real wage and is, under perfect competition, the sum of the marginal physical product of labour curves for each firm. The supply curve of labour is also a function of the real wage (although we shall see in a moment it is more accurate to consider this a function of the *expected* real wage), and arises from the income-leisure trade-off. If we let L^* represent the total labour force, then the supply curve of labour, S_L, rises positively, but cannot exceed $L = L^*$ (i.e., there is some wage w^* at which the supply cure of labour becomes infinitely inelastic). Consider now the real wage $w_1 = (W/P)_1$. At this real wage, those wishing to supply themselves to the labour market are L_1 while the demand for labour by firms is only L_2. The difference, $L_1 - L_2$, is referred to as involuntary unemployment. What is the level of voluntary unemployment? Given the real wage w_1, L_1 are willing to supply themselves to the labour market. Given the total labour force L^*, then this implies that $L^* - L_1$ are voluntarily unemployed.

Figure 2.1 also explains the meaning economists give to the term 'full employment'. If the real wage is w_o then the supply of labour is equal to the demand for labour, both being L_o. This represents the full employment level. In other words, full employment is the situation where there is no excess demand for labour (given a zero inflation rate.)

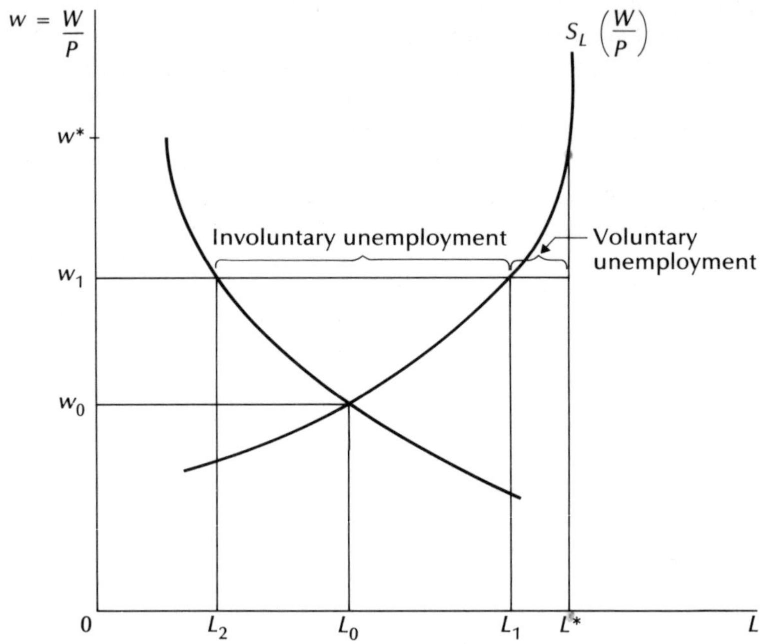

Figure 2.1 Voluntary and involuntary unemployment

Notice that full employment does not mean that there is no unemployment; what it does mean is that there is no *involuntary* unemployment – all the unemployment, $L^* - L_o$, is voluntary when the real wage rate is w_o.

For any given real wage, the level of voluntary unemployment is given by the difference between the working population, L^*, and the supply of labour at that real wage, i.e., the difference between a point on the supply curve S_L, and L^*. Thus, voluntary unemployment refers to people who are capable of working but who, for reasons such as the level of benefits or because they are looking around for another job, choose not to work.

There is a difficulty here that must be appreciated. Suppose the age of retirement is 65 (which at the moment is the case for a man, a woman being able to retire at 60). Consider a man aged 63. He is capable of working – and probably capable of working well into his seventies or later. Now suppose he is made redundant. Then he is classified as being involuntarily unemployed if he actually wishes to work. On the other hand, if he takes on early retirement then he will be voluntarily unemployed. Alternatively, suppose the retirement age is reduced to 60 and he is compulsorily made redundant as a consequence. He is neither voluntarily nor involuntarily unemployed, according to the statistics!

He may wish to work at the ruling wage, but he has in fact been re-classified: he no longer belongs to the 'working population'. Unemployment has not risen, but the number of senior citizens has! The same applies at the other end of the work force – youths. If the school-leaving age is changed then youths become re-classified. The same issue arises under government schemes, such as the Youth Opportunities Programme (YOP). When on the scheme they are not part of the involuntarily unemployed, but once off the scheme they return to the pool of involuntarily unemployed if they do not subsequently get a job.

According to the present analysis, involuntary unemployment occurs when, at the ruling real wage, there is an excess supply of labour. Thus it implies that these people wish to work but cannot find a job. Such involuntary unemployment arises from three basic sources:

(1) There are no opportunities in a particular industry (e.g., in a declining industry such as textiles).

(2) A person's skill or experience is no longer required (e.g., welders in shipbuilding or car plants being replaced by robotics).

(3) A person is not sufficiently qualified although vacancies exist (e.g., in microelectronics and biotechnology).

Figure 2.1 also reveals quite readily the classical view about unemployment. The crucial assumption that must be clearly kept in mind when dealing with classical economics is that money wages are completely flexible. Given this assumption, then the real wage will always change to ensure that the supply of labour is equal to the demand for labour, i.e., a real wage of w_0 and a full employment of L_0 in terms of Figure 2.1. Any unemployment that exists must be only temporary, and occurs while wages in the labour market are adjusting to the equilibrium level. Such unemployment was referred to as 'frictional' and could only be of a short-run nature. In the long run all unemployment is voluntary, in terms of the distinction we made earlier. The Keynesian concept of involuntary unemployment, therefore, rests on explaining how and why the real wage can settle at a level other than that given by the intersection of the demand and supply of labour.

It is important to appreciate that this idea that all unemployment was voluntary and that only frictional unemployment was involuntary was quite widely accepted between the wars. The high levels of unemployment arising during and following the Great Depression were simply ignored as a temporary aberration! As we shall see shortly, the rise of 'new classical economics' once again supports this view, but we shall return to this when we have discussed the meaning of the 'natural rate of unemployment'.

How, then, does the real wage in Keynesian economics occur at a level other than the equilibrium level as specified in the labour market? To appreciate this a fuller model is required which incorporates both the goods market and the money market, along with that of the labour market. This fuller model is now standard analysis in all macroeconomics textbooks.[2]

The situation is captured in terms of Figure 2.2. The goods market and money market are in equilibrium at real income level y_1. This income level is consistent with a demand for labour of L_1 at the real wage w_1. But at w_1 the supply of labour is L_2; hence there arises involuntary unemployment of $U_1 = L_2 - L_1$. But why should this remain?

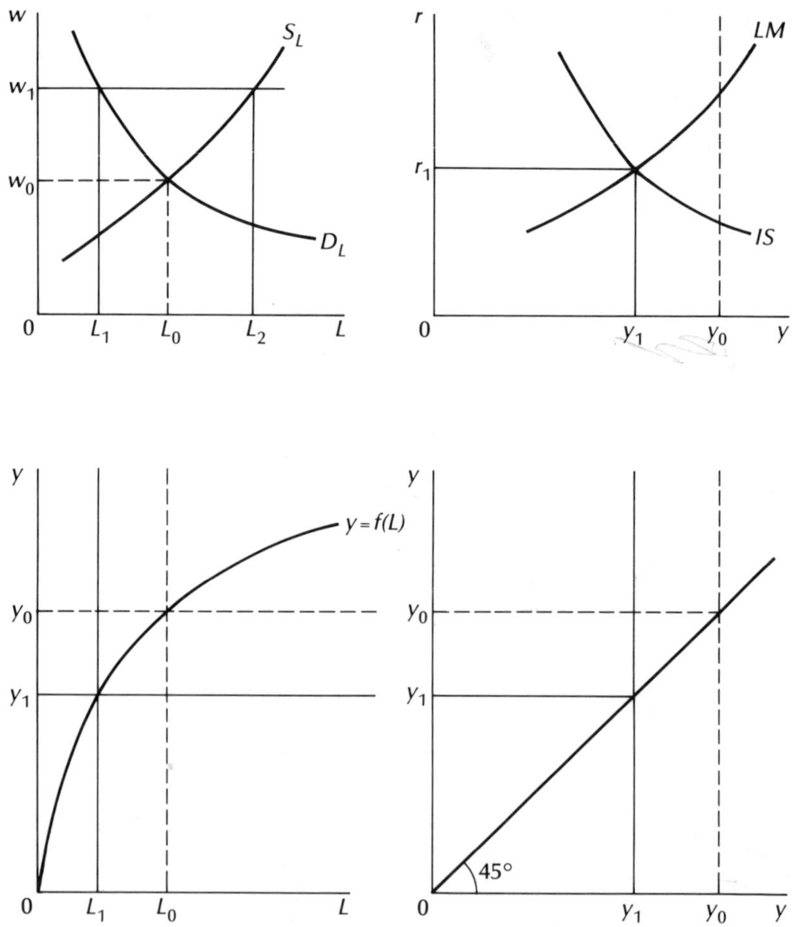

Figure 2.2 Keynesian underemployment equilibrium

The reason given by Keynes is that money wages are inflexible downwards. Where inflation is not under discussion, so that the price level is constant, then real wages remain sticky downwards also. Hence, w_1 will persist. Although we shall not present the analysis in detail, it is clear that the issue here is: *What is an acceptable explanation for the disequilibrium real wage rate,* w_1*, which will persist into the future*? The disagreement is not so much about the non-existence of involuntary unemployment, but rather about how the involuntary unemployment arises.

Having distinguished between voluntary and involuntary unemployment, another classification is useful, and one we shall refer to frequently. First we recognise that unemployment is seasonal. From now on we shall assume that when we refer to unemployment (unqualified) we are referring to seasonally adjusted unemployment. Given this, we can subdivide (seasonally adjusted) unemployment into three component parts:

(1) Demand-deficient, U_d

(2) Frictional, U_f

(3) Structural, U_s

I.e., $U = U_d + U_f + U_s$

To see what exactly these are and how they relate to the concepts of voluntary and involuntary unemployment, we note that the demand for labour can be thought of as the level of employment, E, plus the level of vacancies, V, while the supply of labour can be thought of as the level of employment plus the level of unemployment. Thus:

$$D_L = E + V$$

$$S_L = E + U$$

and $S_L - D_L = U - V$

This excess supply is commonly referred to as 'demand-deficient' unemployment. Thus:

$$U_d = U - V > 0$$

and $U_d = 0$ for $U - V < 0$

In terms of Figure 2.1 this means that demand-deficient unemployment exists only when the real wage is above the equilibrium wage, for in this case $U - V > 0$. When the real wage is below the equilibrium wage then the excess demand simply refers to the number of vacancies.

Frictional unemployment, U_f, refers to the short-run unfilled vacancies in the same occupation and in the same locality. Structural unemployment, U_s, refers to the long-run mismatch arising from unsuitable skills or geographical location – either of firms or of people. Using this classification, one way to define the 'natural rate of unemployment', U_n, is a situation where $U_d = 0$ so that:

$$U_n = U_f + U_s$$

Of course, there is nothing 'natural' about this unemployment level. The term 'natural' is a classical usage – like the 'natural rate of interest' – which usually denotes the level a variable takes when the goods market is in equilibrium. If the goods market is in equilibrium, then there cannot be any demand-deficient unemployment; i.e., $U_d = 0$, and so any unemployment must be structural or frictional. Even in the long run frictional unemployment is zero, so that in the long run the natural level of unemployment denotes the structural unemployment faced by an economy. Notice how this concept of the 'natural rate of unemployment' is very similar to the classical idea that an economy must always be at the full employment situation in the long run and all unemployment is voluntary. The major change here is the fact that in the long run the unemployment is structural rather than voluntary.

One further point is worth noting. Structural and frictional unemployment are assumed to be independent of the real wage, which in turn implies that the natural rate of unemployment is also independent of the real wage. Monetarists usually go one stage further and argue that not only is the natural rate of unemployment independent of the real wage, but it is also independent of the rate of wage (and price) inflation. Under this assumption the relationship between unemployment and price inflation – the long-run Phillips curve – must be vertical.

2.2 The Structure of UK Unemployment

In this section we intend to consider the statistics to see what pattern, if any, they reveal about UK unemployment. One of the difficulties with the concepts outlined in the first section is that they deal with non-observable variables. The three main categories we mentioned – demand-deficient, structural and frictional unemployment – are all conceptual. So too are voluntary and involuntary unemployment along with the natural rate of unemployment. The only statistics we have are those registered at the labour exchange. Notice that this in itself is very limited in denoting the total unemployed. If a married woman decides not to bother registering then she will not be counted as unemployed, even though she may be wanting a job and looking for a job.

In Figure 2.3, taken from Addison and Siebert (1980), we see that

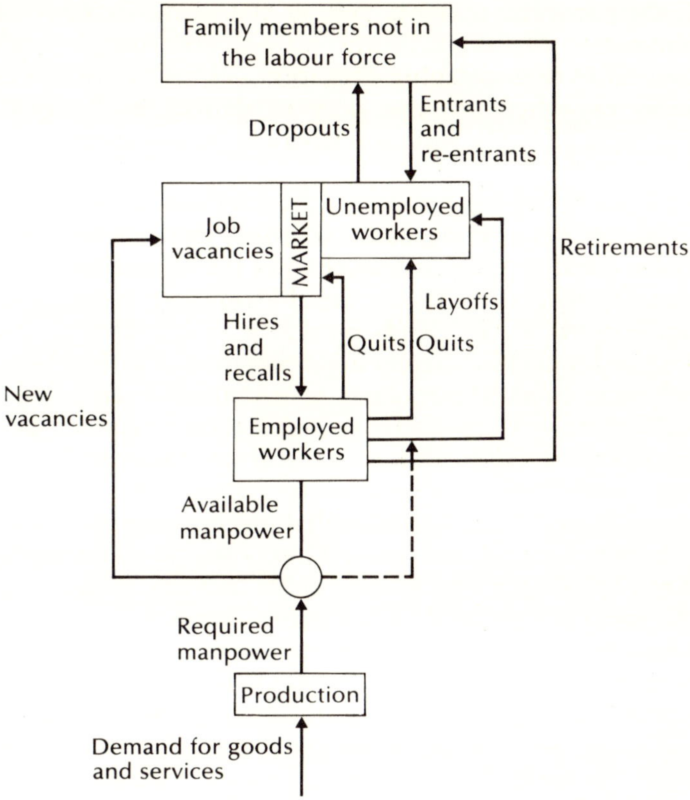

Figure 2.3 Unemployment: stocks and flows (arrows denote flows; boxes denote stocks).
Source: Addison, J.T. and W.S. Siebert, (1980).

there is a considerable inflow and outflow to and from the pool of unemployed and the pool of vacancies. The blocks can be thought of as stocks and the arrows linking the various blocks as flows. To highlight the difficulty in interpreting the statistics let us take an extreme example and follow John Smith through some troubled times. He is presently employed by a shipping company as a welder. He considers, however, that he can do better so decides to go unemployed in order to search for a better job. In this instance he is voluntarily unemployed. Now suppose he gets a job in a small steel firm. But the steel firm finds that the demand for steel has declined on world markets, and so must lay off workers. Unfortunately John is one of these. He now becomes unemployed in the sense of demand deficiency. He tries to get a job, but finds welders are rarely needed because of new automation. Over time, he becomes part of the structural unemployed. This scenario, along with Figure 2.3, illustrates two features:

(1) Unemployment and vacancies coexist (normally in large numbers). This means that unemployment is not a residual.

(2) Flows through the market are not independent of one another; e.g., an increase in vacancies tends to increase both the quit rate and the flow of new workers into the labour force.

The first conspicuous change has been the rise in activity rates for married women (where activity rates are defined as the number in work

Figure 2.4 UK unemployment, 1945-81

or looking for work as a percentage of the adult population). This was especially so in the 1960s, where the activity rate for married women rose from almost 30% in 1961 to almost 50% in 1979. The activity rate for men over this same period declined from 86% to just under 79%. Two other features have changed with respect to the role of women in the labour force. In the past many women had not bothered to register themselves as unemployed, but now far more women are doing so: between 1971 and 1974 females comprised about 15% of registered unemployed and by June 1980 this had risen to almost 30%. The third characteristic of women in the labour force has been their greater employment in the service sector – which has also been the fastest growing sector of the economy. Putting it the other way around, the declining industries have employed relatively more men than women.

The growth in the activity rate for married women also occurred at the same time as the increase in young people arising from the increased birth rate of the 1960s. While the number of school-leavers registered as unemployed was 7.7 thousand in July 1973, this figure rose to 275.4 thousand in July 1981.

In addition to the trends just cited, there has also been an increase in the long-term growth in male unemployment. This has had two characteristics: (1) each peak unemployment has been higher than the previous one, and (2) the duration of male unemployment has risen. The first feature is shown in Figure 2.4, which shows quite clearly the cyclical nature of unemployment in the post-war period.

The second feature is shown in Table 2.1. Although the percentage of the total unemployed for less than 8 weeks is falling, the percentage of the total unemployed for more than 52 weeks has been rising quite sharply. If long-term unemployment is taken to be indicated by unemployment duration in excess of one year, then there is a marked rise in long-term unemployment. However, Table 2.1 does not tell all of the story. It is important to break this down into age groups. When this is done, two groups stand out: the young and the old. The rise in the youth unemployment, although serious, is common to most OECD countries. This is not the case, however, with the old. Furthermore, there are indications that this problem with the old is creeping down the age scale!

This increase in the duration of unemployment is one of the major observable statistics we can use to indicate that there is an increase in structural unemployment. (It could also be interpreted as an increase in the natural rate of unemployment for the UK.) This is an important point in the light of the division we gave in section 2.1. Suppose, by way of illustration, that we concentrate simply on demand-deficient and structural unemployment, and that we consider two situations, labelled

Table 2.1 Unemployment in excess of 52 weeks, 1948-81

Year	Over 52 weeks unemployed	Year	Over 52 weeks unemployed
1948	12.9	1965	16.7
1949	11.6	1966	12.9
1950	12.4	1967	13.7
1951	10.5	1968	18.6
1952	8.5	1969	17.6
1953	10.8	1970	17.8
1954	11.1	1971	15.9
1955	10.3	1972	22.5
1956	8.3	1973	27.7
1957	9.2	1974	20.5
1958	9.7	1975	14.7
1959	15.7	1976	20.0
1960	17.0	1977	22.3
1961	13.5	1978	24.4
1962	12.4	1979	25.9
1963	17.0	1980	19.2
1964	18.8	1981	25.9

Source: Miller and Wood (1982, Table XI): 1948-61, December figures; 1962-81, October figures.

A and B. The figures denote the percentage of total unemployment in each category:

	Demand-deficient	Structural
	%	%
Situation A	90	10
Situation B	10	90

If situation A prevails then a large amount of the unemployment can be eliminated by means of increased aggregate demand brought about by government policy. If, on the other hand, situation B prevails, then such a rise in aggregate demand can only eliminate (at the maximum) 10% of the total unemployed; it may even simply raise the rate of inflation rather than reduce any of the unemployment (and could, then, even raise the level of unemployment). A quite different policy would be required to deal with the remaining 90% – if such an objective were considered to be a role of government! The difficulty is that demand-deficient and structural unemployment are theoretical concepts. We cannot go to the statistics and make an immediate and simple grouping. But clearly it matters whether the situation that prevails is captured by situation A or situation B. One means of seeing this is through the duration of unemployment. If a large element of unemployment is demand-deficient, then during periods when aggregate demand is raised fewer people should be unemployed for long periods. If, however, the unemployment is structural, then, regardless of the level of aggregate demand, it is likely that the number of people in long-period unemployment (those unemployed for more than one year, say) will increase.

Are there any other statistics available that will give us some idea whether it is situation A or situation B? One feature of the present unemployment is the fact that there are jobs available for which people are not available, either because of geographical location or because they do not have the requisite skills or education required. This mismatch means that the difference between unemployment and vacancies has been increasing. This is shown clearly in Table 2.2, which gives the difference, $U - V$, for various occupational groups.

Table 2.2 Occupational unemployment less vacancies, 1975-80

	March 1975	March 1977	June 1980
Managerial and professional	26,715	73,743	80,945
Clerical and related	74,742	159,621	167,137
Other non-manual occupations	15,829	57,008	66,425
Craft and similar occupations	49,448	122,545	123,879
General labourers	243,395	435,018	489,227
Other manual occupations	156,199	254,845	271,215
All occupation	566,228	1,112,780	1,198,828

Source: Hawkins (1979); *Employment Gazette* (September 1980).

Three features stand out from the table:

(1) there are vast differences between occupations in any one year; (2) the highest difference in each year is for general labourers; (3) there has been a consistent growth in demand-deficient unemployment in all occupations.

Even if the difference, $U - V$, indicates a rise in demand-deficient unemployment, it is not the case that market forces alone are sufficient to deal with these mismatches. The point is that they do not simply reflect demand-deficient unemployment. To appreciate this it is important to realise that two mismatches are very important. First, there is the mismatch of unskilled labourers. Second, there is the shortage of skilled workers. Persistently throughout the 1970s and into the 1980s there has been a shortage of skilled labour in some occupations. This has especially come to light since the Manpower Services Commission

(MSC), set up in 1974, has collected statistics on the duration of unemployment and on vacancies. In looking at the mismatch the MSC computes the ratio of vacancies to unemployment (*V/U*) for a given occupation and also for different regions. (Note that a *V/U* ratio of 2 indicates that there are 2 vacancies for every person to fill them, and a *V/U* ratio of 0.33 indicates that there are 3 persons to every vacancy.) Table 2.3 gives *V/U* ratios for severe skill shortage occupations in Britain for June 1979, while Table 2.4 gives the ratio of skilled engineering occupations for June 1979 and June 1980 on a regional basis.

Table 2.3 Severe skill shortage occupations in Great Britain, June 1979

Occupation	*V/U* ratio	Duration of vacancies (weeks)
Tool makers and tool fitters	1.7	18
Engineering draughtsmen	1.3	27
Sheet metal workers	1.2	11
Machine setter operators	1.2	13
Bus and coach drivers	1.2	8
Chefs and cooks	1.1	6
Sewing machinists	1.1	10
Central lathe turners	1.0	11
Ladies' hairdressers	1.0	11
Motor vehicle mechanics (skilled)	0.9	10

Source: Economic Trends (September 1980)

Table 2.4 Regional *V/U* ratios: skilled engineering occupations

	June 1979	June 1980
Great Britain	0.63	0.23
South East	1.36	0.60
East Anglia	1.05	0.38
South West	0.74	0.35
West Midlands	0.49	0.14
East Midlands	0.99	0.29
Yorkshire and Humberside	0.65	0.14
North West	0.35	0.10
North	0.22	0.08
Wales	0.51	0.17
Scotland	0.29	0.17

Source: Economic Trends (September 1980)

The first four categories listed in Table 2.3 denote skilled engineering occupations and these have shown the greatest mismatch. Taking the period 1970-80 for skilled engineering occupations, the *V/U* ratio reached a peak of 2.0 by the end of 1973. For some individual occupations, e.g., machine tool setter operators, press and machine tool setters, etc., the ratio was in excess of 5.0. There was a turn-down in economic activity thereafter and unemployment rose and vacancies fell, so reducing the *V/U* ratio. Since then there has occurred a less dramatic cycle, with a peak in 1979. A similar pattern is shown with a time-series plot of the duration of vacancies in the various occupations.

Another feature of the skill shortage is the regional variations, shown in Table 2.4. In general the worst affected area in 1979 and 1980 (June) was the South East, while skilled labour was relatively plentiful in Scotland and the North for engineering occupations.

In this section we have only scratched the surface of the variety of figures computed in relation to both employment and unemployment. But it is partly the fact that there are so many figures that theory becomes important if we are to appreciate what they mean. It has often been stated that government departments collect statistics whose figures cannot be interpreted without modifying them: but any modification, any meaningful interpretation of the statistics, must involve an underlying theory – even if implicit and heuristic.

2.3 Classical and Keynesian Theories of Unemployment

We have touched on both of these theories in section 2.1, and here we intend to highlight some other features of these models which may help in interpreting the statistics, along with differing views about how to deal with unemployment. We begin with the classical case. In this model no difference arises between expected prices and actual prices; i.e., $P^e = P$, so the real wage is the same as the expected real wage; where the real wage is defined as the money wage, W, deflated by the general price level, P; and the expected real wage is the money wage deflated by the *expected* price level, P^e. Both the demand for labour and the supply of labour are functions of the real wage, w. The demand for labour is a derived demand and hence depends on the demand for goods and services, or real income, y. Since labour employed is related to real income via the production function, we relate the real wage to the level of employment rather than the level of employment to the real wage.[3] Thus, the demand for labour in the classical model can be specified:

$$D_L: \qquad w = W/P = f(L)$$

The supply of labour is determined by individuals' decisions between work and leisure. Since the opportunity cost of leisure is the real wage forgone, then the supply curve of labour is also related to the real wage. Again we write this in its inverse form relating the real wage to labour supplied:

$$S_L: \quad w = g(L)$$

The demand curve can be thought of as denoting the wage at which employers will pay for a specified amount of labour, while the supply curve can be considered as the wage at which individuals are willing to supply a specified amount of labour. In equilibrium the demand price must equal the supply price, for only then will the demand for labour match those willing to supply themselves to the labour market. In the classical model it is assumed that money wages are completely flexible – both upwards and downwards. Any change in the price level is matched by the same proportionate change in the money wage rate, leaving the real wage unaffected.

Let us recapitulate. The demand and supply curves of labour are relationships which depend only on the real wage (equal to the real expected wage). The level of output is related, via the production function, to the level of employment. Since the real wage is independent of the price level, and both money wages and prices are completely flexible, the level of employment is determined solely in the labour market and independent of any other market – specifically the market for goods and services and the money market (not to mention the

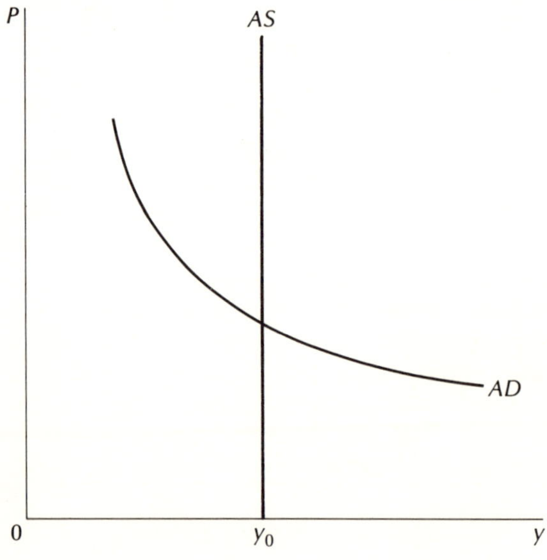

Figure 2.5 Classical situation

foreign exchange market). Put another way, the labour market is segmented from the remainder of the economy. The other variables in the system depend on the wage rate and on the level of employment, but not the other way around. Given, therefore, the level of employment, the level of real income is determined immediately from the aggregate production function. This level of real income occurs regardless of the level of prices. In other words, the aggregate supply (*AS*) curve in this classical model is vertical, as shown in Figure 2.5.

Regardless of the level of demand, therefore, the level of real income will remain at y_0. Any increase (decrease) in aggregate demand will simply lead to a rise (fall) in money wages. In this model, therefore, the only unemployment is the difference between 'full employment' (determined by the equilibrium real wage) and the working population. Using

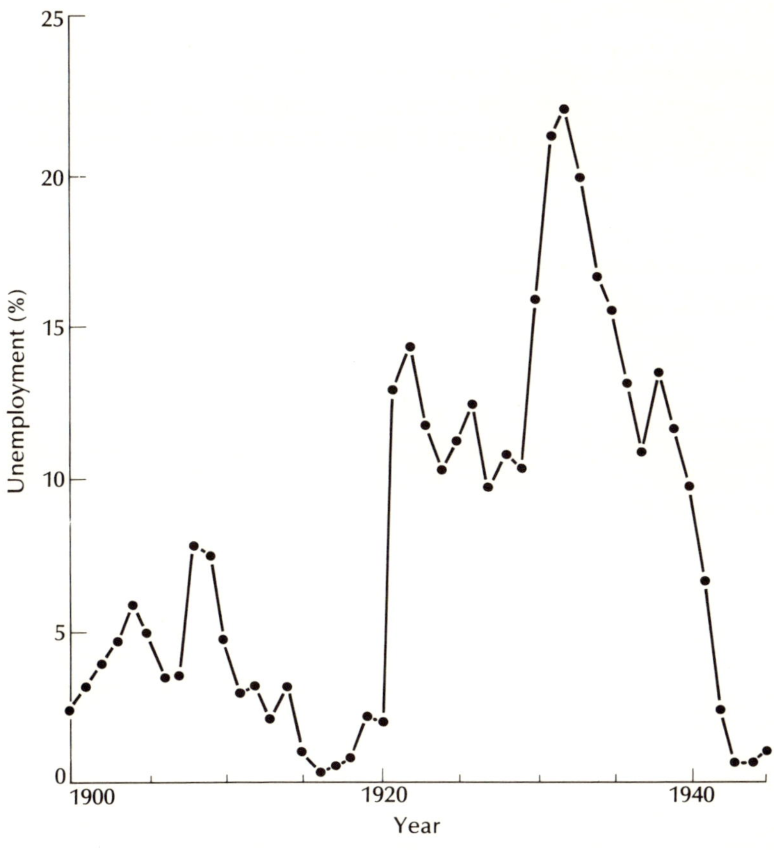

Figure 2.6 UK unemployment, 1900-45

the terminology of Keynes, all unemployment is voluntary unemployment.

The usefulness of theory in large part is to explain real-world observations. The theory just outlined was the one generally accepted until Keynes' ideas were more widely known – which we can take to be in the post-war period. Now consider the graph shown in Figure 2.6, which records the percentage unemployed from 1900 to 1945. Could all the unemployment in the inter-war period be put down to frictional unemployment? In the face of this evidence the theory had to be abandoned. Why it took so long to be abandoned is in part due to the fact that there was no alternative system to replace the classical system of macroeconomics – at least not until Keynes' *General Theory*, to which we now turn.

In introducing the Keynesian theory of unemployment, we must first allow for the actual price level, P, to differ from the expected price level, P^e. When this is done a variety of assumptions is possible. The two adopted by Keynes were:

(1) Employers know the wage charged and can predict prices accurately, so for the demanders of labour we have:

$$w = f(L) \qquad \text{or} \qquad W = Pf(L)$$

(2) Workers are unclear about the price level and base their decisions on the expected price level P^e. Thus they supply labour according to the expected real wage, $w^e = W/P^e$. Hence the supply curve of labour takes the form:

$$w^e = g(L) \qquad \text{or} \qquad W = P^e g(L)$$

In the case of the supply curve for labour in terms of the real wage, w, we must re-define the supply relationship using $w^e = W/P^e$, so that the supply curve is given by:

$$w = (P^e/P)\, g\, (L)$$

In the classical model the assumption is that $P^e = P$, which is a special case under the present model. To summarise so far, the demand curve for labour is based on the real wage while the supply curve of labour is based on the expected real wage.

In this version we immediately see an important implication. Since expected and actual prices are not necessarily equal to one another, then a change in aggregate demand, in so far as it creates or extenuates this divergence, means that the labour market equilibrium is influenced by the level of aggregate demand. The level of unemployment is, therefore, also affected by the level of aggregate demand. But this influence is only on the level of voluntary unemployment.

To see this consider Figure 2.7. Suppose there is an expansion in the money supply which raises actual prices but that there is no revision upwards in the expected price level (we shall return later to the formation of price expectations). In this instance $P^e < P$ and so the supply curve will shift down ($P^e/P < 1$). The result is a rise in the equilibrium level of employment from L_o to L_1, and hence a fall in the level of unemployment from $U_o = L^* - L_o$ to $U_1 = L^* - L_1$. Since both L_o and L_1 are equilibrium levels of employment, the unemployment we have just referred to is voluntary unemployment. The argument so far, therefore, leads only to the result that a change in the level of aggregate demand can result in a change in the level of voluntary unemployment.

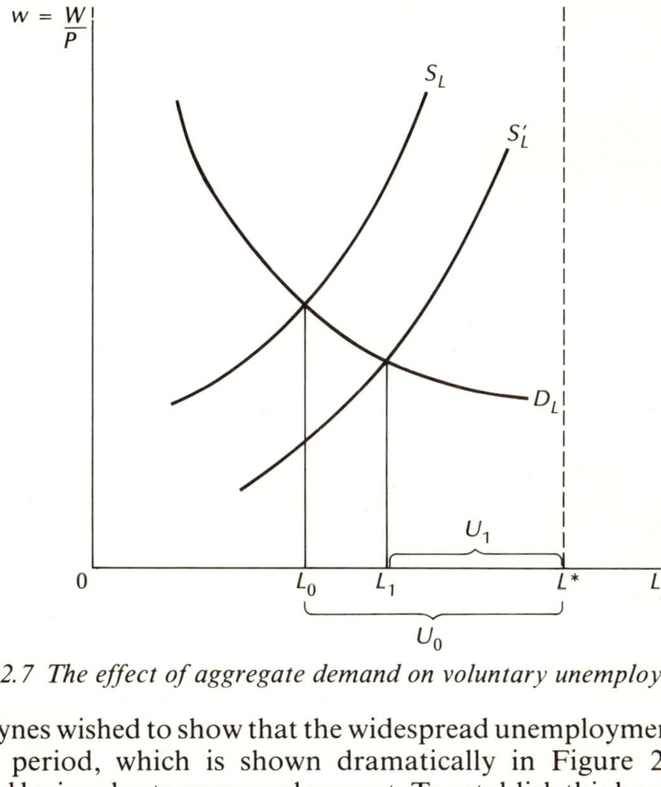

Figure 2.7 The effect of aggregate demand on voluntary unemployment

But Keynes wished to show that the widespread unemployment in the inter-war period, which is shown dramatically in Figure 2.6, was dominated by involuntary unemployment. To establish this he assumed that money wages were inflexible downwards but not upwards. The situation is shown in Figure 2.8, where we have initially a situation of all-round equilibrium at point *A*, with $W = W_o$, $P = P^e = P_o$ and $U_o = L^* - L_o$. We now assume that money wages cannot fall below W_o.

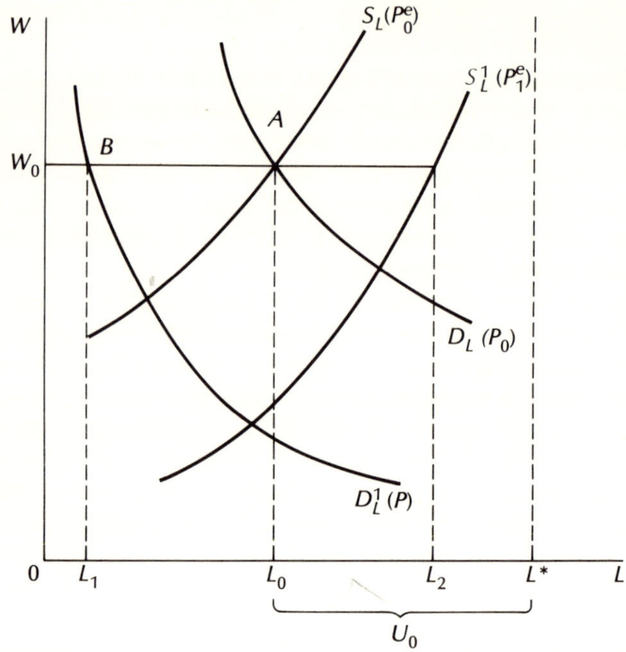

Figure 2.8 Unemployment and money wage inflexibility

Suppose now that aggregate demand falls, because of either monetary or fiscal contraction. This will create excess supply in the goods market which will, in Keynes' model, lead to a fall in the price level. (Notice that Keynes assumes that only money wages are inflexible downwards; the same assumption is not applied to the general price level.) This will result in a shift in the demand curve for labour to D^1 with $W = P_1 f(L)$.

At this point we must assume something about price expectations. Following Keynes for the moment, we assume that expected prices are revised downwards by a smaller amount than the actual price level; in other words, P^e falls but by less than P. The result of this particular assumption is that the supply curve shifts down to $P_1^e\, g(L)$ (and hence less than the shift in the demand for labour curve, $P_1 f(L)$). If P_1 is the new equilibrium price level associated with equilibrium in the goods market and money market (where *IS* intersects *LM*), then employment is now at point *B*, with W still equal to W_0 and $L = L_1$. With money wages rigid, therefore, unemployment is given by $U = L^* - L_1$, which can be broken down as follows:

Voluntary unemployment $= L^* - L_2$

Involuntary unemployment $= L_2 - L_1$

Total unemployment = $L^* - L_1$

If one accepts this line of argument, then solving involuntary unemployment is simply a case of increasing the level of aggregate demand, either through monetary policy or, as Keynes argued, through fiscal policy. Increasing aggregate demand would push up the general price level and so create a fall in the real wage (since $w = W_0 / P$). This would reverse the story portrayed in Figure 2.8 and so reduce the level of involuntary unemployment.

The point can be thought of in a totally different way. Given downward inflexibility in money wages, it is possible for the goods market and money market to be in equilibrium at a level of real income less than the full employment level of income. If this is so, and the difference in real income arises from the involuntarily unemployed, then it can be eliminated by raising the level of demand in the goods market (expansionary fiscal policy) or by raising the money supply (expansionary monetary policy). Although these have different implications for the rate of interest (and even more for the real rate of interest), they have in the short run the same qualitative result on real income and employment.

We are now in a position to discuss the new classical view in the light of the analysis just presented. Two interrelated assumptions were made in the Keynesian model:

(1) The supply curve of labour depends on the expected real wage.

(2) Price expectations are revised but not all the actual price change is anticipated; i.e., P does not equal P^e.

Crucial in the argument of explaining involuntary unemployment is the assumption about the formation of price expectations. In the new classical view it is assumed that expectations are rationally formed: they are based on the 'best' available information and participants in the market are assumed to know the 'best' model relating the economic variables.[4] Such an assumption implies that market participants are efficient in their use of information so that they make unbiased estimates of, for instance, prices. This does not mean that they do not make mistakes; it means only that they do not make mistakes consistently in one direction and that each mistake is independent of others. If there are no other distortions (to be explained in a moment) then the assumption of rational expectations implies that in the long run the only rationally expected price is that equal to the actual price; i.e., $P^e = P$. But this is exactly the classical assumption we discussed at the beginning of this section.

The new classical model will have employment settling down at the equilibrium rate, and this rate will always be the same regardless of the level of aggregate demand since in the long run all inflation is anticipated and $P^e = P$, and hence the expected rate of inflation equals the actual rate of inflation, $\hat{P}^e = \hat{P}$. This level of employment is now called the 'natural level', and the unemployment associated with it is called the 'natural rate of unemployment'. In comparison with the Keynesian case, it is clear that all unemployment in the new classical model, at least in the long run, is voluntary unemployment.

How then do new classical economists account for the rising unemployment depicted in Figure 2.4? The deductions of economic theory never rest on just one assumption, they arise from the interrelationship between a whole variety. New classical economists, besides assuming that expectations are rationally formed, also assume that markets, if left to themselves, will clear. In other words, free markets are efficient and equilibrium will always be achieved. With this in mind it immediately follows that those who accept this view will see the rising unemployment as a consequence of inefficient markets which arise from distortions. These distortions include trade unions, social security benefits, etc. Thus, in their view, in order to reduce the level of unemployment the labour market must be rid of these distortions which impede the free market from working. It is, therefore, quite consistent to hear monetarists argue for a curb on trade union power and a reduction in unemployment benefits. A rise in aggregate demand will simply lead to higher prices.

2.4 Search Theories of Unemployment - ON YOUR BIKE!

We noted in the previous section that the new classical economists accounted for some of the unemployment as arising from market distortions. Another totally different view has also emerged in the literature, namely the relationship between search time and unemployment, more specifically on the *duration* of unemployment.[5] The basic idea is that a rise in the level of aggregate demand will raise the equilibrium employment of labour because of the differential effect the price level change has on the demand and supply of labour curves. The money wage will accordingly rise and those seeking jobs perceive an improvement in job opportunities. In other words, a rise (fall) in the level of aggregate demand will reduce (increase) the search time required in finding a new or suitable job.

There are two features in this model:

(1) There exists a pool of unemployed (namely, the natural unemployed).

(2) There is uncertainty about the price level; i.e., price changes are not fully anticipated.

Search theories, since there are more than one, basically amount to an explanation of unemployment as a result of uncertainty from lack of information. There is a lack of information on both the demand and the supply side. Employers may not take on a person from the first round of appointments if they believe that they can acquire someone who is better suited – either in skill, education, or social suitability – from the pool of unemployed. On the supply side, an unemployed person is not fully acquainted with all the wages being offered by a multitude of firms – even in the same field. Thus, an unemployed person may not accept the job offered if she feels that she can, with some searching around, improve on that offer, where the 'improvement' refers to a higher wage and/or better working conditions. On the supply side uncertainty surrounds the skill and suitability for the job, while on the demand side the uncertainty is about the wage and working conditions.

This type of unemployment, and it obviously does not account for all unemployment (the theory was never meant to), is voluntary in nature. Notice also that the uncertainty on the supply side alters the level of unemployment while the uncertainty on the demand side alters the level of vacancies.

Search theorists argue that the bulk of the natural rate of unemployment can be explained by this uncertainty and the need to search. A reduction in the natural rate of unemployment, therefore, requires improvement in methods of search; namely, improved information about the job market. It also focuses attention on (1) the quitting, re-entry and entry into the job market, as shown in Figure 2.3, and (2) the institutional arrangements which prolong search time, e.g., unemployment benefits.

It is apparent that search theorists are a sub-group of the new classical economists. The reduction in the uncertainty is a means of increasing the efficiency of the labour market. Although they do not take a position on trade union power, they do advocate similar policies with regard to unemployment benefits – namely, to reduce them.

2.5 Policies for Curing Unemployment

The basic aim of the above sections has been to find out the cause of unemployment. Like any disease, it is possible to give a general treatment without knowing the true cause of the problem – but then, it is not clear why the cure works and whether it will, therefore, work on the next occasion. A cure, although not inevitable, has a greater chance of being effective if the cause is known and understood. The most obvious observation that can be made from the earlier sections is that *there is no single cause for UK unemployment.* Nor is there agreement on what the causes are. Given this lack of knowledge and differences of opinion, it is useful first to list what we have learnt from our analysis so far.

There are sixteen observations:

(1) There is no single cause for UK unemployment.

(2) There is no agreement among economists or politicians about what is/are the causes of unemployment.

(3) Governments differ as to whether they believe they should have full employment as a major policy objective, or even whether it is within their power to do so.

(4) An explanation of unemployment based on aggregate demand alone or aggregate supply alone is almost certain to be deficient.

(5) Although economists agree on voluntary unemployment, they differ as to whether involuntary unemployment exists; or, if it exists, the reason for its occurrence.

(6) Price expectations (and hence the expected rate of inflation) play a significant part in modern theories of unemployment.

(7) There is a significant difference between the statistics on unemployment and the theoretic concepts used by economists. This will make any testing of theories most difficult.

(8) In the post-war period unemployment in the UK has shown a cyclical pattern around a marked rising trend.

(9) There has been a significant rise in the activity rate of married women, coinciding with a rise in youth unemployment (from the increased birth rate of the 1960s) and more women registering as unemployed.

(10) In the post-war period long-term unemployment (i.e., being unemployed in excess of 52 weeks) has shown a cyclical pattern around a rising trend.

(11) The two major categories of people in the unemployment pool are the very young and the very old. The former is common to most OECD countries but the latter is particular to the UK.

(12) There is a growing mismatch for a number of occupations,

especially for general labourers and for some specialist skilled occupations.

(13) There is a wide variation in total unemployment and occupational mismatch on a regional basis.

(14) Keynes' theory of unemployment depends not only on the assumption of downward rigidity in money wages but also on the assumption about price expectations.

(15) The new classical theory of unemployment rests on the assumptions of rational expectations and markets that clear in the absence of distortions.

(16) Search theory is one explanation for the growing level of voluntary unemployment.

With such a diversity of observations it would be remarkable that a simple solution, such as raising the level of aggregate demand, would deal with all these aspects. The list highlights the point that unemployment must be approached *by means of a policy package*. Furthermore, this policy package must contain policies which are largely microeconomic rather than macroeconomic.

Of course, this presupposes that a government considers that it should in fact do something. Removing constraints, and no more, *is* a policy. It is a policy consistent with the new classical economics because it deals with market efficiency. But its success rests on whether the assumption of market-clearing in the absence of distortions will in fact take place. It is not possible to conceive of *all* distortions being removed, since this would mean no government taxes. Also, its success rests on the belief that most of the UK unemployment is voluntary.

Rather than state monetarist solutions versus Keynesian solutions, I will present here a package. Each element in the package will tackle one or more of the points made in the list at the beginning of this section. This, it seems to me, is a sensible approach given our ignorance of the labour market. A scheme such as the Youth Opportunities Programme (YOP) cannot, by design, deal with the growing long-period unemployment of the over-50s.

Policy Package

(The list in this package is in no specific order.)

(1) Government investment in high technology.

(2) Government guaranteeing demand for products of new technology for up to two years.

(3) Training schemes in high technology industry.

(4) Shorter working week. (?)

(5) Youth opportunity schemes.

(6) Greater employment of the young and over-50s in welfare services.

(7) Over-50s used in training schemes for youths (i.e., link the two groups in some positive way).

(8) Mechanism for processing job applications so as to avoid unnecessary escalation of entry requirements.

(9) More positive regional incentives (to prevent polarisation).

(10) If greater location of labour is required, subsidise relocation.

(11) Create consumer demand for 'information'.

(12) A more positive attitude towards 'unfair' competition from abroad.

(13) An avoidance of using the exchange rate to bring about domestic adjustment.

(14) A clear idea by the government of what constitutes adjustment and what does not, in order to concentrate their effort on the fundamental problems.

(15) Easing of trade union practices.

(16) Cooperation rather than conflict with the trade unions.

(17) A thorough investigation into wage differentials; clear and open statement on comparability.

(18) A change in male/female attitudes.

(19) A means of keeping the long-term unemployed 'functioning' members of society so that apathy, etc. does not set in.

Questions

1. Why did the Conservative Party decide to abandon the objective laid out in the 1944 White Paper on Employment? Could it be argued that they have not abandoned it, but have merely redefined the period of concern?

2. Comment on the view that 'full employment is not a gift that governments can bestow: it should neither be promised nor provided.'

3. 'Since we cannot observe or measure voluntary and involuntary unemployment, these concepts are of no use to economists.' Discuss.

4. If the government re-introduced conscription would this solve youth unemployment?

5. Critically assess the benefits or otherwise of the Youth Opportunities Programme.

6. Will a shorter working week reduce the level of unemployment in the UK?

7. Analyse the concept of 'demand-deficient' unemployment. In the absence of statistics, why would the Labour Party tend to argue that this is the major element in our present unemployment, while the Conservatives would not? What statistics would help in coming to some view of the extent of demand deficiency in the present unemployment?

8. Critically assess the concept of the 'natural rate of unemployment'. Is this rate a function of the level of inflation?

9. What would you say have been the main changes in UK unemployment in the post-war period?

10. Account for the fact that unemployment *and* vacancies can exist at the same time. Is there any relationship between unemployment and vacancies?

11. In what way has the changing role of women led to increased male unemployment?

12. Analyse as fully as you can the trend in long-term unemployment presented in Table 2.1.

13. Look up regional unemployment figures in *Economic Trends* and the *Monthly Digest of Statistics.* Do these data substantiate the claim that a polarisation is occurring between North and South in the UK?

14. Would you agree that the introduction of price expectations in macroeconomic models has led to major insights into present UK inflation and unemployment?

15. Give a possible explanation of how the demand for labour can depend on the exchange rate. What significance has this for the aggregate supply curve?

16. Are there any employment policies which can deal with both youth unemployment and unemployment of the over-50s?

17. Indicate how search theories explain some of the features in Table 2.1. Do such theories support:
   (a) A reduction in unemployment benefits?
   (b) A reduction in trade union power?
   (c) An increase in job centres?
   (d) Youth opportunities programmes?

18. Critically assess the contribution of rational expectations to the explanation of unemployment and to its possible cure.

19. If the unemployment of the over-50s is particular to the UK, does this suggest that some major structural changes are taking place?

20. Will the 'information revolution' worsen or reduce present UK unemployment?

21. Can the unemployment of the inter-war period be usefully compared with the unemployment of the early 1980s? What features are:
   (a) Similar?
   (b) Different?

22. According to the income-leisure trade-off of microeconomics, work is treated as a 'bad' (undesirable); only leisure is 'desirable'. Then why should governments try to achieve full employment?

23. Discuss the contention that unemployment arises because of imperfections in the labour market and, therefore, that any reduction of these imperfections will raise employment.

24. Can full employment be equated with clearing in the labour market?

25. 'Unemployment benefits, far from increasing the search duration, actually match particular employees with the appropriate jobs and are therefore beneficial to society.' Discuss.

Notes

1. For an elementary introduction to this comparison see Donaldson (1980) , who presents this as a major theme of his book.
2. See, for example, Gordon (1981), Dornbusch and Fischer (1981), Parkin and Bade (1982), and Levacic and Rebmann (1982).

3. This is because for a profit-maximising firm that operates in a perfectly competitive product and factor market, the demand for labour satisfies the condition:

$$w = W/P = MMP_{L}$$

where MPP_{L} is the marginal physical product of labour. With a given technology and given capital stock, MPP_{L} is a function only of labour. Hence, the demand for labour is:

$$w = W/P = f(L)$$

a form we shall use in chapter 11. This curve can be interpreted as giving the demand price of labour for a given quantity of labour employed. (The supply curve, $w = g(L)$, will give the supply price of labour for a given quantity of labour employed.)

4. For an introduction to the new classical view see Maddock and Carter (1982), Gordon (1981), Kantor (1979), Begg (1982), T. J. Sargent (1973), Parkin and Bade (1982), Colander and Guthrie (1980-81) and Tobin (1980).
5. See, for example, Stigler (1962), Akerlof (1979), Lucus and Prescott (1974) and Solow (1980).

CHAPTER 3

What are the costs of inflation?

Much has been written about inflation, especially about what causes it. But a look through standard macroeconomic textbooks will indicate that little is said about its costs. This is surprising. At the present time most governments have made a reduction in the rate of inflation a central objective of their economic policy – and the British government could be said to be determined to bring it down 'at all costs'. This unanimous objective of governments would suggest that inflation is truly a problem bearing obvious detrimental consequences. Why, then, is so little said about these consequences in standard textbooks? If an economist states that inflation is a problem and that we must cure it, discussion then abounds on what causes inflation, because this gives insights into how to cure it. But *is* it a major problem? Does it deserve to become the overriding objective of government policy? Or have we all been brainwashed into believing that inflation is undesirable because the government says so? To answer these questions we must establish the costs of inflation in some detail.

There are basically two ways of doing this:

(1) Considering the direct effects of inflation on various sectors of the economy

(2) Considering the opportunity cost of reducing inflation.

We shall consider both of these in this chapter. The direct effects are relatively easy to consider, but the opportunity cost of reducing inflation is not so obvious. To establish that inflation has detrimental effects does not imply that it should be reduced. It may be that reducing inflation has even greater costs, although possibly not direct ones. In other words, the cure may be worse than the disease!

Why worry about inflation? If wages are rising at the same level as prices, then real wages remain constant. If money income is rising as fast as prices, then real income remains constant. Such a simplistic statement, however, involves a number of assumptions; none of which is true. These include:

(1) All inflation is anticipated.

(2) All income comes from wages and all income is spent on consumption goods.

(3) All inflation is distributed evenly across goods and services so that all sectors are equally affected and all people are equally affected.

(4) There are no distortions, e.g., taxation.

(5) All wage contracts are uniform across sectors and are negotiated to come into force at the same time and for the same duration.

(6) All debt contracts are the same.

First, therefore, we shall consider the costs of anticipated inflation. For instance, does it matter whether inflation is 2% or 10%, so long as the rate is fully anticipated? In section 3.2 we take up the issue of unanticipated inflation. As we shall note, anticipated inflation can be incorporated into contracts but unanticipated inflation cannot. In section 3.3 we consider how inflation affects firms' decisions. Although more microeconomic in its emphasis, effects must be felt at the microeconomic level. In the final sections we turn to the opportunity cost of reducing inflation.

Before discussing these costs in greater detail, it is important to be clear about whether we are concerned with the *level* of inflation or with its *rate of increase* – the acceleration (or deceleration) in the inflation rate. (The analogy with a car is useful here. The speed of a car is the distance travelled over a given time interval; its acceleration is the change in the speed over a time interval.) The costs attached to bringing inflation down to a certain level, or simply to a lower level, are not necessarily the same as the costs attached to bringing the rate down quickly. (One may agree on reducing one's speed from 50 mph to 30 mph, but not necessarily on the manner in which this is done – the time interval over which it is accomplished.)

3.1 The Costs of Anticipated Inflation

Does it matter whether the rate of inflation is 2% or 10%, so long as it is fully anticipated? A fully anticipated inflation rate means that there is no discrepancy between the actual rate of inflation, $\hat{P}$, and the expected rate of $\hat{P}^e$., i.e., $\hat{P} = \hat{P}^e$. In this instance all lending and borrowing can take account of the inflation rate in the contracts agreed. The same applies for wage claims. Does this mean, then, that there is no implication of the actual level of inflation? The answer is, 'No!'

To see why the answer is no, it is important to distinguish between a variety of interest rates. In order not to lose track of the argument we shall list here all the interest rates which are relevant in the discussion (and one reason why inflation is such a difficult topic):

(1) The *nominal* (or *market*) rate of interest, r.

(2) The *real rate of interest,* defined as the nominal rate of interest less the rate of inflation. Since we have two alternative inflation rates, the actual and the expected, so we have two real rates of interest:

(a) the *actual real rate of interest:*

$$r^{a} = r - \hat{P}$$

(b) the *expected real rate of interest:*

$$r^{e} = r - \hat{P}^{e}.$$

(3) The *natural rate of interest,* r_n. This rate is a concept introduced by Wicksell and denotes the real rate of interest at which there is no excess demand in the market for goods and services.[1]

When inflation is fully anticipated, then the actual rate of inflation is equal to the expected rate of inflation; this in turn means that the actual real rate of interest is equal to the expected real rate of interest.

We can see the result of a higher rate of inflation that is fully anticipated in terms of Figure 3.1. We assume that initially there is no inflation, so $\hat{P} = \hat{P}^{e}=0$. In this case the actual rate of interest, the expected real rate of interest and the nominal interest rate are all equal. Let us take it that this is 5%, which we shall also take to be the natural rate of interest. Now suppose for some reason that everyone expects the rate of inflation to go up to 5% and that these expectations are fulfilled. What is the result?

The initial position is point A, where $r = r^{a} = r^{e} = r_n = 5\%$ and $\hat{P} = \hat{P}^{e} = 0$. This *IS* curve, it must be noted, is based on the real rate of interest, but in Figure 3.1 it is drawn with *nominal* interest rate on the vertical axis. Thus, with a fully anticipated inflation of 5%, the nominal interest rate is the original real rate of 5% plus the rate of inflation of 5%, equalling 10%. Thus IS^1 denotes a curve consistent with an anticipated inflation of 5%. The economy moves to point *B*, which we shall assume gives rise to a nominal interest rate of 7.5%. But this is not the final equilibrium.

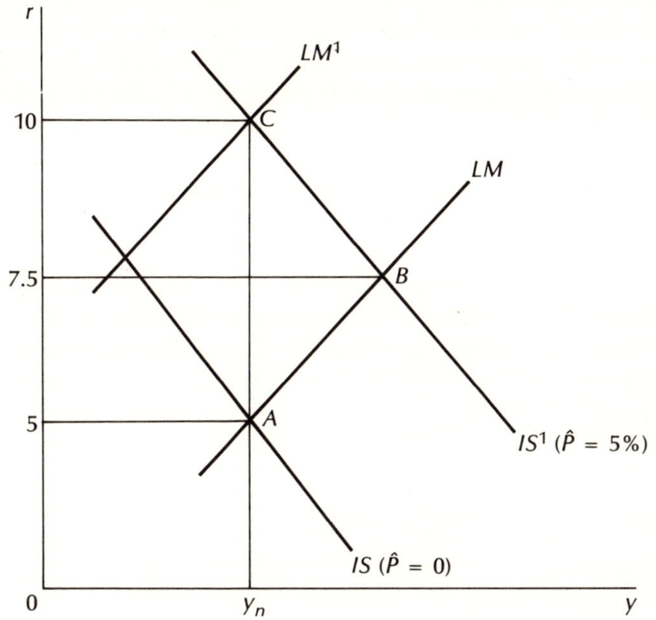

Figure 3.1 Inflationary expectations

The rise in the actual inflation rate from zero to 5% means a fall in real money balances, *M/P*. This results in a shift in the *LM* schedule to the left. But by how much? It is here that the real natural rate of interest enters the analysis. With a nominal interest rate of 7.5%, the real interest rate (actual and expected) is 2.5%, which is lower than the natural rate of interest which stands at 5%. People will move out of money and into other things. The situation will settle down when the *LM* curve shifts to LM^1, giving a nominal interest rate of 10%, because at this nominal interest rate the natural rate of interest is equal to the actual (and expected) real interest rate. This is denoted by position *C* in the figure.

We see, therefore, that the result of a higher rate of inflation which is fully anticipated is to raise the nominal rate of interest by the increase in the inflation rate. In other words, the economy will settle down in the long run at a position where the nominal rate of interest is equal to the real rate of interest plus the rate of inflation (where the real rate of interest is equal to the natural rate of interest and actual inflation is equal to expected inflation).

The fact that nominal interest rates tend to rise with the rate of inflation, even when fully anticipated, has important consequences for an open economy – especially one with a high interest elasticity of net capital flows, such as the UK. Suppose we begin with two economies with the same nominal interest rates and zero inflation. Now suppose that both economies experience inflation which is fully anticipated – but different. Then nominal interest rates will also be different. Generally speaking, the greater the inflation differential, the greater the nominal interest rate differential. Let us assume, by way of example, that the UK is inflating at a greater rate than the USA, and that these inflation rates are fully anticipated. The result will be a net inflow of capital into the UK. This will lead to adjustments either in the foreign exchange market, where exchange rates are floating, and/or in the domestic economy, especially where the exchange rate is fixed. Furthermore, it is almost certain to raise the money supply in the UK, which may aggravate the situation even further. With open economies, long-run equilibrium cannot be established until their inflation rates are equalised.

Some costs associated with anticipated inflation are associated not so much with the level of inflation *per se*, but rather with the method, or success, of the index-linking (escalation) procedure that may be adopted (Flemming, 1976). If inflation is to be fully anticipated then contracts would have to have escalation clauses built into them. To the extent that these were inappropriate or deficient, certain costs would be involved. In addition, it would mean that compensation would be required to holders of notes and coins and other non-interest-bearing assets. Since this is most unlikely, a higher inflation rate which results in a higher nominal interest rate would mean a move out of currency and into interest-bearing assets. Since less currency would then be held for transactions purposes, the result would be more frequent visits to the bank and other financial institutions to withdraw currency as and when needed. Such a cost is considered to be small when inflation is at a 'reasonable' level but more significant when hyperinflation is reached.

Even when inflation is fully anticipated it must be remembered that inflation denotes a *persistent* increase in the price level. Individual prices do not rise by the same extent. The inflation rate is determined by a basket of goods and services (or as a GDP deflator). Relative prices are still changing even though the inflation rate may be constant. This involves changing consumption patterns, which may be small but still involve some cost.

Another cost arises from tax distortions where the escalation may not be complete, or lags behind the rise in inflation. Notice here that this should not occur where inflation is constant but is more likely to occur where inflation is accelerating – even when fully anticipated. If tax allowances and tax brackets are not adjusted with the rate of inflation, then as money incomes rise people will move into higher tax brackets, even when their real income may be constant.

Although these do not account for all the costs of anticipated inflation, they do indicate the most significant ones. But these costs do not seem to be too great, and certainly not so great as to warrant the importance that governments seem to have attached to the reduction of inflation. This would suggest that the concern lies with other costs, most likely those of unanticipated inflation.

3.2 The Costs of Unanticipated Inflation

If inflation is unanticipated, the actual rate of inflation, $\hat{P}$, is different from the expected rate of inflation, $\hat{P}^e$; i.e., $\hat{P} = \hat{P}^e$. This immediately implies that the actual real rate of interest and the expected real rate of interest are also different. Suppose that the actual rate of inflation exceeds the expected rate of inflation, $\hat{P} > \hat{P}^e$; this implies that the actual real rate of interest is less than the expected real rate of interest. For the saver the return on his savings is less than he expected, while the borrower pays back less than he expected. The following illustration indicates the unanticipated loss and gain respectively. In this illustration we suppose individual 1 saves £x while individual 2 borrows £x. At the end of the period the situation is:

Individual 1 (Saver)

Actual saving $= (1 + r^a)x$

Expected saving $= (1 + r^e)x$

Unanticipated loss $= (1 + r^a)x - (1 + r^e)x$

$= (r^a - r^e)x$

$= (\hat{P}^e - \hat{P})x < 0$

Individual 2 (Borrower)

Unanticipated gain $= (\hat{P} - \hat{P}^e)x > 0$

If individual 1 and 2 happened to be the same person, then the net position is one of zero unanticipated gains and losses. An individual (or company) will experience a net gain from actual inflation exceeding expected inflation only if he (or it) is a net borrower. In practice, this conclusion would have to be amended to take account of the fact that different securities would be involved, each with different interest rates; that the gains and losses would depend on the original distribution of savings/debt; and that lending rates are not the same as borrowing rates.

The most significant net borrower in the country is the government!

A positive inflation rate, whether anticipated or not, leads to an increase in the money supply in the case of a government that wishes to retain a constant debt in real terms and does not wish to finance this debt from taxation. Suppose the debt is £1000m. With an inflation rate of 10%, in the next period the government debt must be £1100m in nominal terms to retain a real value of £1000m. If the additional £100m is not to come from taxation, then the money supply must increase by this amount. The time path is shown in Table 3.1, where it can be seen that with a constant inflation rate the nominal money supply must constantly increase by an increasing amount. This increase in the money supply can itself fuel further inflation.

Table 3.1 Inflation and money supply growth

Period	0	1	2	3
Net debt	1000	1100	1210	1331
Change in M_s	0	100	210	331

If we concentrate purely on unanticipated inflation, it would appear that the main effect of this is a redistribution of wealth from creditors to debtors. This is both true for individuals and true when we consider sectors of the economy. This in turn can mean a redistribution of income. Inflation, therefore, is embedded in the issue of class and questions of wealth distribution. Some have argued that, since actual inflation exceeds expected inflation with unanticipated inflation, then price rises exceed wage rises. The result of this, so the argument goes, is that profits rise. This is difficult to test. In the UK nominal profits (and real profits) have been falling. But the obvious question is why? To be consistent it would have to be demonstrated that profits would in fact have fallen more than they have done and that the reason they have not is because of unanticipated inflation. This raises the typical counterfactual question so common in economics. Such counterfactual questions are extremely difficult to quantify satisfactorily.

Before leaving this topic it must be remembered that the arguments also apply for a reduction in the rate of inflation. In this case creditors gain at the expense of debtors. Given our complex credit system, it is highly likely that this will be symmetrical; i.e., a move from 5% inflation to 10% inflation will alter the distribution of wealth; but it is unlikely that a move from 10% inflation to 5% inflation will establish the original distribution of wealth. This does raise the question of whether, in order to return to the original distribution of wealth, the rate of inflation would have to be reduced substantially below its former level. It is impossible to come to any conclusion on this given our present knowledge of the workings of the economy.

3.3 The Costs of Inflation to Firms

It has sometimes been said that a little inflation is a good thing. By 'little' is usually meant about 2% per annum. But why is 2% a 'good' thing but higher rates, especially those which have been experienced in the 1970s, a 'bad' thing? The argument, not generally substantiated with any formal analysis, is that during a period of gently rising prices there is greater business confidence and a more willingness to invest. In addition, during the upswing of the business cycle marginal costs tend to rise relative to average costs, so shifting the distribution of income away from wages and interest to profits. But even those who may argue such a case would not argue it for an inflation of, say, 10% per annum. The order of magnitude is quite different.

In sorting out some of the costs of higher inflation on firms it is useful to ask whether we are concerned with:

(1) The *level* of inflation, anticipated or not?

(2) *Variations* in inflation around a trend?

(3) The *acceleration* in the inflation rate?

We are, in fact, concerned with all three. It is useful, however, to have set these out because the costs associated with each are not the same. By not distinguishing them there is a tendency to associate all the costs with the level, rather than with either the variations around a trend or the acceleration in the rate of inflation. Let us assume for a moment that all costs are associated with (2) and (3). If this is so, then the government cannot argue that its desire to reduce the level of inflation is because it will be good for industry. If the costs are very much associated with (1) and (3) then the government can claim that reducing inflation is (possibly) a 'good' thing. But it would not support a policy of a quick reduction in the inflation rate. The issues are therefore relevant to whether we are interested in a rise in the rate of inflation or a fall in the rate of inflation, the latter of which is engineered by the government.

A high level of inflation makes long-term investments uncertain. It raises labour and raw material costs. If, however, such inflation is anticipated, then investment should not be adversely affected, even in the long run. Rising costs of production also should not be a problem if the inflation is fully anticipated. All wage contracts will incorporate the correct adjustment for inflation, as will other contracts. All decision-making can incorporate adjustment for price rises. Again we come to the practical point that, where inflation is anticipated, the costs of inflation surround the difficulties of incorporating indexation appropriately into all the manifold cost, production, and investment decisions that must be undertaken. The debate over inflation accounting is a good example of this. Where inflation is unanticipated, however, there is uncertainty, and many decisions can be affected by such uncertainty. This will especially be true of long-run investment decisions.

When inflation is accelerating the costs are associated more with frequent changes in prices and costs of production. Wage contracts will need to be settled more frequently and this may lead to greater militancy if there is disagreement over the appropriate adjustment. This will especially be so when the inflation rate is not only accelerating but is also at a high level. The rapid rise in prices may not be able to be matched by tax changes and other government controls, so leading to an even greater divergence between actual and expected inflation. Again, the actual level of inflation is relevant here. When the level of inflation is high the government is more likely to impose controls of one kind or another. These will inevitably create distortions and so decisions will be different from what they otherwise would have been.

The conclusion we come to from these brief comments is that in the case of firms the major difficulties of inflation surround the high level (whether anticipated or not) and the acceleration in the rate of inflation.

3.4 Conceptual Difficulties in Measuring the Opportunity Cost of Reduced Inflation

At the time of writing unemployment has reached over 3 million. Is this the cost of the policy to reduce inflation? Is it really the case that the government will reduce inflation 'at all costs'? How do we measure the cost of reducing inflation? Is the cure worse than the disease? If the cost is worth bearing, should it be borne quickly or gradually?

These are difficult questions to answer, but some answers are called for. The reason they are difficult to answer is because they involve the counterfactual question: 'What would the economy have been like if the present policy had not been pursued?' When such a question is posed it is usual to assume that the economy will move along a path determined by the policies at the moment the policy under question was implemented, or about to be implemented – in other words, assuming nothing else is undertaken.

To highlight this approach, suppose we calculated that, if the government had pursued no deflationary policy and had left the economy to move along a path determined by circumstances from the moment it took office, then the unemployment would be 2 million. With an actual unemployment of, say, 3 million, the cost of the policy could be measured in terms of 1 million unemployed. Alternatively, it could be measured in terms of the lost output that could have been achieved had this additional 1 million people been working. Although this argument is appealing, however, it is misleading. It is misleading because we have not specified any time period. If the present policy is successful, then the economy will settle down at the natural rate of unemployment. Let us take this to be 1 million (purely for illustrative purposes). In order to consider a quick policy as compared with a more gradualist one, let us specify the policy-on as Policy-on 1 for a *quick* solution, and as Policy-on 2 for a *gradualist* policy. We shall refer to the economy following its path without such a policy in terms of Policy-off.

Table 3.2 Alternative unemployment costs to reduce inflation

Period	0	1	2	3	4	5	6
Policy-off	2	2.5	2	2.3	1.8	2.5	1
Policy-on 1	2	3	3.5	2	1	1	1
Policy-on 2	2	2.5	3	3	2.8	2.6	1

By way of illustration, suppose the unemployment figures under these different configurations are those given in Table 3.2. The table reveals that by period 6 all alternatives reach the natural level of unemployment. Would this suggest that all three policies are equal in terms of their cost? Clearly not. But how do we compare the three alternatives? One possibility is simply to accumulate the unemployment figures over the seven periods. If this is done then the 'Policy-on 1' option comes out best, with a sum of 13.5. If, however, we measure the cost in terms of the sum of the squared deviations from the natural rate,[2] then the 'Policy-off' option comes out best. These figures are given in Table 3.3. They are purely illustrative, and the aim is simply to show that the ranking of alternative policies depends on how you go about measuring 'failure' (or 'success').

Table 3.3 Alternative measures of 'success'

	Sum	Squared deviations
Policy-off	14.1	8.83
Policy-on 1	13.5	12.25
Policy-on 2	16.9	17.05

One of the methods of measuring 'success' was in terms of the sum of the squared deviations from the natural rate of unemployment. Even if we do not know the natural rate of unemployment we can replace this with the desired level of unemployment, denoted U^*. Ignoring time periods for the moment, this would suggest a measure:

$$W = (U - U^*)^2$$

But this ignores the fact that inflation itself may not be at its desired level. It is possible for U to equal U^* at zero inflation or 10% inflation. Let $\hat{P}^*$ denote the desired rate of inflation. Then an alternative measure is:

$$W = (\hat{P} - \hat{P}^*)^2 + (U - U^*)^2$$

We require one final adjustment. As it stands, both unemployment and inflation are given equal weight. This may be the case, but it is unlikely to be generally true. To take account of differing weights we can write the measure in the form:

$$W = a(\hat{P} - \hat{P}^*)^2 + \mathrm{b}(U - U^*)^2 \qquad 0 \leqslant a, b \leqslant 1$$

This result is not so much measuring the costs as measuring the objective of the government; it gives an explicit expression to the meaning we attach to the term 'success'.

If the government intends to reduce inflation to its desired level 'at all costs', then this implies that a = 1 and b = 0. If the government argues that, in the long run, its policies will achieve a low inflation and unemployment at its natural level, then 'success' is when $U = U_n$ and $\hat{P}^*$ is achieved. Of course, if $\hat{P}^*$ is not announced then it is difficult to know when 'success' is or is not being achieved. If the policy itself alters the value of U_n (assuming it is known in the first place!), then this too will make it difficult to assess 'success.'[3]

Even if we accept this as a means of measuring policy, as it stands it does not define the time period over which it is to apply. Our numerical illustration in Tables 3.2 and 3.3 highlighted the importance of this. Do we wish to minimise the squared deviations of the terminal period only, or do we wish to minimise the sum of the squared deviations – thus taking into account all periods? In either case we need to agree on the terminal period; or, in the second case, on the period we consider appropriate. Economic theory cannot supply this information. From a practical point of view it depends on whether concern is about the short, the medium or the long run. But how long is the long run? Monetarists, who are the economists who generally advocate policies which are long-run, very rarely specify this period. It may be true that in the long run the desired inflation rate can be achieved, but what if this takes 50 years? If unemployment does not come into the government's reckoning (i.e., if $b = 0$) then the path of unemployment over this period is irrelevant. If unemployment does come into the reckoning, then the path of unemployment over this 50-year period is relevant in assessing the 'success' of the policy. We shall take up this point in chapter 7.

3.5 The Costs of Alternative Strategies

It is Mrs Thatcher's policy to reduce the rate of inflation by reducing the money supply. Because of the government constraint, discussed more fully in chapter 8, this implies a reduction in the Public Sector Borrowing Requirement (PSBR). The reduction in the money supply, in so far as it leads to a rise in nominal interest rates, and the reduction in the PSBR both lead to a fall in income. One question we must address ourselves to is whether this reduction in nominal income comes about because of a fall in prices or a fall in output. Nominal income, Y, is equal to Py, where P is the general price level and y is real income. Consequently a change in nominal income is the sum of a change in the price level (inflation) and the change in real income (output); i.e.,

$$\hat{Y} = \hat{P} + \hat{y}$$

To see the alternative strategies we shall use the less familiar demand pressure and short-run Phillips curve analysis.[4] In the past the issue was considered solely in terms of the Phillips curve. But this supply-side argument was clearly deficient, simply because it concentrated only on the supply side of the problem. The analyses of inflation in terms of demand pull were also incomplete, simply because they concentrated on the demand side of the problem. A more complete account of inflation is achieved by combining demand and supply considerations. This is done in Figure 3.2. Notice that the horizontal axis represents real income and the vertical axis represents inflation (and not the price level). The SPC curve (an abbreviation for the short-run Phillips curve) is derived from a set of three relationships:

(1) A wage equation

(2) A price equation (which itself involves the wage equation under (1))

(3) A reaction function relating unemployment to real income (Okun's law).

By means of these three equations a positive relationship between inflation and real income can be established, and is shown in Figure 3.2 by the upward-sloping SPC curve. Although straightforward to draw, it is not a simple relationship and involves a great many assumptions – most particularly about the formation of price and income expectations, the response of wages to unemployment, the (empirical?) relationship between unemployment and real income, and finally assumptions about price and wage setting. Although these assumptions are numerous, they will affect the position and slope of the SPC curve but are not likely to affect the basic point that it is upward-sloping.

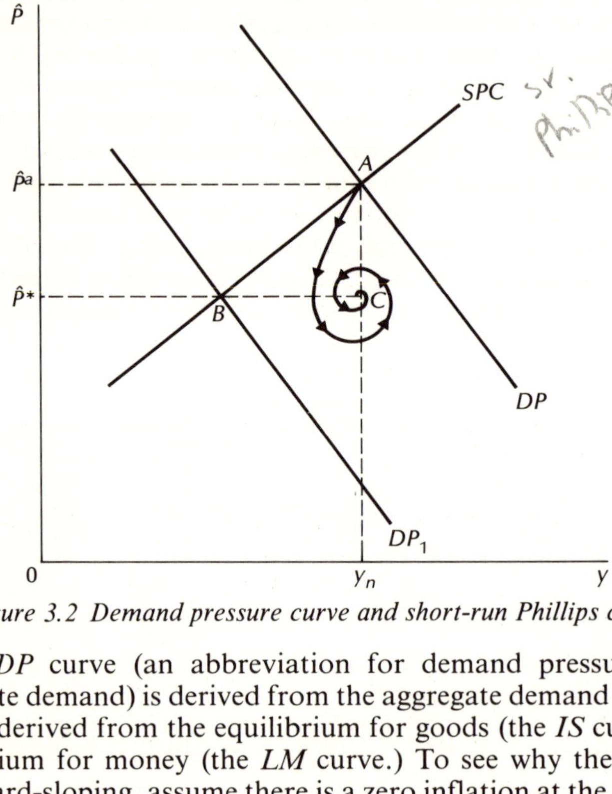

Figure 3.2 Demand pressure curve and short-run Phillips curve

The *DP* curve (an abbreviation for demand pressure, and not aggregate demand) is derived from the aggregate demand curve, which itself is derived from the equilibrium for goods (the *IS* curve) and the equilibrium for money (the *LM* curve.) To see why the *DP* curve is downward-sloping, assume there is a zero inflation at the current price level. Prices now rise, giving a positive rate of inflation. The rise in the price level lowers real money balances and shifts the *LM* curve to the left, which results in a lower equilibrium level of real income. The *DP* curve not only involves monetary policy but also incorporates fiscal policy. Although once again the assumptions are many, they do not detract from the result that the *DP* curve is downward-sloping.

In Figure 3.2 y_n denotes the natural level of real income, which is associated with the natural rate of unemployment, U_n. In the long run, so monetarists argue, the Phillips curve is vertical at the natural rate of unemployment – or, as in the figure, at the natural level of real income.

We are assuming, for simplicity, that the economy is at point *A*, with inflation at $\hat{P}^a$ and real income at its natural level. The aim of the government is to achieve a target inflation rate of $\hat{P}^*$ and unemployment at its natural level, U_n, i.e., a level of real income of y_n.

A reduction in the growth of the money supply along with a reduction in the PSBR will shift the *DP* curve to the left. One drastic policy is to reduce the money supply growth and the PSBR necessary to achieve the target inflation rate $\hat{P}^*$. In this case the economy will move to point *B*, at least in the short run (and probably in the medium term also). The mechanism that moves the economy to point *B* is subsumed in the *SPC* curve itself. It involves reducing output, thereby reducing aggregate demand, which brings pressure on firms to lower prices, and creates unemployment, and so brings pressure on the labour market to accept lower wage increases. A deep recession is caused in order to 'cure' inflation. Once *B* is achieved the aim is then to move to point *C*, maintaining inflation at the desired level and raising real income to its natural level. Although the move from *A* to *B* may be achieved, it is not clear that a move from *B* to *C* can be achieved without once again fuelling the inflation. It is clear from the diagram that a rise in demand pressure alone cannot be used to move the economy from *B* to *C*, since this will raise the rate of inflation. What is required is a combined shift in both the *DP* curve and and the *SPC* curve. It is difficult to see, however, how to bring about a downward shift in the *SPC* curve. On the other hand, it does direct attention to the supply side of the economy – 'supply-side economics', as it is now becoming known. The point about this strategy is that, although the move from *A* to *B* will be accomplished, the recession may be so great that the move from *B* to *C* may take very long or may not even come about! For this reason a number of economists have advocated a more gradualist strategy.

Under a gradualist strategy the aim would be to reduce the money supply growth by a certain percentage each year. At the same time other supply-side measures can be implemented. The type of path envisaged is that shown by the curve linking *A* to *C*. Under this strategy, in comparison with the first, real income (and hence unemployment) does not fall by as much. On the other hand, it could take longer to reach point *C*. Unemployment, although less in each period, may, when taken over the whole adjustment period, be at a greater cost. We saw this in the previous section.

Figure 3.2 directs our attention to another difficulty which must be appreciated. A policy of reducing the money supply growth and the PSBR will reduce both the rate of inflation and the level of real income. Thought of another way, such a strategy reduces both the rate of inflation and the rate of growth of real income (output), *y*. This can be

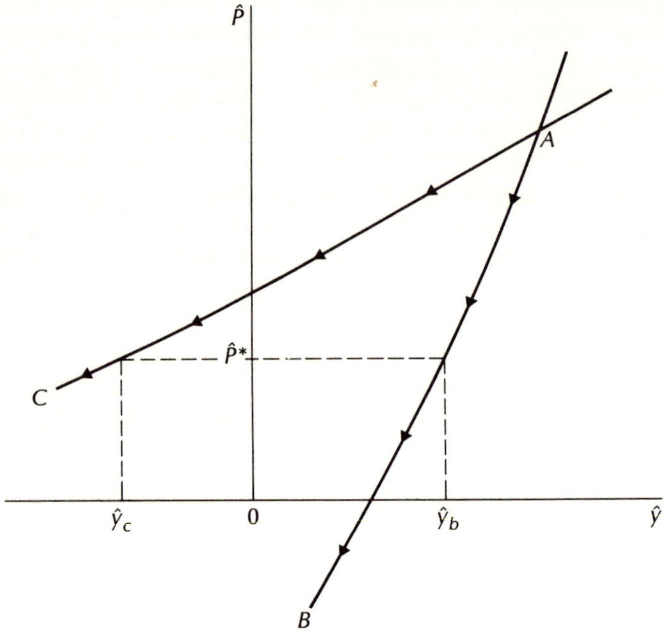

Figure 3.3 Consequences of reducing the growth of the money supply

appreciated by considering the money market equilibrium condition $M_s = kPy$. With k constant, then in terms of changes we have:

$$\hat{M}_s = \hat{P} + \hat{y}$$

A reduction in the growth of the money supply, a fall in M_s, must be matched by a fall in either $\hat{P}$ and/or in $\hat{y}$.

Assume that the economy is at point *A*, as shown in Figure 3.3. The question now arises as to which path the economy will move along; path *AB* or path *AC?* Path *AB* assumes that, with a reduction in the money supply growth and the PSBR, most of the adjustment falls on prices rather than output. But as Hicks (1976) argues, this may not in fact be the path that the economy follows: it may follow the path *AC*. In this case output responds relatively more than prices. The economy is brought to a collapse before inflation reaches the level desired by the government. Here the cure is worse than the disease.

We simply have too little information on adjustments to know which of these two paths the economy is likely to follow. Monetarists would tend to argue that path *AB* is closer to the truth, while neo-Keynesians would probably argue that it is path *AC*. No government is a fully fledged monetarist or Keynesian. The present UK government, however, is following a very monetarist strategy. If it wishes to reduce inflation 'at all costs' then it will not be concerned whether it is path *AB* or path *AC* that is followed. Political credibility, however, will demand that the path is monitored. It must gauge the extent to which output falls and unemployment rises, and then adjust its policies accordingly. This uncertainty about which is the most likely path for the economy to follow also gives some support for the gradualist strategy, which would allow for some 'fine tuning' along the way.

Questions

1. What is meant by 'inflation'? Would you agree with the contention that it is everywhere and at all times a monetary phenomenon?
2. In what way is anticipated inflation a problem?
3. Suppose you agree on a reduction in the rate of inflation. Compare and contrast a gradual reduction with a quick solution.
4. What is the 'natural rate of interest'? Has this rate any bearing on the issue of inflation?
5. Why do nominal interest rates and inflation tend to follow similar paths? Is this significant for open economies?
6. Comment on the proposition that 'since for the economy as a whole net borrowing equals net saving, then unanticipated inflation is of no consequence.'
7. Has inflation anything to do with the decline in UK profits?
8. Do you consider that the asymmetry arising from a move from 5% inflation to 10% inflation, in comparison with a move from 10% inflation to 5% inflation, is important?
9. Which is more significant to a firm:
   (a) The level of inflation?
   (b) The variation of inflation around a trend?
   (c) The acceleration in the inflation rate?
   Would you say the same for the government?
10. How would you measure the cost of reducing inflation?
11. Analyse in detail the formula:

$$W = a(\hat{P} - \hat{P}^*)^2 + b(U - U^*)^2$$

How would you adapt this to deal with a comparison between two periods consisting, say, of T_1 periods and T_2 periods respectively?

12. In the text we considered $\hat{Y} = \hat{P} + \hat{y}$. Taking data either from the *Blue Book* or *Economic Trends,* obtain this breakdown. Can you conclude anything from your results? (Plot $\hat{P}$ against $\hat{y}$ and compare this with Figure 3.3.)

13. Does increased inflation lead to increased trade union militancy? Would you consider this a cost or a benefit?

Notes

1. Although the natural rate of unemployment has attracted much attention, this is not true of the natural rate of interest – yet this latter concept is an important feature of the adjustment mechanism. 'By the "money rate" is meant the rate of interest actually prevailing in the loan market. By the "natural rate" is meant not a rate quoted upon a market, but the investors' rate of return on capital in the commodity market. Equilibrium can exist only when these two rates are equal ' (Patinkin, 1966, pp. 367-8).
2. See Theil (1966, ch.2).
3. The policy would affect U_n if U_n where related to the rate of inflation, i.e., if the long-run Phillips curve were not vertical.
4. This is now the more modern treatment outlined in Dornbusch and Fischer (1981) and Gordon (1981). The treatment here follows the former.

CHAPTER 4

How effective are price and wage controls?

In the previous chapter we considered the costs that are involved in inflation. Governments throughout history have usually taken it upon themselves to curb inflationary pressure. Even if we simply take the post-war period (1945 to the present), various UK governments have repeatedly turned to price and wage controls of various kinds as a means of dealing with inflation.

Does this suggest that a price and wage policy, then, is the 'right' policy? Does it mean that such a policy has been so successful that no other policy has even been considered? The answer to both of these questions is a resounding, 'No'. Then why is it that governments, both in Europe and the United States, have repeatedly turned to such a policy? We try to answer this question in the first section of this chapter before we even attempt to look at particular price and wage controls that have been implemented in the UK. It is an important question. Many macroeconomics textbooks argue against a price and income policy. If the reader is convinced by such arguments then the issue still remains as to why governments persist in their use! In section 4.2 we consider in brief some aspects of those price and wage controls which have operated in the UK since 1945. This will allow us to highlight some important features of price and wage controls and so lay the foundation on which to discuss them in more detail. In section 4.3 we turn to the issue of exactly what a price and wage control policy is trying to do. We cannot possibly consider whether such a policy is successful if we do not know exactly what its aim is. There is little point in stating that a policy does not do x when it was never designed to do x in the first place. Once we have the aims clearly specified, we then turn in section 4.4 to the difficulties there are in carrying out these aims. In the final section then we can turn to the issue which opens this chapter: 'How effective are price and wage controls?'

4.1 Why Do Governments Turn to Price and Wage Controls?

In discussing this topic it is important to state quite explicitly that a stated objective of governments has been to curb excessive price inflation. Given that we are presently in what is considered by many to be a high-inflation period (see column (3) of Table 7.1), we can simply state the objective as a reduction in the rate of inflation. Even this is vague. Will a reduction of 2% be acceptable, or must the rate finally be below 10%, or even below 5%? Will a reduction be acceptable 'at all costs'? Is there any time limit set on achieving the aim? All these questions, and more, indicate that the very vagueness of the final objective leads to difficulties in assessing any policy which may be used to achieve the stated aim.

In attempting to find a policy solution to inflation, it very much depends on what you believe to be the cause of inflation in the first place. A variety of reasons have been advanced for the cause of inflation and no one reason is necessary and sufficient – unless you insist on purely (very?) long-run analysis. The reason for this is not hard to grasp. In the short and medium term all shocks to the system are temporary. Only one shock can persist through the short and medium term and into the long run – namely, the printing of more money by the government. Given this, it is not surprising that such people as Milton Friedman have argued that inflation is a monetary phenomenon and that everywhere and at all time a persistent inflation is caused by excessive growth in the money supply. But what about the short and medium term, where we take the medium term to be about five years? Detailed analysis of inflation indicates that in the short and medium term other factors contribute to inflationary pressure, besides excessive growth in the money supply. Simply controlling the money supply may not, then, be a policy solution. In fact, five policy solutions have been advocated over the years:

(1) Reduction in the growth of the money supply

(2) Price and wage policy

(3) Indexation

(4) Restriction of aggregate demand through fiscal policy

(5) Exchange rate policy.

It is not my intention here to discuss all these alternative policies; what I wish to highlight is why governments have persistently turned to a price and wage policy rather than one of the others.

The answer reduces down to policy degrees of freedom. Post-war policy in the UK can be thought of in terms of targets and instruments, a framework introduced by Tinbergen (1956). First let us approach the problem purely abstractly. Suppose a government has three objectives and only two instruments at its disposal. It is necessary that the two instruments be independent of one another (a difficulty when it comes to monetary and fiscal policy, as we shall outline in chapter 8). Let us assume that the two instruments are independent of one another. How are the three objectives achieved? Tinbergen demonstrated that you require as many independent instruments as you have objectives. In this illustration this condition is violated. What can be said is that any two of the three targets can be chosen and the instruments used to achieve these, but the third target must be abandoned. There is no policy degree of freedom. Now consider the opposite situation. Suppose there are only two objectives and the government has three independent instruments with which to achieve them. In this case the government can take any two instruments to achieve the two targets. It has one policy degree of freedom – one spare policy instrument.

Now let us be more specific. Following the Second World War governments had a number of objectives, but three stood out:

(1) Full employment

(2) Stable prices

(3) A balance of payments equilibrium.

Under the Bretton Woods system the exchange rate was held fixed, which meant that the exchange rate was generally ruled out as a policy instrument. Effectively the government had but two instruments: the Budget deficit (fiscal policy) and interest rates (monetary policy.) In fact, for most of the early post-war period, the governments relied almost exclusively on fiscal policy. During this period inflation was not a problem and so the only objectives the government had to contend with were full employment and the balance of payments deficit. Even so, Tinbergen's analysis did show that the two objectives could not be achieved with a *single* instrument. Either full employment could be achieved or balance of payments equilibrium, but not both. As we shall note later, this led to the typical 'stop-go' policies of the late 1950s and early 1960s.

What about the late 1960s and later? In 1967 the pound was devalued as a means of dealing with the balance of payments, leaving fiscal policy to deal with full employment. But devaluation is a one-off event. Furthermore, from the late 1960s inflation began to take off, and it became a major problem in the 1970s. What is more, it became clear that monetary and fiscal policy were not in fact independent of one another (a point we shall develop in chapter 8). Being oversimplified, in the 1970s the pound sterling was floated, so allowing the exchange rate to deal with the balance of payments and fiscal policy to deal with full employment. But what about inflation? Monetary policy could not be used to deal with inflation because this was constrained by the fiscal policy that was being implemented. (Alternatively, monetary policy could be pursued and then the fiscal policy would be constrained.) What was required was an independent policy instrument to deal with inflation. But what policy instrument was available to the government that was under its control and also independent of monetary and fiscal policy? The only instrument available was a price and wage policy. Whether effective or not, and this we shall discuss later, the point was that the government lacked an independent instrument for dealing with inflation. It had three objectives but only two independent policy instruments at its disposal.

We have avoided discussing the issue of which instruments should be paired with which targets (the *assignment problem*). Whatever the assignment, the government lacked enough instruments for its various objectives. If we consider Mrs Thatcher's policy there appears no lack of instruments. This is not so. The exchange rate is being used to deal with the balance of payments, and monetary policy is being used to deal with inflation (although as we shall show in chapter 6, money supply and the exchange rate are not independent of one another). But what about full employment? This objective has been relinquished. For the first time since the Second World War, the objective of maintaining full employment has been abandoned. Hence, Mrs Thatcher has not merely reassigned instruments and targets, she has abandoned one of the three targets we listed above: namely, full employment (at least in the short and medium term). In the long run, however, the aim is to achieve both a low inflation and employment at the natural level. This is supposed to be possible with just the one policy instrument: monetary policy. The Thatcher government is making a similar conceptual mistake as previous governments – trying to achieve too many objectives with too few instruments.

What we conclude from this analysis is that, while governments maintained the objective of full employment along with their other stated aims, they lacked an independent policy instrument to deal with inflation. The only possible one at their disposal was a price and wage policy. To avoid a price and wage policy a different assignment of instruments and targets was called for. The one chosen by the Thatcher government also meant that full employment in the short and medium term had to be abandoned. But the simultaneous achievement of low inflation and a natural rate of unemployment is unlikely to be achieved with only one policy instrument. The present government too has one instrument still to find which is independent of those it is already using – the only difference is that this instrument must deal with unemployment rather than prices and wages?

4.2 Brief History

Ever since 1948 Britain has experienced virtually every form of price and wage policy, from the complete freeze to the voluntary restraint. In the case of voluntary restraint the government seeks co-operation from the unions and employers in limiting wage settlements and price increases. Statutory control, on the other hand, invokes the law as a means of enforcing wage and price rules. In the latter case the rules must be fairly clear if the law is going to be invoked, while in the case of voluntary restraint no such precision is necessary.

The first post-war incomes policy was implemented in 1948 by Sir Stafford Cripps (the Labour chancellor) and took the form of a voluntary wage standstill. It broke down in the aftermath of the sterling devaluation of 1949 and the rise in raw material prices during the Korean war. It was abandoned when the Conservatives took office in 1951, but by 1956 pressure again led the government to contemplate an income policy. The TUC, however, was unwilling to co-operate in any voluntary restraint. As it turned out, the Conservative government resorted to taking a firm line on public sector pay claims, over which it had more direct control. In 1961 the UK economy faced another sterling crisis which resulted in a 'pay pause' on public sector pay being implemented by Selwyn Lloyd. It was hoped that this would set an example to the private sector. It met with little success, and was followed by a pay norm – the 'guiding light', which remained until the fall of the Conservative government in 1964.

The newly installed Labour government was very much in favour of a voluntary income policy. Under the direction of George Brown (who at the time headed the Department of Economic Affairs) a 'Declaration of Intent' was signed by unions and management. It involved the acceptance of a 3–3½% wage norm, the establishment of a Prices and Incomes Board (PIB), and a promise by the TUC to vet wage claims. It failed completely. In 1966, when a further sterling crisis occurred, the Labour government implemented the first statutory wage controls, which involved a six-month wage and price freeze. This was followed by a period of 'severe restraint' and later by even less severe controls. But in 1970 wages exploded as free collective bargaining once more became the means for wage settlements.

A Conservative government was elected in 1970 which was very much against such controls. It also abolished the Prices and Incomes Board. Wage settlements continued to lead to rapidly rising wages and by 1972 the government felt that it had to do something, and so implemented a statutory wage control. This was in three stages. Stage I involved a six-month freeze; stage II a limit on pay increases to £1 per week plus 4% with a limit of £250 per year per person; and finally, stage III involved a limit of pay increases to the larger sum of £2.25 a week or 7%, with a maximum of £350 a year per person. The miners refused their pay increase limit during stage III and this resulted in British industry going on a three-day week. Mr Heath, the then Prime Minister, called for an election in support of his policy, but lost.

When Labour took office in 1974 the government abandoned the statutory wage controls but retained the price controls. A squeeze on profits resulted and so the price control was eased towards the end of 1974. The main policy was referred to as the 'social contract'. Stage I was implemented in 1975, which involved a maximum flat rate increase on wages of £6 a week, with no increase for those earning more then £8,500 a year. Although voluntary in nature, the government did implement some policing. Stage II began in 1976 allowing for larger wage increases and a relaxation of the price code. Although a Stage III was originally conceived, it was never implemented. It was rejected by the unions, and in its place the government announced 'guidelines'. The situation came to a head in 1978-79 during the 'winter of discontent', which contributed to the fall of the Labour government in 1979. When the Conservatives took over under Mrs Thatcher's leadership in 1979 they abandoned the wage and price controls and chose a totally different approach to deal with inflation.[1]

Ten features arise from this brief history. The first three involve elements that any price and wage control must contain, while the remainder involve consequences of the policies themselves:

(1) The voluntary/involuntary form the policy takes, i.e., the rules under which it operates

(2) Penalties for violation of the rules, i.e., the form of policing

(3) Monitoring agency – a Prices and Incomes Board or some existing agencies

(4) The upsurge in wage claims after the controls are removed

(5) The need to get the unions' co-operation (which is necessary but not sufficient)

(6) The distortions that result

(7) The differential impact between public and private sector pay

(8) The possibility of misjudging public sympathy – by both unions and government

(9) The short-lived nature of a number of the policies

(10) The small number of years when no form of price or wage control was operating.

4.3 What Is Their Aim?

The aim of price and wage controls is to limit inflation. Easily stated, but exactly *how* does it do this – if at all? On the face of it this may appear an easy question to answer, but far from it! To appreciate the difficulty let us once again employ the demand pressure (*DP*) curve and the short-run Phillips curve (*SPC*), which we introduced in the last chapter. (It may help to re-read section 3.5 before continuing.)

There is no obvious reason why a price and wage control should affect the demand pressure curve – other than the possible increase in

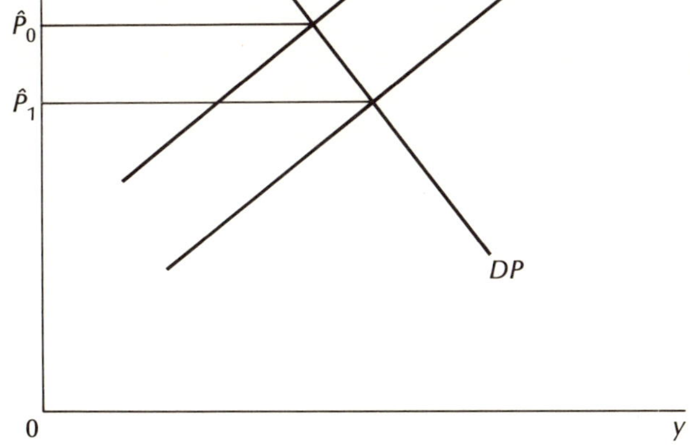

Figure 4.1 Result of price and wage controls

government finance to administer the policy, which we shall ignore. It would appear that the aim of price and wage controls is to do something to the *SPC* curve (the mirror image of the traditional Phillips curve). But there seems to be a difference of opinion on this. Gordon (1981) argues that such a policy shifts the *SPC* curve downwards. This is shown in Figure 4.1, where the new curve is labelled SPC_1. On the other hand, a recent textbook by Parkin and Bade (1982) argues that it does no such thing! The difference of opinion rests on the derivation and interpretation of the *SPC* curve.

We pointed out in the previous chapter that the SPC curve is derived from a set of three relationships:

(1) A wage equation

(2) A price equation, which itself involves (1)

(3) A reaction function relating unemployment to real income (Okun's law).

By means of these relationships we can establish a relationship between price inflation, $\hat{P}$, and the level of real income, y. It will aid the discussion greatly if we specify a particular relationship so that we can discuss some of its properties. This is taken from Dornbusch and Fischer (1981) and is of the form:

$$\hat{P} = \hat{P}^e + ah[(y/y_f) - 1]$$

In considering this equation it is important to realise the meaning of the parameters a and h. Both a and h are reaction coefficients. The coefficient a relates wage inflation to unemployment; i.e.,

$$\hat{W} = -aU \qquad 0 < a < 1$$

while the coefficient h relates unemployment to real income (this relationship is known as Okun's law); i.e.,

$$U = h[1 - (y/y_f)] \qquad h > 0$$

These two reaction functions are drawn in Figure 4.2.

We are now in a position to consider a price and wage control. First, let us abstract from price expectations by assuming $\hat{P}^e = 0$. In this case the *SPC* curve intersects the horizontal axis at $y = y_f$. One such curve is marked SPC_0 in Figure 4.3. Now consider that a wage control is implemented. It is quite possible for this control to lower the value of a.

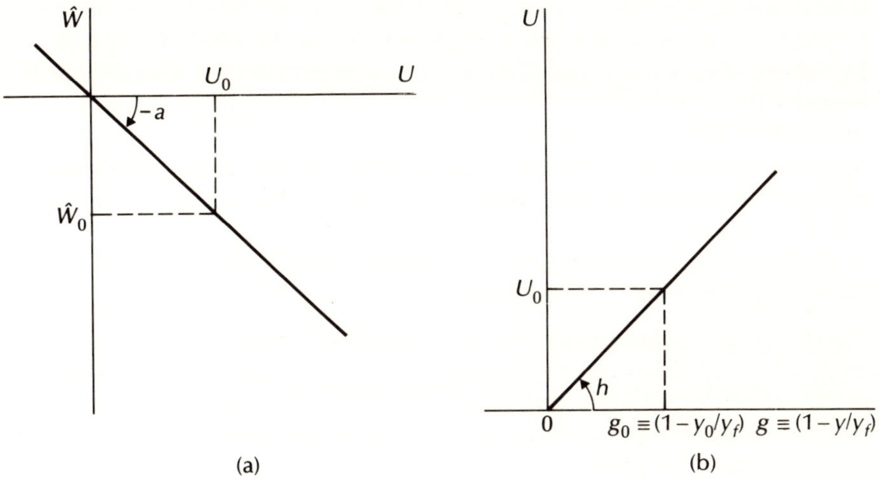

Figure 4.2 Reaction functions in constructing SPC

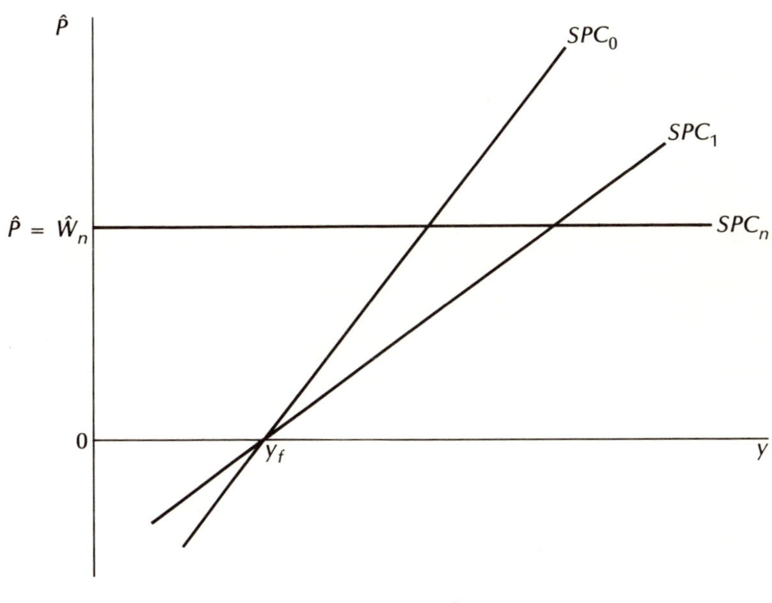

Figure 4.3 Price and wage controls and their result on the SPC curve

In other words, for any given level of unemployment the control means that wages do not rise as fast as when no such controls are in operation. Let the initial value be a_0 and the new value a_1, where $a_1 < a_0$. This will in fact pivot the *SPC* curve at the point $y = y_f$ on the horizontal axis (assuming $\hat{P}^e = 0$). This is shown in Figure 4.3 by the curve SPC_1. It is quite possible that the relationship between wage inflation and unemployment is not as simple as we have stated, nor is it likely to be proportional. Suppose, by way of illustration, that

$$\hat{W} = c - aU$$

Then c may be related to trade union bargaining strength. If wage controls can reduce c, then the *SPC* curve will shift bodily downwards and tilt simultaneously. We simply do not have enough information about the relationship between wage inflation and the rate of unemployment when account is taken of trade union power and the structure of wage bargaining.

Before we continue the argument, Figure 4.3 also shows the result of a wage norm. Suppose wage increases are not allowed to exceed $\hat{W}_n$. Then with mark-up pricing, which is what is implied in the form of the inflation equation given at the outset, price inflation equals the wage norm; i.e., $\hat{P} = \hat{W}_n$. This gives a horizontal *SPC* curve, which in Figure 4.3 is marked SPC_n.

Now let us return to the price inflation equation:

$$\hat{P} = \hat{P}^e + ah\,[(y/y_f) - 1]$$

We immediately see from this equation that there are two elements to consider when deciding on the effect of a price and wage control. First, there is the effect on price expectations. Second, there is the effect on the second term.

Parkin and Bade argue, in the case of price expectations, that a price and wage control cannot alter the value of price expectations. Their argument rests on rational expectations. If expectations are rationally formed, then $\hat{P}^e$ at its initial value is based on all the information, including the fact that controls will not work! Hence, there is no reason for the *SPC* curve to shift because the price expectations are correctly formulated in the first place. This is either circular or empty. One problem with rational expectations is the point at which the information becomes available. It may be that SPC_0 is rational and is based on information ruling at the time – which does not include the possibility of an income policy. Once an income policy is implemented then new rational expectations are formed. When this is so why should the new *SPC* curve be the same? To argue that it must be the same and that such information was known from the beginning reduces (raises?) all economic agents to omnipotent beings – omnipotent with respect to past, present and future!

Furthermore, the argument just presented rests on the belief (or assumption) that expectations are rationally formed. What if they are not? Suppose, for instance, that expectations take the form of adaptive expectations, so that:

$$\hat{P}^e = a\hat{P} + (1-a)\hat{P}_{-1} \qquad 0 < a < 1$$

In this case price expectations do depend upon the actual rate of inflation. If, as we indicated above, a wage and price control tilts the *SPC* curve, then $\hat{P}$ will fall, given a downward-sloping *DP* curve. Consequently so will $\hat{P}^e$. The argument reduces to one of the formation of price expectations.

To conclude, a wage and price control can tilt or shift the short-run Phillips curve (the *SPC* curve) downwards by altering the reaction function relating wage inflation to the level of unemployment. Since very little is known about this particular relationship it is very difficult to predict precisely what will happen to the *SPC* curve. In addition, the *SPC* curve can shift if a price and wage control alters price expectations. Whether such price expectations are altered depends largely on the assumption about how price expectations are formed: whether rationally or by some other means.

4.4 Difficulties of Implementation

There are basically three difficulties in implementing a price and wage control policy:

(1) Distortions

(2) Policing

(3) Wage explosion when controls are removed.

All controls distort the workings of the price mechanism. In the case of price controls, if they are effective then relative prices alter and so there is a shift in resources from that which would have taken place if the controls had not been imposed. And the distortions in price are not the only effect of controls. It is probable that businessmen will find alternative ways of maximising their utility – whether this be in terms of profits or some other elements. The most obvious is a change in quality. A price control is not a control over the whole commodity; it is, as its name implies, simply a control on price. A manufacturer who cannot raise the price of his chocolate bar can alter the composition of the ingredients, or he can make it smaller but sell it for the same price as the original.

Similarly, in the labour market a control on wages leads to a misallocation of labour. One difficulty encountered is the narrowing of differentials between the pay of the skilled and less skilled. Again, such controls can be circumvented by internal promotions, bonus schemes, etc. There is also a sector problem. Since public sector pay tends to be more under the control of the government, then during such controls (and certainly over long periods of time) public sector pay can lag behind private sector pay.

It is worth pointing out in this regard that one of the great failings of economics is not being able to establish a convincing theory of wage differentials. There is no 'right' wage differential. Even so, society as such has some idea of what it thinks is an 'acceptable' differential. Suppose we begin with a set of wages which society finds 'acceptable' in terms of the differentials that this entails. Now suppose that over time a series of price and wage controls has been implemented, just as described in section 4.2. Then these differentials will be destroyed. Now it is clear that the original set was probably not suitable either. But after so many controls, and given that the differentials have changed, *who decides what they should be and when they are to be brought about?* Is it the role of government to decide who gets what in relation to someone else, or should this be left simply to collective bargaining, or even to some independent Commission?

One obvious difficulty with price and wage controls is how to police them. There are literally trillions of prices and it is simply not possible to monitor every single one. One solution is to set up a Prices Board which can deal with complaints about 'unfair' price increases – depending on the public to put in the complaint. Of course, if there are too many complaints then this too is not feasible. It is possible for a company simply to ignore the price limit. What happens then? This depends upon the legal powers the government advanced when it set up the controls. The same problems arise on the wages side. If a manufacturer wishes to give a wage increase above the agreed limit will he do so? In part it will depend on why the increase is being given, but it also depends on what legal sanctions were set up when the controls were implemented. Furthermore, who is to undertake this policing of companies?

In section 4.2 we outlined a brief history of post-war controls in the UK, and it is clear from this history that on some occasions a special organisation was set up to monitor prices and wages, and at other times this was left to existing institutions. This is not a trivial point. When we consider government policy-making in terms of instruments and targets, one way to do this is to associate one of the instruments with a given institution in order to deal with one objective. This was suggested by Meade (1978) in his Noble Prize lecture. When we think of monetary policy we naturally associate this with the Bank of England, and when we consider fiscal policy we associate this with the Treasury. But when we come to inflation, what institution do we associate this with? The main point about this suggestion of Meade's is that it gives some specific institution the *responsibility* for a particular target. When it fails we know whom to blame!

The third major difficulty in implementing a price and wage control is the fact that after the control is removed it is probable that there will be a burst of wage claims – and this has certainly been the case in the UK. To what extent this is so depends in theory largely on the assumption about how expectations are formed. If expectations are rationally formed, then there should be no shift in the *SPC* curve, either down when the controls are put on, or up when the controls are removed. For rational expectations theorists to be consistent, they cannot argue for a shift in the *SPC* curve once the controls are removed. (How they do account for the observed behaviour is not at all clear.) If expectations are not formed rationally, or if, as we argued in the previous section, the *SPC* curve tilts and/or shifts down as a result of the controls, then it will tilt and/or shift upwards when the controls are removed. It is possible for the upward shift in the *SPC* curve to go beyond what it was before the policy was implemented. This is shown in Figure 4.4. The original curve is SPC_0. After the policy is implemented we suppose it shifts to SPC_1. When the policy is removed, rather than shifting back to SPC_0, it shifts to SPC_2, with a higher rate of inflation and a higher rate of unemployment than before the controls were implemented!

These difficulties are very real. They have led to such policies being only short-lived, and have even brought down governments. But it should not be presumed that just for this reason they should not be implemented. Monetarists repeatedly point out these difficulties with regard to such controls, but they give the impression that their suggested policy of monetary control involves no such difficulties. This is simply not true. All policies lead to distortions of some kind. Take Mrs Thatcher's monetary policy, which is an alternative to price and wage controls. The reduction in the growth of the money supply means a cut in the PSBR. This in turn has led to cash limits being imposed, either arbitrarily or by Cabinet decision. But do not these create distortions? The rising unemployment and bankruptcies are not obviously leading to a more efficient allocation of resources; and to the extent that efficient companies are going bankrupt, it could easily be argued that a misallocation of resources is also the case for a monetarist solution to inflation. Even when we consider policing, although much

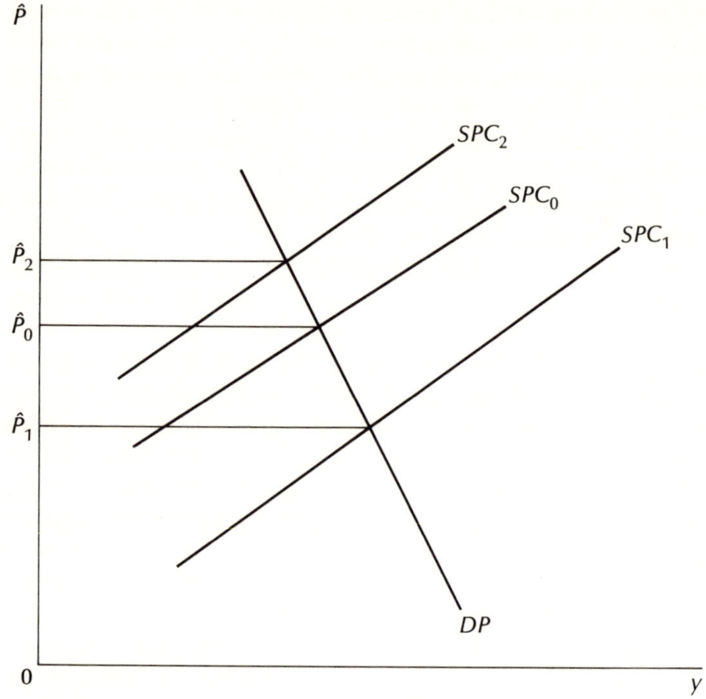

Figure 4.4 Result of removing price and wage controls

easier – since the Bank of England clearly has responsibility for the money supply – it has not exactly been successful (as we shall see in chapter 5).

The point to be made is a cautionary one. It is not sufficient for economists to point out the difficulties and deficiencies of a wage and price control; it must be demonstrated that any alternative policy's net benefits are greater than those of the price and wage control. To say simply that there are costs to a policy is only the beginning of analysis, not the end.

4.5 How Effective Are They?

We are now in a position to consider the main issue which is the title of this chapter: 'How effective are wage and price controls?' In one sense, the issue can be resolved by considering whether a wage and price control policy is effective in shifting and/or tilting the *SPC* curve and ensuring that when the controls are removed the inflation rate is less than it would have otherwise been. Put this way, there are two elements to the discussion. First, have such controls led to a downward shift in the *SPC* curve? Second, after the controls have been removed, has the inflation rate settled down at a rate less than it would have been without the controls? These are two totally different questions, but each has a bearing on the effectiveness of such controls.

Let us take the first question: have wage and price controls led to a downward shift in the *SPC* curve? In section 4.3 we discussed the features of the *SPC* curve which would lead to such a move. We concluded there that, if a price and wage control changed the value of the reaction coefficient relating wage inflation and unemployment (the coefficient a), then this would tilt and/or shift the *SPC* curve. But this relationship in practice is not so well specified. It subsumes a very complex institutional bargaining process which has built up over a long period of time. It implicitly, if not explicitly, assumes a uniform or interlinking wage bargaining process across industry. Although wage settlements are related, 'the links are not simple, clear-cut, or permanent' (Brown, 1980).

In section 4.3 we also discussed the formation of expectations. If expectations are rationally formed, there is no reason for price expectations to be altered and so no reason, on this account, for the *SPC* curve to shift. On the other hand, if expectations are not rationally formed, e.g., if they are formed in some adaptive manner, then the *SPC* curve can shift down. The formation of price expectations is a very recent development in macroeconomics (see Begg, 1982), and here we shall simply say that, depending on how expectations are formed, the *SPC* curve may or may not shift.

It is possible to approach the problem from a totally different perspective. The short-run Phillips curve was originally constructed in the $\hat{W} - U$ space; i.e., it was a relationship between *wage* inflation and unemployment. Later it was replaced by the relationship between *price* inflation and unemployment. The *SPC* curve in earlier diagrams related price inflation to real income. But by Okun's law, there is (supposed to be?) a relationship between unemployment and the gap between real income and full employment income. If there does exist a one-to-one relationship between unemployment and the real income gap, then we can equally specify the *SPC* curve as a relationship between price inflation and unemployment – what is traditionally known as the Phillips curve. This alternative specification is shown in Figure 4.5.

Thus a shift in the *SPC* is matched by a shift in the *PC* curve of Figure 4.5 and vice versa. It is now possible to investigate, by means of econometrics, what happens to this relationship when a wage and price control policy is applied. In simple terms one obtains two curves, one for the policy-off and one for the policy-on. Let Figure 4.6 represent such a situation.

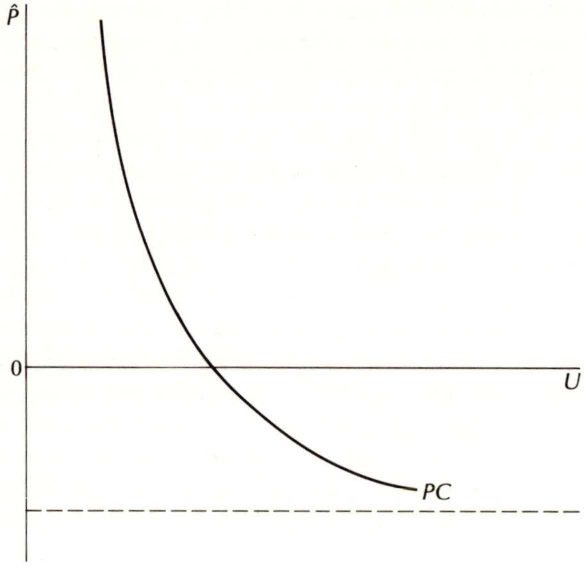

Figure 4.5 Phillips curve

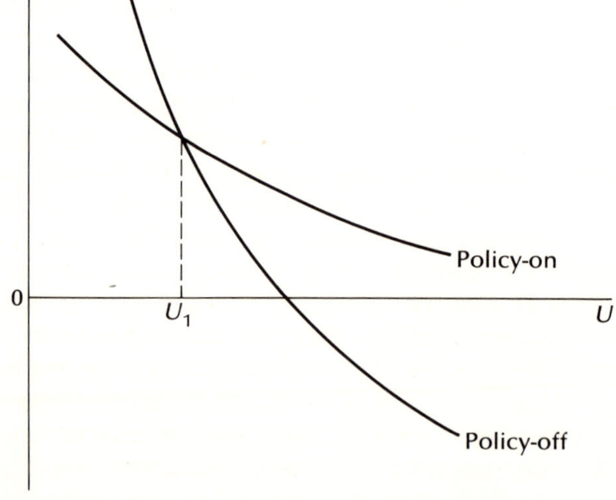

Figure 4.6 Policy impact on the Phillips curve

Now ask the question, 'Has the policy been successful?' There is no unambiguous answer to this question, since it depends on what the level of unemployment is. If the level of unemployment is greater than U_1, the answer is 'No'. If, however, the level of unemployment is below U_1 then the answer is 'Yes'.

Now let us turn to the second question: 'After the controls are removed does the inflation rate settle down at a rate less than it otherwise would have been?' To put this question in perspective, it is asking whether, when the controls are lifted, the *PC* curve with the policy-off remains the relevant curve or whether it has shifted as a consequence of the policy. This issue we dealt with in the previous section, and is highlighted in Figure 4.4. If when the controls are removed there is a rush for large wage claims, then it is possible that the *SPC* curve shifts from SPC_1 to SPC_2. Since this new curve is above the original curve, denoted SPC_0 in Figure 4.4, then the policy has made things worse. The evidence for the UK would suggest that, although the policy has had some effect while it operates, it has had no *lasting* effect on price inflation or has possibly made things worse (Batchelor *et al.*, 1980).

It should now be clear why we opened this chapter with a discussion of why governments seem to turn to wage and price controls. All the evidence seems to point to the fact that they tend to be effective while they operate but do not help in the long run – and possibly make things worse. Given such evidence, it does appear strange that they have so frequently been resorted to. The answer, as we pointed out at the beginning, arises from the fact that there does not exist any alternative independent policy instrument for dealing with inflation, if full employment is to remain as one of the objectives. True, a totally different assignment can be followed, as Mrs Thatcher is doing. But this simply shifts the problem of finding an independent policy instrument for dealing with unemployment. At some point the present government must pursue some form of employment policy. If not, it too will be forced to try some form of wage and price control – which the government is totally against.

Whether a policy of wage and price controls or an employment policy is pursued, one aspect is clear: they are microeconomic rather than macroeconomic. They both involve government intervention, but of a different kind. Although the Conservative government is against government intervention, it will at some point in time have to decide to intervene. The only question is in what manner. But one question remains for the future: *Will an employment policy be any more effective than a policy of wage and price controls?*

Questions

1. If P_t and M_t denote inflation and money supply growth at time *t*, why would you expect a poor correlation between them? Using quarterly data in *Economic Trends*, compute the following two equations:

$$P_t = a + bM_{t-6}$$

$$M_t = c + dP_{t-6}$$

   Comment on the results you obtain.

2. Is the Conservative government's strategy an abandonment of a target so as to have consistency between instruments and targets and/or a new assignment of traditional instruments and targets?

3. If it is important to have independent instruments to achieve a number of targets, can it be argued that where insufficient macroeconomic instruments are available, the government should turn to microeconomic means for achieving macroeconomic objectives?

4. Would you agree with the proposition advanced here that governments turned to a price and income policy because (assuming the objective of full employment) they had no independent policy instrument to deal with inflation?

5. Why is there a difference of opinion by economists as to whether a price and income policy shifts the *SPC* curve? Is this difference of opinion important?

6. Critically assess the two reaction functions:

   (a) $\hat{W} = -aU \qquad 0 < a < 1$

   (b) $U = h\,[1 - (y/y_f)] \qquad h > 0$

7. Discuss the proposition that the only fundamental difference between adaptive expectations and rational expectations is the *actual time path* of the economy towards its long-run equilibrium position.

8. Is it the role of government to decide on wage differentials, or should this be left simply to collective bargaining, or even to some independent Commission?

9. Under what conditions will a wage norm lead to a higher rate of

wage inflation? Are these conditions likely to hold in practice?

10. 'By replacing a price and income policy by a control of the money supply to control inflation, the government has no more than replaced a price and income policy with an employment policy.' Discuss.

Note

1. For a more detailed look at price and income policies implemented in the UK, see Dawkins (1980) and Blackaby (1978).

PART III
Monetary Policy

CHAPTER 5

Can the government control the money supply?

The present government has a deliberate policy of money supply control as a means of curbing inflation. This *intermediate* target has become a corner-stone of its policy and in this chapter we wish to consider the issue in more detail. Although we have posed one question as the heading to this chapter, it is clear that in order to answer it we must consider other related questions, such as:

(1) Does the definition of 'money supply' matter?

(2) Why does the government wish to control the money supply?

(3) Does the institutional framework have an important bearing on the issue of control?

(4) What form can control take?

(5) Does the fact that the UK is an open economy make control more or less difficult?

We shall deal with the first four of these questions in this chapter, leaving question (5) to the next. With some answers to these questions we can then turn to the issue of whether or not the government can control the money supply and how successful it is.

To give some coherence to a very elaborate debate we shall in the first section take up the issue of definition. In the next section we shall present a brief sketch of banking reforms that have taken place in the UK. This is necessary if we are to answer question (3) in the list above. In section 5.3 we consider why control is thought desirable. The fact that governments talk about an issue does not mean that it is important or even desirable. The government's emphasis on money supply control needs justifying. In section 5.4 we consider the alternative methods of control, and finally we shall return to the basic issue and see if the attempt has been, or even can be, successful.

5.1 Definition of Money Supply

In no other area of macroeconomics is the definition of a variable so important as it is in monetary economics. It must be recalled that economic variables are theoretical constructs and that if we are to test a theory we must find, or define, its operational counterpart. Normally the choice is not too difficult, but this is not the case with 'money supply'. A look at the official publications on money supply figures will readily indicate that quite a number of variables exist. To name but the most important; there are: M1, sterling M3 (denoted £M3), PSL1, PSL2, and most recently (a revised) M2. These are stock figures. There is also domestic credit expansion (DCE), favoured by the International Monetary Fund (IMF), which is a flow.

If there were little difference in practice between these various money supply figures then it would not matter too much which we chose. But this is not the case. Figure 5.1 shows the growth of M1, £M3 and PSL2.

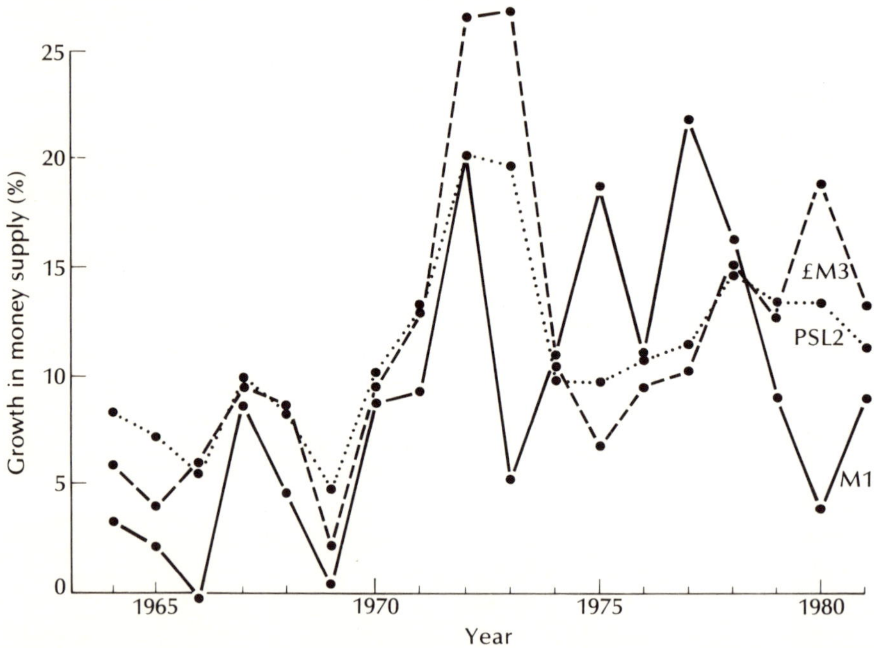

Figure 5.1 UK money supply growth rates, 1964-81

This graph indicates quite clearly that the behaviour of the various series differs. The obvious question to raise, then, is 'Which do we choose for "the" money supply?' Certainly if the intention is to control 'the' money supply then it is paramount that the one chosen (1) can be controlled, and (2) is the right one to be controlled.

It is not our intention here to become too involved in the intricacies of various definitions, but it is important to have some notion of what is included in the various definitions to see why some economists prefer one definition over another. The different variables listed above form a series of more general concepts. We begin with the narrow definition of money, M1, which is contained in the next, £M3, which in turn is contained in M3. M3 itself is contained in PSL1, which in turn is contained in PSL2. Hence, PSL2 is the broadest of the official definitions of 'money supply'. DCE is related to the *change* in £M3 (and hence to the change in M3) as we shall see later. The latest British series, the *new* M2, fits into the list between M1 and M3.

M1 consists of currency and notes in circulation outside the banks and sterling 'sight' deposits held by the UK private sector. It is the definition of 'money supply' which comes closest to the theoretical concept of money supply as a medium of exchange. It does, however, have its limitations as an indicator of the medium of exchange. First, only about four-fifths of M1 is non-interest-bearing. Second, since not all accounts which can be used for transactions purposes are included in M1, when interest rates rise there is a move out of M1 and into interest-bearing deposits which may also have a transactions element. This difficulty is to a large extent overcome with the new definition of money supply, M2. A broader definition of money supply is that of sterling M3, which includes M1 plus UK private residents' sterling deposit accounts with banks and discount houses along with the public sector's deposits with the banks. It is basically the total of sterling deposits of the domestic sector with the banking sector plus notes and coins in circulation with the public. This broader definition of money involves money (strictly sterling) not only as a medium of exchange, but also as a store of value. M1 and £M3 are by far the most common definitions used for 'the' money supply. If deposits of other currencies are also included along with £M3, then this gives M3.

One issue that has always been of concern in monetary economics is whether 'money' or 'liquidity' is the most suitable concept. This, of course, partly depends on what your main interest is in. The Bank of England has, since 1979, compiled a liquidity series, Public Sector Liquidity, which itself takes two forms: PSL1 and PSL2. The series PSL1 consists of private sector holdings of £M3 plus money market instruments (bills, deposits with local authorities and finance houses) and certificates of tax deposits. On the other hand, PSL2 consists of PSL1 plus building society and other savings deposits. Of particular interest is PSL2, since this includes for the first time building society and other savings deposits which are competing very strongly with commercial bank deposits and are very substitutable for them.

Before finishing this section a word about domestic credit expansion (DCE). In broad terms, DCE is the sum of the increase (decrease) in the money supply plus the deficit (surplus) on the balance of payments. It is a liquidity concept relevant for an open economy and for that reason is favoured by the IMF. Where loans from the IMF are sought, as Britain did in the 1976 crisis, the IMF imposes DCE targets rather than money supply targets. The reason for this will become clearer after we discuss the relationship between the money supply and the exchange rate, which we do in the next chapter.

To summarise, there is a spectrum of definitions for 'money supply' from the narrow definition, M1, to the broadest liquidity definition, PSL2. The different series do not show the same pattern over time. The present government, however, has chosen to concentrate its control largely on £M3 – more particularly, on the growth of £M3.

5.2 Reforms

British banking is based on a branch banking system, unlike the Federal Reserve system in the United States. In addition, there exist in the UK a number of non-bank financial intermediaries (NBFIs). These play a major role in the financial structure of the market, and are especially significant in the issue of control. It is useful to think of the banking structure as a pyramid, as shown in Figure 5.2 – which is certainly the case when attention centres on the supply of credit.

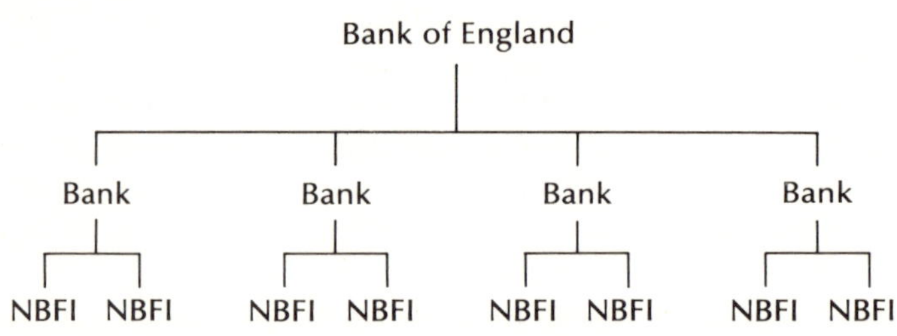

Figure 5.2 UK banking structure

The system of control between 1946 and 1971 remained virtually unchanged – it merely became more comprehensive in its influence. Initially there was a cash and liquidity ratio of 8% and 30% respectively (the latter reduced to 28% in 1963). From 1961 Bank rate (later the minimum lending rate – MLR) was continually used by the Bank as a means of influencing the financial system. This rate was the minimum rate at which the Bank of England would re-discount Treasury bills. Since clearing bank rates were linked to Bank rate, all interest rates were ultimately linked to Bank rate. The Bank of England also influenced the market in one other significant way. The Bank of England is the manager of the national debt and does this by operating in the gilt-edged market, where it influences yields of all maturities on government securities.

Throughout the period 1946-71 requests were made to the deposit banks to follow particular policies. Also, in 1960-61 a Special Deposits Scheme was introduced. In this scheme the commercial banks were requested to deposit with the Bank of England a certain amount of their reserves and these would not be included in their liquidity ratio. This was basically the only major quantitative control, the remaining being qualitative – such as letters sent from the Bank of England to the deposit banks suggesting priority and non-priority loans. Generally, however, the type of assets and the type of institutions that were involved was widened on each subsequent tightening of credit. One important result of these controls was that, as more and more became operative on the commercial banks, other non-bank financial institutions grew in importance. As a consequence the deposit banks became relatively uncompetitive. These developments led to the reforms of 1971, under the title of *Competition and Credit Control* (CCC) (see Gowland, 1978).

Competition and Credit Control fell into three main parts:

(1) Most of the distorting controls were abolished. Quantitative restrictions on bank advances were removed and the interest rate cartel was abandoned.

(2) Other controls were lightened and also were extended to other institutions. The 8% and 28% ratios were replaced by a 1½% cash reserve ratio and 12½% reserve asset ratio. These new ratios applied first to all banks and were later extended to finance houses.

(3) A commitment to competition and market forces was agreed.

There was also a switch to the broader monetary aggregate M3.

By 1973 requests concerning advances were once again made and a ceiling was placed on interest rates for retail deposits. Also a Supplementary Special Deposit was introduced which imposed a rising marginal cash reserve requirement on the growth of banks' interest-bearing liabilities from a base date, later referred to as the Corset. This led to a distortion in the market and to a less potent monetary control. By 1979 the Bank of England was extending its supervisory role over a larger number of financial institutions in an attempt to have greater influence (control?) over those institutions which were involved in 'money' as a medium of exchange. A number of later developments were directed at *prudential* control rather than monetary control; i.e., they were designed to ensure the solvency of the authorised and licensed financial institutions.

The main reforms began in 1980 and continued into 1981. These may be summarised as follows (Dow, 1982):

January 1980: The Bank of England released the special deposits which had been called from banks and larger finance houses, initially as a temporary measure. They have not so far been called, although the facility to do so has been retained.

June 1980: Supplementary Special Deposits (the 'Corset') were abolished: these had penalised excessive growth of interest-bearing deposits during three successive periods since December 1973.

October 1980: The Bank of England ceased to announce dealing rates for eligible commercial bills of over one month to maturity (which banks could hold as reserve assets).

January 1981: The Bank ceased to announce dealing rates for Treasury bills (also reserve assets). Reserve assets ratio reduced from 12½% to 10% of eligible liabilities, and temporarily to 8% from 2 March to 30 April.

August 1981: Reserve asset ratio was abolished:

- 1½% cash ratio reduced to ½% of eligible liabilities, but coverage extended from London clearing banks to all authorised banks and licensed deposit-taking institutions;
- 6% of eligible liabilities on average to be held as secure money at call, subject to a daily minimum of 4%;
- the monetary aggregate 'eligible liabilities' to be broadened by the inclusion of deposits of all authorised banks and licensed deposit-taking institutions, but with deposits between this wider range of institutions, and most secured money at call, netted out;
- the Bank to extend the range of bills in which it will deal to those issued by additional banks, particularly foreign banks (subject to various conditions);

the minimum lending rate (MLR) no longer to be announced, but to be replaced by an unpublished target range for an MLR-equivalent.

The result of the 1980 measures was to leave interest rates as the sole remaining monetary instrument for achieving monetary control. The Bank did feel, however, that this might be inadequate and so considered the possibility of monetary base control. This we shall take up later.

5.3 Why Controls?

So far we have given a largely descriptive account of banking practice and monetary control in the past and the reforms now taking place. These are essential if we are to answer the question, 'Can the government control the money supply?' But before we turn to this question it is important to ask, 'Why does the government want to control the money supply?'

Although Keynes did not underestimate the importance of money, neo-Keynesian analysis stresses the importance of fiscal policy as a means of managing the economy. As we shall see in later chapters, such a Keynesian demand management has not been altogether successful. As the previous two sections indicate, however, the various UK governments came to rely on monetary policy. In terms of the static *IS-LM* analysis it did not matter from a qualitative point of view whether the demand and/or the supply of money was interest-sensitive. In either case the *LM* curve was upward-sloping (only its position and slope would be affected by interest sensitivity). A rise (fall) in the money supply, prices constant, would shift the *LM* curve to the right (left) and so raise (lower) income and lower (raise) interest rates. But it soon became clear that this textbook analysis was either too simplistic or simply wrong.

With the rise in 'monetarism', led by Milton Friedman, a debate soon ensued. One outcome of this debate was that we came to realise how little we understood the money supply process. On the other hand, monetarists, being concerned largely with the long run, played down such an institutional consideration. To see this point consider the Cambridge quantity equation:

$$M_d = kPy$$

where M_d is the demand for money, k the reciprocal of the income velocity of circulation, P the general price level and y real income. If the money market is quick to adjust, then $M_s = M_d$ so that

$$M_s = kPy$$

In the long run k is constant and y is at the 'natural' level. Thus, any increase in the money supply will simply lead, in the long run, to an equal increase in the price level; i.e., in the long run $\hat{P} = \hat{M}_s$. If follows immediately from this analysis that inflation is a monetary phenomenon and that to control inflation it is necessary to control the money supply!

It is this link between inflation and the money supply which is the basis for arguing control of the money supply, since by so doing inflation can be brought under control. The primary objective, at least of the present Conservative government, is to bring down the rate of inflation. The present analysis would suggest, therefore, that this can be achieved by controlling the money supply. It is now that we see how important it is to keep in mind that the money supply is not a primary objective but an *intermediate* target. Why is this so? If inflation is not so closely linked with money supply growth, then controlling the money supply will not necessarily bring down the rate of inflation. If the primary objective is to bring down the rate of inflation, and supposing this poor association is true, then control must be directed elsewhere and not to the money supply. It is, of course, possible to argue for monetary control for prudential reasons, but this is not what is being argued by the present government.

We can conclude from this analysis, therefore, that the crux of the argument for monetary control is the strong link between money supply growth and inflation. But there is a difficulty here. The theory, as just outlined, is a long-run theory. Monetary control tends to be concerned with the short and medium term. Even if the link between money supply growth and inflation is strong in the long run, this does not mean that it is strong in the short or medium term. Furthermore, in the long run it is true that institutional considerations play a less significant role. But, again, this cannot be said of the short and medium term. Even if we accept for the moment the need to control the money supply, the mechanics of such control will almost certainly differ for different time periods. Suppose, for example, we consider money base control. It may be that this type of control is suitable for the long run but is totally ineffective for short and medium-term control. We shall deal with this in the next section.

To summarise, the reason for controlling the money supply (other than for prudential reasons) is because of the belief in a strong link between money supply growth and increased inflation. Given that the primary objective is to reduce inflation, then according to monetarists this can be achieved by controlling the growth in the money supply. Whether this is true depends on what is the cause (or causes) of inflation, and whether interest is in the long run or the short and medium term.

5.4 Alternative Methods of Controlling the Money Supply

Analysis of the money supply process has historically begun with the money multiplier. Since this is the basis of money base control it is worth beginning with this analysis. We start with the definition that the money supply, M_s, is a multiple expansion of the money base; B; i.e.,

$$M_s \equiv mB$$

where m is the multiplier coefficient. This definitional equation directs our attention immediately to three things:

(1) The definition of M_s

(2) What constitutes the money base, B?

(3) What does the multiplier, m, depend upon?

Let us first consider the multiplier, m.

The money supply stock is the sum of the total currency in circulation, C, and total bank deposits, D; i.e., $M_s \equiv C + D$. The money base, B, is the sum of the total currency in circulation, C, and total bank reserves, R; i.e., $B \equiv C + R$. From the definitional equation we have that $m \equiv M_s/B$. Substituting, we get:

$$\frac{M_s}{B} \equiv \frac{1 + C/D}{R/D + C/D} \equiv \frac{1 + c}{r + c}$$

or

$$M_s \equiv \left(\frac{1 + c}{r + c}\right) B$$

where c is the currency/deposit ratio and r the reserve/deposit ratio.

Ten observations are worth making with regard to this final equation.

(1) The money base, B, is often referred to as 'high-powered money'.

(2) If m is reasonably stable, then the money supply is dependent on the money base. Also we immediately have:

$$\hat{M}_s \equiv \hat{m} + \hat{B}$$

a form we shall find useful when discussing control.

(3) Although this formulation deals only with the banking sector, it can be, and has been, elaborated to incorporate non-bank financial intermediaries (e.g., Coghlan, 1980, ch.9 and Dow and Earl, 1982, ch.5).

(4) Until assumptions are made about c and r, the final equation is still *definitional* – just as the first is.

(5) It is crucial for analysis that the money base, B, is autonomous and independent of r and c.

(6) The multiplier, m, is larger the smaller the currency/deposit ratio, c, and the smaller the reserve/deposit ratio, r.

(7) Since $0 < r < 1$, then $(1 + c) > (r + c)$ so that $m > 1$.

(8) Dow and Earl (1982) derive multipliers for M1, M2 and M3 with respect to the money base, B (which they label M_o).

(9) Such multipliers suppose that M_s rises to its maximum allowed under the formulae, regardless of the level of the demand for money.

(10) Such multipliers are determined institutionally and are independent of the rate of interest.

By means of this analysis we can now discuss money base control. Base money, or high-powered money, consists of those assets which are used by the banking system to settle inter-bank debts and by the public as non-deposit money. It is possible to define the base either from the assets or the liabilities side of the accounts. When defined in terms of assets, money base is considered from the point of view of its 'sources'; if it is defined in terms of liabilities, the money base is considered from the point of view of what 'uses' it can be put to. The 'uses' are notes and coins held by the public and the banking system (excluding the Bank of England) plus bankers' deposits at the Bank of England (excluding special deposits) plus public sector deposits at the Bank. In terms of 'sources' the base shows three main ways the monetary authorities can create or destroy base money:

(1) Lend to the private sector

(2) Lend to the public sector

(3) Lend to the foreign sector.

From $M_s \equiv mB$ it follows that the money base forms the foundation of money supply creation. Regardless of the demand for money, if the cash within the banking system is limited then so is the expansion of credit. Furthermore, the money base is what is 'produced' by the monetary authorities and by no one else; i.e., the authorities have a monopoly for the supply of base money. Since, therefore, the money base is under the complete control of the authorities, control is much easier and more predictable than other forms of control. Since B is under the government's control, then to predict M_s all that must be predicted are the banks' excess cash reserves (for computing r) and the public's demand for cash (for computing c). Alternatively, to achieve a target rate of growth of money supply, $\hat{M}_s^*$, the government would forecast $\hat{m}$ and set $\hat{B}$ equal to $\hat{M}_s^* - \hat{m}$. Money base control, therefore requires a 'good' forecast of m. One rather elaborate procedure has been adopted in the past by the Swiss National Bank (Schiltknecht, 1981).

One other reason has been advanced for monetary base control. Money base is considered by some to be an accurate measure of the monetary implications of the combined actions of the government and central bank. Basically, when the combined action of the authorities is expansionary the money base will rise, and when it is contractionary the base will fall. Furthermore, the money base depends only on the actions of the authorities and not on the private sector. In this sense, the money base is a superior control method to the minimum lending rate or any other indicator – *if attention is focused on the authorities alone*. Even for an open economy, the actions of the monetary authorities in the foreign exchange market are also reflected in the money base.

One important implication of money base control, especially in comparison with interest rate control, is that the adjustment mechanism falls on the banks by means of profit-maximising responses rather than interest rates being chosen by the authorities. Thus, money base control imposes a *quantitative* restriction upon banks' intermediation – it is a control over the 'input' into the banking system.

Before setting down some of the difficulties with money base control let us first consider the system of interest rate control operated by the Bank of England up to 1980. This begins with a demand for money function, which we shall simply take to be $M_d = M(r,y)$ – the exact form is not essential to the argument. In the short run, which is the major period of concern to the Bank, income is taken as constant, say at $y = y_o$. The Bank then estimates the demand for money function and how it shifts.

The situation is shown in Figure 5.3. $M_d = M(r, y_o)$ is the estimated equation for given income, $y = y_o$. Suppose the government wishes the money supply to be M_o: then it moves the interest rate to r_o. The problem is that the Bank of England does not know the demand for money for a given level of income and interest rate; i.e., the demand for money schedule is not likely to be stable. Suppose the demand for money schedule can shift between M^* and M^{**}. Thus, even for a given interest rate $r = r_o$, the government may still announce a *range* for money supply, viz., M_1 to M_2. The greater the variation in the demand for money schedule, the greater the variation in the money supply for any given

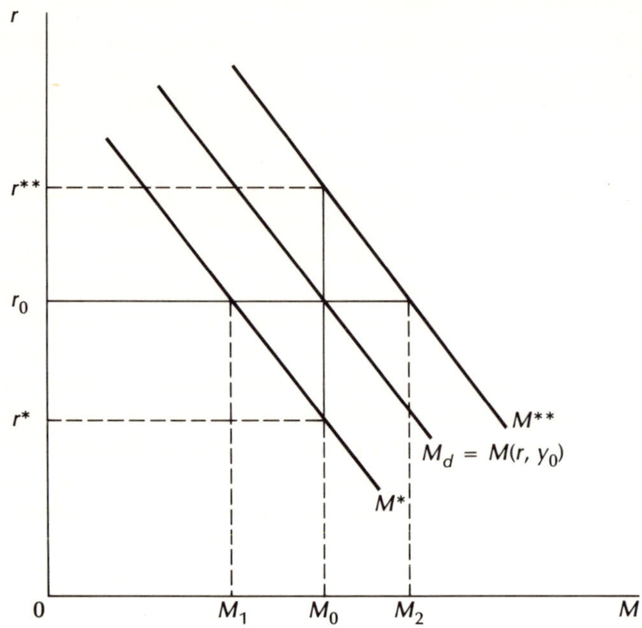

Figure 5.3 Unstable demand for money

interest rate. For this reason controlling interest rates may not lead to a control of the money supply.

This was exactly the situation in the 1970s. The demand for money schedule was unstable, and although the Bank of England attempted to control the monetary system by means of interest rate control, the growth in the money supply was not brought under control. It was at this time that the Bank began to consider the composition of the growth in sterling M3. It first broke £M3 down into its component parts, and then considered the growth in each separately, and finally amalgamated the results to see the impact on the growth of £M3. But even so, the Bank still retained control by means of the interest rate. All this did was supply information as to why the money supply targets were not being achieved.

Given the difficulties encountered by interest rate control, why has the Bank of England not taken up money base control? The reason is that money base control has difficulties of its own. Four stand out:

(1) The resultant fluctuations in interest rates

(2) The possibility of the Bank relinquishing its role as 'lender of last resort'

(3) The institutional change involved

(4) The fact that it would lead to intermediation through the Euro-sterling market.

Briefly, let us take each in turn.

1. This is the mirror image of the interest rate control discussed above, and highlighted in Figure 5.3. Suppose there is money base control; then M_s is also fixed if the relationship $M_s = mB$ holds true (now a behavioural equation). Suppose the money base is B_0 with the money supply M_0. Then, given the same variation in the demand for money schedule (from M^* to M^{**}), the interest rate will vary from r^* to r^{**}. This does not necessarily mean large fluctuations in interest rates, but it does imply frequent and small changes in them. The obvious question to ask in this regard is, 'Which is more detrimental to the economy, (1) variable money supply, or (2) variable interest rates?' Not only variation: if the trend is for increased growth we must also ask, 'Which is more detrimental to the economy, (1) a growing money supply or (2) rising interest rates?' On these two issues (variability and trend movements) the Green Paper on Monetary Control (HM Treasury, 1980) was most hazy.

2. The Bank of England would need to relinquish its role as 'lender of last resort', or at least it could not always act as lender of last resort without defeating the object of its money base control. Since loans from the Bank as 'lender of last resort' are for seven days, if this does operate in some form or other it would mean that the Bank would have to determine the money base from week to week.

3. The introduction of base control would require a change in the definition of reserve assets, which, it appears, would lead to a loss of business for discount houses. This in turn would result in mergers and a desire to diversify their businesses. Other institutions to be affected would be jobbing firms, which deal with gilt-edged stocks (see Foot *et al.*, 1979).

4. Money base control would lead to commercial banks seeking funds in the Euro-sterling market (i.e., from sterling held by non-UK residents). This would give a stimulus to the growth of the Euro-sterling market, just as regulation Q has done (imposed in the USA) to the growth of the Euro-dollar market. It need not necessarily mean, however, that the Euro-sterling market will expand, except to the extent that the authorities impose controls on the banking system.

In the light of these remarks about money base control, exactly what method of control have the authorities adopted in terms of the reforms outlined in section 5.2? They do not constitute a money base control, nor do they lead to the old method of interest rate control. Herein lies the difficulty. The Bank has gone partway to monetary base control, but only so long as interest rates do not vary too much. Although the minimum lending rate (MLR) has been abolished, the Bank has retained the right to announce a minimum rate that would apply to its lending in the market if the need arose. In other words, there is a range for interest rate variations which the Bank will allow – but this range is unknown!

The present system, as indicated by Tew (1981), can be seen in terms of Figure 5.4. Suppose the government decides on high-powered money of B_0. So long as the demand curve for money intersects this vertical supply curve between r_1 and r_2, the Bank will not step in. If, however, the demand curve shifts so that an equilibrium interest rate falls outside the band $r_1 - r_2$, then the Bank will step in and announce a minimum interest rate. In other words, at interest rates r_1 and r_2 (both unknown!) the

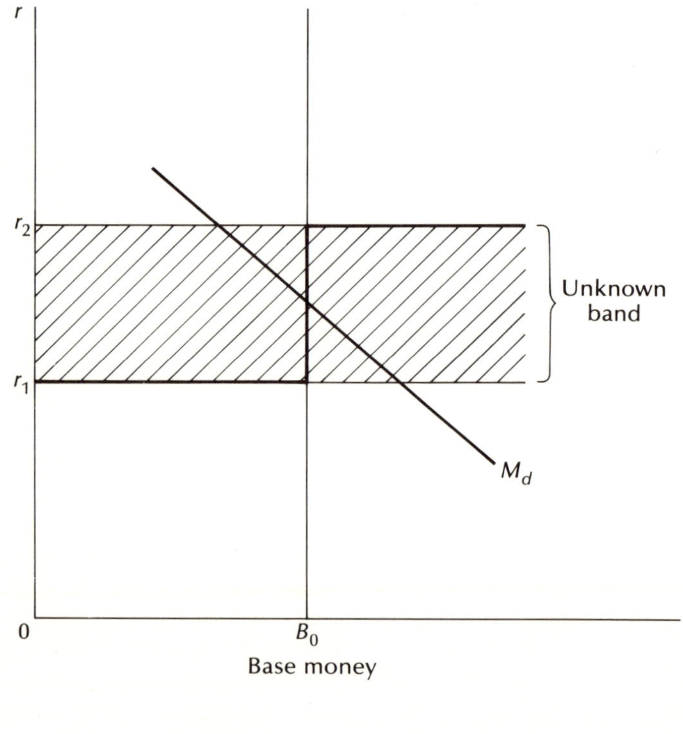

Figure 5.4 Money base control with interest rate band

supply curve of high-powered money becomes infinitely elastic.

Whether this system of control is any different to the interest rate control operating prior to 1980 depends largely on the width of the interest rate band. If, as Tew suspects, the band is not very great, then the system will operate largely as in the past. Furthermore, the fact that the band is unknown will introduce an element of uncertainty. This is surprising. The authorities, in line with the rational expectations argument, seem to believe that, if there is a smooth growth of money supply from quarter to quarter, this will establish confidence in government policies and expectations will be favourably influenced. Given that they believe this, will an unknown band for interest rate variations, and hence an unknown variation in the growth of money supply, favourably influence market expectations? Surely not!

Questions

1. Why is there so much concern over the appropriate definition of money? Has this concern anything to do with the three functions of money?
2. Is there any difference between 'money' and 'liquidity'? Which series of money stock published in the UK do you consider comes closest to the former (the latter)?
3. Why were the reforms of 1980-81 considered desirable after having implemented major changes under Competition and Credit Control only 10 years earlier?
4. If $M_d/P = f(y, r)$ then explain why, in the long run, the rate of inflation equals the growth in the money supply only where income is at its natural level *and* the rate of interest is at its natural level. What significance has the natural rate of interest in establishing this result?
5. Distinguish between interest rate control, quantitative control and prudential control which the Bank of England can exercise over banks and non-bank financial institutions.
6. 'Interest rate control versus money base control is simply a question of controlling the price or the quantity.' Do you agree?
7. Criticise the four reasons given in the text for the Bank of England not taking up money base control.
8. Would you support the Bank's decision to abandon MLR and not to announce the limits for interest rate movements?

9. Distinguish between an intermediate target and a final target. Why is the growth of the money supply an intermediate target? Is it possible to fail to achieve an intermediate target but yet achieve a final target?

10. 'All you have to do is control the money stock and inflation will disappear.' Why, then, has Britain's inflation not disappeared?

11. Rational expectations theorists argue that wage demands (and hence costs and prices) would rapidly slow down if people believed that the government really was controlling the money supply. How does this fit in with the wage bargaining process?

12. Goodhart's 'law' states that any statistical regularity will tend to collapse once pressure is placed on it for control purposes. What implications has this for money base control? Does it give support for the Bank's view not to announce the range for interest rate movements?

13. 'The reduction in UK inflation in late 1982 and 1983 was not the result of money supply control but because of recession, high sterling and low world commodity prices. Money control should therefore be abandoned.' Discuss.

14. Monetarism has proved to be 'merely an extreme form of the old Keynesian stop, whereby a restrictive demand management policy attempts to control both the main elements in cost-push inflation, and does so in the messiest and costliest way' (*Guardian,* 10 March 1983). Discuss.

CHAPTER 6

Money target or exchange rate target?

When the Conservatives took office in 1979 they made a policy decision to control the money supply as a means of achieving a reduced rate of inflation. Some of the difficulties encountered we have already dealt with in chapter 5. Put simply, however, the government aims to reduce the growth in the money supply by reducing the PSBR. Thus a reduced PSBR is a means of achieving the *intermediate target* attached to the growth in the money supply. It must not be forgotten that the target for money supply growth is not a final objective – or a *primary target*. The primary target is a low and stable rate of inflation.

There has at the same time been little concern about the exchange rate. Sterling was floated in June 1972; and prior to 1976 there was an objective to keep the dollar/pound rate at a competitive level. In June 1977 this 'target' was changed to the effective rate for sterling, but this was abandoned almost immediately (October 1977). Since then a policy of smoothing has been implemented. But does the government have to worry about the exchange rate? One of the major reasons for floating is to isolate the domestic economy from external influences. But this textbook theory is far from true in reality. There is a rather complex link between exchange rates, the money supply and the price level; and it is this that we are concerned with in this chapter.

It could be asked whether concern about these links is important. It must be recalled that in the UK monetary targets are a fairly new phenomenon in government policy-making. As we pointed out in chapter 5, the British government has found it difficult to achieve its stated target. This has also been true in other countries – so much so, that Austria, Belgium and Sweden abandoned their monetary target in favour of an exchange rate target; while Switzerland and West Germany encountered considerable pressure on their exchange rates (to appreciate). The basic point is that the government has only one policy degree of freedom: it can set a target for the money supply growth or the exchange rate or some combination of the two. Whichever it chooses, the PSBR must then be chosen consistent with it. The essential question, then, is: 'Which target, if any, should be the object of government policy?'

In order to answer this question we set the scene in section 6.1, which shows the links between all the variables. These are largely definitional and so do not give much insight into the impact of changes in the economy. We therefore discuss in section 6.2 the causations involved and the transmission mechanisms. We can then turn more directly to the issue. In section 6.3 we find that the answer depends on shocks to the economy and where they originate.

Before we begin, one analytical point is worth mentioning. Ever since Tinbergen's classic work (1956), policy models have been discussed in terms of instruments and targets.[1] In these models the 'targets' referred to final objectives or primary targets. The present interest in controlling the money supply has led to a problem of terminology, but this can be dealt with by referring to such 'targets' as 'intermediate targets'. The literature has developed in terms of considering the number of instruments and targets and the rules for assigning instruments to targets. In the following analysis a different policy framework emerges. Rather than link instruments to primary targets, *instruments are linked to disturbances.* Although simple to state, this view has profound implications for policy-making and directs attention very much to the form and source of disturbances that an economy is prone to. This different emphasis should be kept in mind throughout.

6.1 Definitional Relationships

We begin with the definition that the money stock, M, equals the stock of domestic credit, D, plus the stock of foreign exchange reserves, R; i.e.,

$$M \equiv D + R \tag{1}$$

Or in terms of flows:

$$dM \equiv dD + dR \tag{2}$$

Suppose we identify dR with 'official financing' – namely the currency transactions which need to be accommodated by the authorities after all private current and capital transactions have been taken into account.[2] To crystallise this, let $X - M$ denote the balance on current account, where X and M denote the value of exports and imports of goods and services respectively. Further, let K denote net capital inflows so that the balance on current and capital account is given by:

$$B \equiv (X - M) + K \tag{3}$$

This looks at the balance of payments accounts from 'above the line'. The 'official financing' then is the negative value of this balance (ignoring errors and omissions). Thus:

$$B \equiv (X - M) + K \equiv -dR \tag{4}$$

Thus, the accounts sum to zero, $B + dR \equiv 0$, as they must. We can now consider (2) in the form:

$$dM \equiv dD - B \tag{5}$$

Although the monetarist approach to the balance of payments concentrates on (2), this can be misleading, and how misleading is shown by considering (5). Monetarists assume that domestic credit is exogenous and largely determined by the authorities. If this were true then dD and dR would be totally independent of one another. However, the more credit that is available, the more consumers can spend on imports and the greater the change in reserves has to be. It is simply not the case that the change in domestic credit and the change in reserves are independent of one another. Furthermore, as we pointed out in chapter 5, the change in domestic credit is not exogenous and this also leads to interdependence between the terms.

To see the problem in perspective, consider a UK exporter who is paid in dollars. The exporter could convert all dollars into sterling. Alternatively, he could open a dollar account at a UK bank. But now suppose the exporter's bank on-lends the dollars to a second bank which then converts part of these dollars into sterling. The effect on the sterling component of the money supply, therefore, depends ultimately on how much overseas credit is converted into sterling.

A more detailed breakdown is required. This is involved, and various interdependencies are discussed in Coghlan (1980), Goodhart (1975), Artis and Lewis (1981) and Cobham (1981). Here we shall simply state that:

$$\begin{aligned} \text{DCE} &= \text{PSBR} - \text{gilt sales} + \text{increase in bank lending} \\ \Delta\text{£M3} &= \text{DCE} + \text{net external flows} \\ &\qquad - \text{increase in non-deposit liabilities} \\ \text{M3} &= \text{£M3} + \text{deposits in other currencies} \end{aligned}$$

where DCE denotes domestic credit expansion, PSBR denotes the public sector borrowing requirement and £M3 denotes the sterling components of M3. It is worth noting that, if we ignore the increase in non-deposit liabilities, then:

$$\Delta \text{£M3} = \text{DCE} + \text{net external flows} \qquad (6)$$

which is the working equivalent of equation (2). The point to be made, however, is that the terms are not independent – most especially components of DCE and net external flows. We cannot say that a rise in net external flows of £*x* million leads to an increase in the money supply of £*x* million because it can be offset by movements in the opposite direction of components in DCE. What we have shown is that Δ£M3, the PSBR, DCE and net external flows are definitionally linked.

We have one more complication. The rate of interest can be altered by changing the money supply. But this may also lead to a change in the exchange rate, which in turn will lead to a change in net external flows. In addition, the change in interest rates could lead to a change in the PSBR (because of, say, interest repayment). All components of equation (6) are accordingly changing and interacting. The same is true if we begin with a movement of the exchange rate.

What can we conclude? We can conclude that Δ£M3, PSBR, DCE and the exchange rate are all closely linked and there is no one-to-one relationship between any of them. To highlight this latter point, the relationship between Δ£M3 and the PSBR and between Δ£M3 and the change in the effective exchange rate, Δ*E,* for the period 1970-1981 (annual data) are:

$$\Delta\, \pounds M3 = \underset{(1.71)}{2404.01} + \underset{(2.32)}{0.4033}\, PSBR \qquad R^2 = 0.35$$

$$\Delta\, \pounds M3 = \underset{(6.81)}{5836.95} + \underset{(1.76)}{218.36}\, \Delta\, E \qquad R^2 = 0.24$$

The first equation is only just significant while the coefficient of Δ*E* in the second equation is not (*t*-values are in brackets). Also note that the coefficient of the PSBR is not unity; and although it has the correct sign, it is significantly different from unity.[3] The conclusion to draw from these results, and the comments above, is that no simple linear relationship exists between the stated variables and so any control of any one will not have simple predictable effects on the remainder.

6.2 Causation and the Transmission Mechanism

Definitional equations can never give us insight into the causation that lies behind economic variables and precisely how changes in one variable get transmitted through the economy. These aspects more than any other are clouded in confusion. Why is this? Causation and the transmission mechanism specify more precisely how an economist views the economic system. The model employed, whether explicit or implicit and whether verbal or mathematical, embodies the methodology of the analyst. The early debate between monetarists and Keynesians was confined in large part to the elasticities of various schedules which led to different quantitative predictions. This is, however, a very mechanical view of the difference. This approach relegates the methodological differences to obscurity. When causation and the transmission mechanisms are discussed, however, it is here that the methodological differences show themselves. Furthermore, it must be appreciated that such questions involve dynamic considerations – the path of variables over time – and it is in the dynamics, and not in the comparative statics, that one of the major differences between Keynesians and monetarists lies.

Causation

Keynesian analysis rests on the *stability* of the consumption function (or more strictly, on the expenditure function), which allows the generation of multipliers, which in turn allow predictions to be made concerning the effects of changing exogenous variables. For instance, given the expenditure multiplier k (which depends on a variety of propensities), a change in equilibrium income, dY, arising from a change in government spending, dG, is $dY = kdG$. Even where the monetary sector is incorporated, as in the *IS-LM* framework, the basic point remains valid – it is only the value of k which has to be adapted. Monetarists, on the other hand, begin with the basic premise that the crucial equation is the demand for money equation, which they consider to be the *stable* relation in the economic system. Given equilibrium in the money market, so that the supply of money is equal to the demand for money, there exists a link between the (assumed) exogenous money supply and the endogenous variables of the system. Thus, $dY = mdM_s$, where m is the money multiplier. If m is more stable than k then the money equation is considered to be a 'better' predictor of dY and other endogenous variables in the system.

The problem was how to test this proposition formally. An initial attempt was outlined by Friedman and Meiselman (1963) which sparked off quite a controversy.[4] The controversy involved their statement of the Keynesian and monetarist positions and the *ad hoc* procedures that they adopted. What came out of the controversy is that money had a role to play in analysing the economic system, a point played down by Keynesians (although not by Keynes himself). How important a role money has to play has not yet been resolved.

The controversy was, and still is, not simply academic. In the British context Keynesian economics dominated policy-making throughout the 1950s and 1960s, and to some extent the 1970s. The emphasis was very much on fiscal policy, with monetary policy being purely accommodating. It is important to realise that it was not until the Radcliffe Report of 1958 that even some vital monetary statistics were compiled. The impact of this report was not as great as it might have been, however, and one reason for this was the Radcliffe Committee's concentration on the concept of 'liquidity' rather than on a narrower definition of money – the former of which they never defined explicitly.

One crucial aspect of the causation debate is whether changes in the money supply *cause* changes in output and prices or whether the changing money supply is a *consequence* of output and price changes. One reason for wanting an answer to this arose from another aspect to the debate which ensued, namely, 'Is monetary policy more effective (in changing output) than fiscal policy?' The importance of monetary policy rested very much on the money supply being a cause and not a consequence of income (and output) changes. The same applies in the more recent inflationary period: 'Is money supply growth a cause of the accelerated inflation or a consequence of it?'

To justify changes in the money supply causing changes in either output, prices or both we need a link between the variables. This leads us directly into the issue of the transmission mechanism.

The Transmission Mechanism[5]

The transmission mechanism is concerned with dynamics and so we must establish what in fact changes in the presence of excess demands. There are basically three markets:

(1) Goods and services

(2) Money

(3) Bonds.

Let *EG, EM* and *EB* denote excess demand in the three markets respectively. By Walras' law we have that, taken together, all excess demands must sum to zero – in the sense that an excess demand in one market must show up as an excess supply in one or the other markets.[6] Thus:

$$EG + EM + EB \equiv 0$$

which is identically true. Equilibrium in any market is defined to be where there is no excess demand. It is clear, then, that if any two markets are in equilibrium the third must also be in equilibrium; e.g., if $EG = 0$ and $EM = 0$, then it follows from Walras' law that $EB = 0$. This means that we only need to consider any two markets at any one time. Let these be the goods market and the money market. (This explains the emphasis on the *IS-LM* model, which denotes equilibrium in the goods market and the money market respectively. Here, however, we are more concerned about *disequilibrium* states.)

If there is a positive or negative excess demand in any market (where a negative excess demand denotes excess supply), what changes to establish equilibrium? In such a situation two broad choices are possible as to the engine of force that brings about changes: (1) 'price', and (2) 'quantity'. Which of these it is depends not only upon assumptions about the economic system but also on methodological considerations – especially when we come to adjustment in the money market. Let us take first the goods market.

We have two situations to consider: (1) less than full employment and (2) full employment. Given either of these, we assume in the case of (1) that all adjustment falls on output, y, which is a *quantity* adjustment, while in case (2) all adjustment falls on the consumer price index, P, which is a *price* adjustment (see Table 6.1).

Table 6.1 Adjustment in the goods market

Goods market	Less than full employment	Full employment
$EG > 0$	$\Delta y > 0$ or $y \uparrow$	$\Delta P > 0$ or $P \uparrow$
$EG < 0$	$\Delta y < 0$ or $y \downarrow$	$\Delta P < 0$ or $P \downarrow$
$EG = 0$	$\Delta y = 0$	$\Delta P = 0$

Table 6.2 Adjustment in the money market

Money market	Interest rate adjustment	Price level adjustment
$EM > 0$	$\Delta r > 0$ or $r \uparrow$	$\Delta P < 0$ or $P \downarrow$ $(r_n < r_m)$
$EM < 0$	$\Delta r < 0$ or $r \downarrow$	$\Delta P > 0$ or $P \uparrow$ $(r_n > r_m)$
$EM = 0$	$\Delta r = 0$	$\Delta P = 0$ $(r_n = r_m)$

In the money market a similar situation prevails. First, what is the analogy with 'full employment'? It is the natural rate of interest, since, following Wicksell, this is the rate of interest at which there is no excess demand for goods and services. Let r_m denote the market rate of interest and r_n the natural rate of interest. In deriving the adjustments we need only note that we are concerned with real money demanded and supplied. Real money balances is M_s/P. We now have the situation shown in Table 6.2.

The two versions for the money market are shown in Figure 6.1. In part (a) of the figure the excess demand for real money balances causes a rise in the interest rate to the equilibrium market rate r_m. In Figure 6.1(b) the market rate r_m is a temporary equilibrium rate and denotes an excess of money demand at the natural rate, r_n. In this instance the price level falls from P_o to P_1 and so raises real money balances to M_s/P_1.

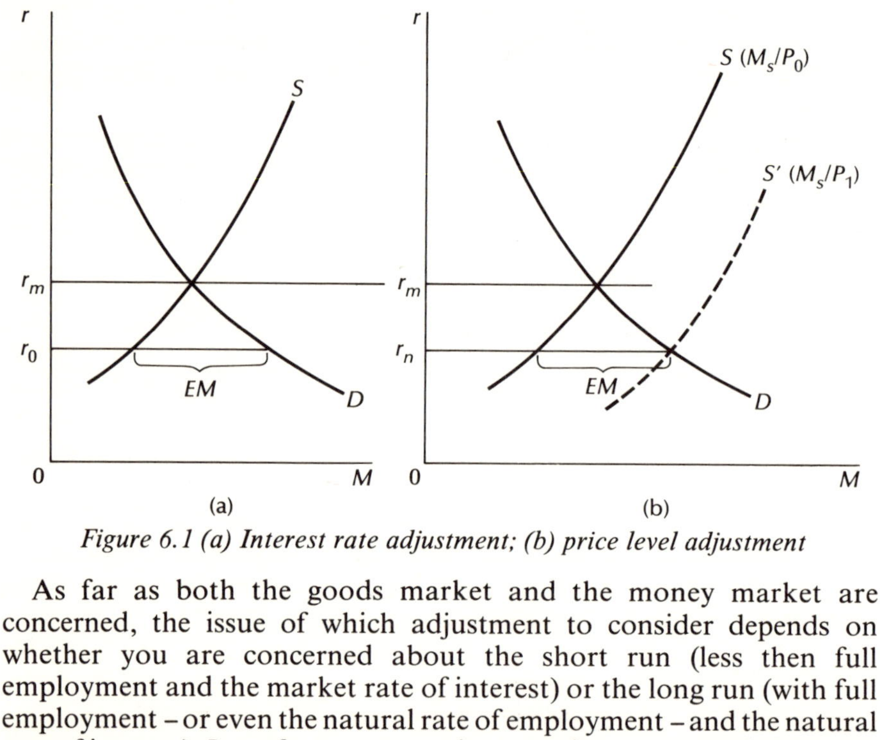

Figure 6.1 (a) Interest rate adjustment; (b) price level adjustment

As far as both the goods market and the money market are concerned, the issue of which adjustment to consider depends on whether you are concerned about the short run (less then full employment and the market rate of interest) or the long run (with full employment – or even the natural rate of employment – and the natural rate of interest). In so far as monetarists are often concerned about the long run, their methodology is one which concerns itself with 'natural' rates of employment and interest. Keynesians, on the other hand, are generally concerned about the short run – following Keynes' dictum that 'in the long run we are all dead!' It is important, therefore, that the reader be constantly aware of which time period he or she has in mind. There is no 'right' time period; it is simply a matter of emphasis.

Before we consider some final points about the transmission mechanism we must consider one other excess demand, viz., the foreign trade sector. Consider the market for foreign exchange. The spot price is in terms of domestic currency, so that S is the pound/dollar rate (e.g., \$1 = £0.5). Using our earlier notation we have $K \equiv K_x + K_m$, i.e., net capital inflows is the sum of net capital exports plus net capital imports, and $BP \equiv (X - M) = K$. We now have *three* choices for adjustment, depending on the exchange rate regime. With a freely floating rate system, a balance of payments deficit ($BP < 0$) leads to a depreciation of sterling (a rise in S) and vice versa for a surplus. This is shown in Figure 6.2(a).

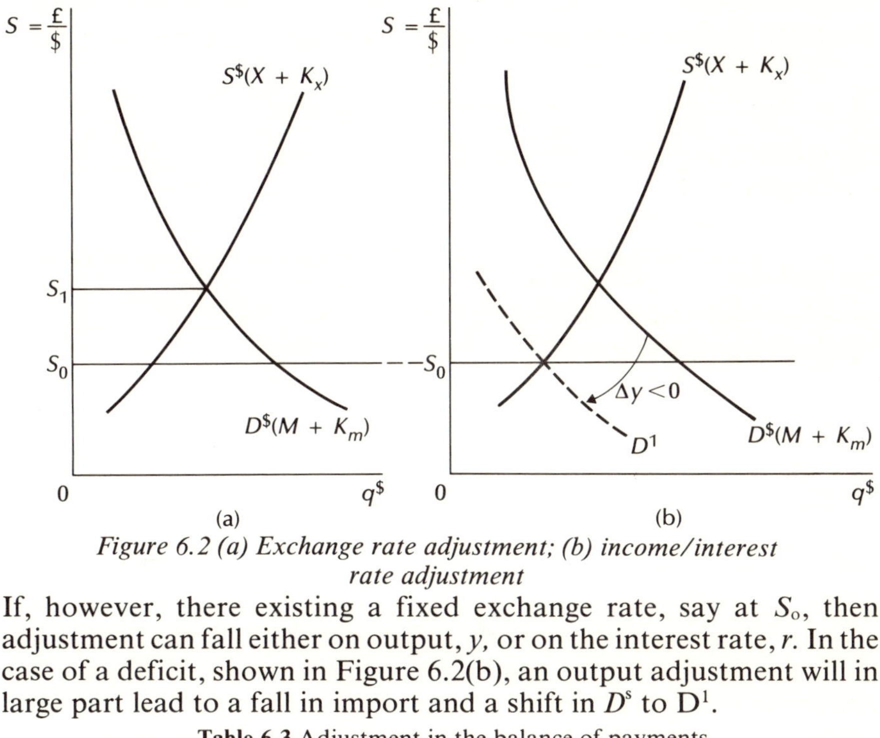

Figure 6.2 (a) Exchange rate adjustment; (b) income/interest rate adjustment

If, however, there existing a fixed exchange rate, say at S_o, then adjustment can fall either on output, *y*, or on the interest rate, *r*. In the case of a deficit, shown in Figure 6.2(b), an output adjustment will in large part lead to a fall in import and a shift in D^s to D^1.

Table 6.3 Adjustment in the balance of payments

Balance of payments	Floating system $S(=£/\$)$	Fixed exchange rate: Income adjustment	Fixed exchange rate: Interest rate adjustment
$BP > 0$	$\Delta S < 0$ or $S\downarrow$	$\Delta y > 0$ or $y\uparrow$	$\Delta r < 0$ or $r\downarrow$
$BP < 0$	$\Delta S > 0$ or $S\uparrow$	$\Delta y < 0$ or $y\downarrow$	$\Delta r > 0$ or $r\uparrow$
$BP = 0$	$\Delta S = 0$	$\Delta y = 0$	$\Delta r = 0$

In the case of an interest rate adjustment (see Table 6.3), a deficit can be eliminated by attracting more overseas capital, which can be achieved by raising the interest rate. This will lead to a rise in K_x and a fall in K_m, i.e., to a rise in net capital inflow, K.[7]

Also note that Walras' law now takes the form:

$$EB + EM + EB + BP \equiv 0$$

Again we choose to ignore the bond market. Now, however, bond market equilibrium is automatic only when $EG = 0$, $EM = 0$ and $BP = 0$.

We are now in a position to conclude our discussion. In the case of the Keynesian system the transmission from an increase in the money supply to output and/or prices is as follows:

$$M_s + \rightarrow r- \rightarrow I + \rightarrow Y +$$

That is, a rise in the money supply lowers interest rates, which in turn stimulates investment, which, through the multiplier process, raises nominal income. The rise in nominal income can occur because of either a rise in real income, y, and/or a rise in the price level. This arises from the identity $Y \equiv Py$, so that $\hat{Y} \equiv \hat{P} + \hat{y}$; i.e., the percentage change in nominal income is the addition of the percentage change in the general price level plus the percentage change in output.

The monetarist transmission mechanism rests solely on the stable demand for money equation, which for simplicity we shall take to be $M_d = kPy$ or $M_d = kY$. Since $M_s = M_d$ for equilibrium in the money market, then:

$$M_s + \rightarrow Y +$$

where again $\hat{Y} \equiv \hat{P} + \hat{y}$, and so the rise in nominal income can occur from a rise in prices and/or a rise in output.

There is, however, one important neglect in these simple transmission mechanisms. *They are for a closed economy*. A look at Table 6.3, which indicates adjustment in the foreign exchange market, shows that, whether we take the Keynesian transmission mechanism or the monetarist transmission mechanism, the foreign exchange market will be affected, which in turn will lead to adjustments. What type of adjustment depends on which of the above mechanisms we consider and which exchange rate system is operating. Only in the case of a freely floating exchange rate does it appear that adjustment in the foreign exchange market is independent of the internal transmission mechanism. But this is not so. First, interest parity establishes a link between interest rates at home, r, and abroad, r^*, and the forward premium/discount, π.[8] In simple terms this says that there will be a net capital inflow ($K > 0$) if the interest rate differential, $r - r^*$, is greater than the cost of forward cover, π; i.e., if $r - r^* > \pi$ then $K > 0$

if $r - r^* < \pi$ then $K < 0$

if $r - r^* = \pi$ then $K = 0$ (interest parity)

In the case of the Keynesian transmission mechanism there is a clear link between the influence of M_s on Y and responses in the foreign exchange market. This is less true of the monetarist transmission mechanism, but we have assumed a demand for money which is totally interest-inelastic (by assuming only a transactions demand for money equation). Many monetarists would accept some interest rate sensitivity, in which case we again have an interconnection between the internal transmission mechanism and the foreign exchange market.

This association between the markets makes the causal chain less precise. It is very much this problem which has led to difficulties in managing the UK economy: difficulties not only for Keynesian demand management but, as we outlined in chapter 5, also for monetary control for fighting inflation. A floating exchange rate does not segregate the foreign sector from the domestic sector. This would be true only if the balance of payments were a function of the exchange rate alone; but in fact interest rates play a major role (especially in the UK) in net capital flows. The basic link, which is generally unspecified, is that net capital flow, K, are not simply a function of the domestic interest rate but are strictly a function of the covered interest rate differential; i.e.,

$$K = K\,[(r - r^*) - \pi]$$

Since π involves both the spot and forward exchange rates, all these interact to determine net capital flows, K. Since any change in K involves changes in $(X - M) + K$, the 'above-the-line' imbalance changes and hence so does the 'below-the-line' change in the reserves, dR. This in turn changes the domestic money supply, as noted in equation (6) above.

This complex interlinking of the markets even under a floating exchange rate became clear in the two exchange crises of November 1982 and January 1983. The latter in particular led to a rapid and large depreciation of sterling and put in jeopardy the government's fight to bring down the rate of inflation.

6.3 Monetary Targets versus Exchange Rate Targets

In the introduction we raised the question, 'Which target (if any) should be the object of policy?' – where this was directed at monetary targets and/or exchange rate targets. First we must be clear what the intention is with regard to final objectives in setting intermediate targets. It is important to distinguish *levels* from *changes*. Let us be more specific. We have basically two final objectives: output, y, and the price level, P. We can specify as an objective the level of real output (e.g., the natural level) and the level of the general price index. These together would also imply an objective for the level of nominal income – since $Y \equiv Py$. Alternatively, we can be concerned about changes – or what some economists loosely call stabilisation. In this case we are concerned about the level of $\hat{y}$ and $\hat{P}$. It is of course possible to have an objective about the level of real income, y, and about the level of inflation, $\hat{P}$. The point of emphasising this is that an instrument appropriate for a level, say y or P, is not necessarily suitable for dealing with changes, say $\hat{y}$ and $\hat{P}$. In particular, when dealing with levels such as y or P, instruments are assigned to these targets, while in the case of changes, such as $\hat{y}$ and $\hat{P}$, the objective is to keep these as small as possible – usually around some desired level – and so instruments are assigned in such a manner as to reduce these variations; i.e., *instruments are assigned to disturbances*.

There are two questions we can ask:

(1) What matters in achieving Δ£M3 and why may it be difficult to achieve?

(2) Why have an M_s target at all, and what other intermediate targets are available for achieving the primary objective of a reduced rate of inflation?

We have to some extent dealt with (1) in chapter 5. The material there, and that to be discussed, is also relevant in answering question (2). Although the material is the same for each question the focus of attention is quite different. Here we shall concentrate on the second question.

In dealing with the second question we shall take the primary objective to be a low and stable rate of inflation. Monetary analysis has argued a strong link between the growth in the money supply and inflation. But it has also become apparent – most especially for the UK – that a changing exchange rate can also affect the rate of inflation. In general, a sterling depreciation raises the general price level while an appreciation lowers it. One point is worth stressing. Suppose we are talking of an $x\%$ change in the exchange rate. Let us further suppose that an appreciation of sterling by $x\%$ reduces the price level by $z\%$. Can we say that the relationship is symmetrical, in the sense that an $x\%$ depreciation will raise the price index by $z\%$? The evidence suggests not.

The relationship is asymmetric. Prices rise more readily than they fall and also much more quickly, so that an $x\%$ depreciation gets transmitted to the price level more readily and in a greater magnitude than an $x\%$ appreciation of sterling.

The causation just mentioned is from the money supply to inflation and from the exchange rate to inflation. But we noted in the earlier sections how a change in the exchange rate affects not only external flows but also other elements in the components of Δ£M3. Hence we have a two-way link between the money supply and the exchange rate. The same is true of the inflation rate and the exchange rate. Although changes in the exchange rate can cause changes in the price level, it is also true that a change in the rate of inflation can lead to a change in the competitive position of the country, which will influence its exports and imports and, most likely under a freely floating exchange rate system, lead to a change in the exchange rate. We have then the links shown in Figure 6.3. As we pointed out in connection with the link between the exchange rate and Δ£M3, this is neither simple nor predictable. This point in fact applies to all the links in this schema.

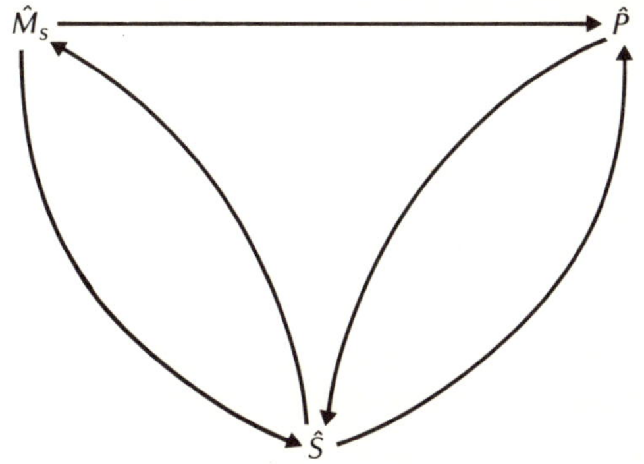

Figure 6.3 Causal links between money supply, inflation and the exchange rate

Having set out the difficulties, we still need to ask which is the stronger and more predicable link:

(1) That between $\hat{M}_s$ and $\hat{P}$, or

(2) That between $\hat{S}$ and $\hat{P}$?

Furthermore, if the government concentrates on (1) alone then it may result in undesirable changes in *S;* while if the government concentrates on (2) alone then this may result in undesirable fluctuations in the money supply. This obviously begs the question of which has the least undesirable consequences. It also raises the question of whether we can in some way deal with both (1) and (2) in combination. We have, then, three possible rules:

(1) A money supply rule

(2) An exchange rate rule

(3) A conditionality rule (combining in some way rules (1) and (2)).

In chapter 5 we pointed out difficulties that the UK government has been having in controlling the money supply. But this difficulty arises from two sources. First, there is no simple link between the PSBR and Δ£M3, for a variety of reasons which we have discussed. Second, the economy has received a number of shocks (or disturbances) in the 1970s, both internal and external. This leads us to ask:

> *Is the choice between a money supply rule and an exchange rate rule determined by the fact that there is not a one-to-one relationship between the money supply and the exchange rate; or is it determined by the fact that the economy is prone to disturbances, which leads to a preference for one rule over the other – or even some conditionality rule?*

Suppose the choice is determined by a disturbance. In this instance the strategy for a government is not to link the money supply with inflation but rather to find an instrument suitable for reducing the effects of the disturbance. Clearly, the disturbance itself is largely unpredictable and so the aim would be to find instruments suitable for dealing with various classes of disturbances. The strategy, then, is the following:

> *To each disturbance attach one or more instruments (intermediate targets) in such a way that the effects of the disturbance are minimised (i.e., the assignment rule).*

Consider a disturbance originating with a rise in US interest rates– which happened early in 1982. The first thing to note is that a money supply rule would deal only with the influence this has on £M3. But a rise in US interest rates lowers the covered interest differential and reduces any net inflow of capital (or increases the net outflow). Also, it will lead to a depreciation of sterling and may also lead to UK interest rates being raised. The disturbance, therefore, gets transmitted to many sectors of the economy and not only to the money supply. In this case if the above assignment rule is followed what is required is an instrument, or set of instruments, to minimise the effects of the changes emanating from the foreign exchange market. If any rule is suggested in this instance it would be an exchange rate rule. But no simple rule can deal with the manifold disturbances. This leads us to the obvious question:

If a rule (or instrument) is to be attached to disturbances, does it matter from where the disturbances emanate?

The simple answer is, 'Yes.'

Although we shall here be concentrating on disturbances, it is worth stressing that there are a number of issues that must be considered in choosing any rule. These are:

(1) The type and sources of disturbances

(2) The pricing behaviour of firms

(3) The formation of price expectations

(4) The degree of association between the PSBR, M_s and the exchange rate

(5) The speed and form of the transmission mechanism.

Four other observations are worth making. First, if we turn our attention to rules for dealing with disturbances it is not clear that the objective should be a low and stable inflation rate. Certainly once inflation is down to some acceptable level then the objective may very well be that of stabilising real output. The rule may then be quite different. In what follows, however, we shall retain the objective of a low and stable inflation rate. Second, the number of instruments (intermediate targets?) need not equal the number of disturbances, and so more than one instrument at any one time can be used to deal with a particular disturbance. This Artis and Currie (1980) referred to as the *conditionality rule*, which can itself take two forms:

(1) A monetary rule along with a floor and ceiling on the effective exchange rate

(2) A combinatorial rule with specified trade-offs; e.g.,

$$W = a\hat{M}_s + b(E - E^*)$$

where a and b are specified weightings, and E is the effective exchange rate while E^* is the desired effective exchange rate. (Note that, in the present case followed by the Conservative Party, $a = 1$ and $b = 0$.)

Third, a decision on the time period must be made, making a clear distinction between the short-run and the long-run effects. In particular, a policy decision must be made as to whether it is the short-run or the long-run disturbances which are to be minimised. Fourth, and very importantly, under what conditions should an intermediate target be abandoned?

This has become an obvious issue in the case of the UK. The government has decided on one intermediate target 'at all costs'. Yet the same intermediate target has had to be abandoned or trimmed in other countries. There is evidence that *de facto* the UK government abandoned its money supply target in 1980-81 when the real exchange rate for sterling was appreciating, a situation similar to Switzerland's experience.

We said above that the rule depends on the source of the shock. A variety of disturbances have been analysed by Artis and Currie (1980). Here we shall outline a simple version of their analysis. Since they are concerned about price and income stabilisation, they first set up equilibrium in the goods market (*GM*), the money market (*MM*) and the aggregate supply market (*AS*). The reader may be familiar with goods market and money market equilibria discussed in terms of the *IS-LM* diagram. Given, however, that our interest is in the price level, *P,* and real income, *y,* we set up the equilibria in the *P-y* plane. This is shown in

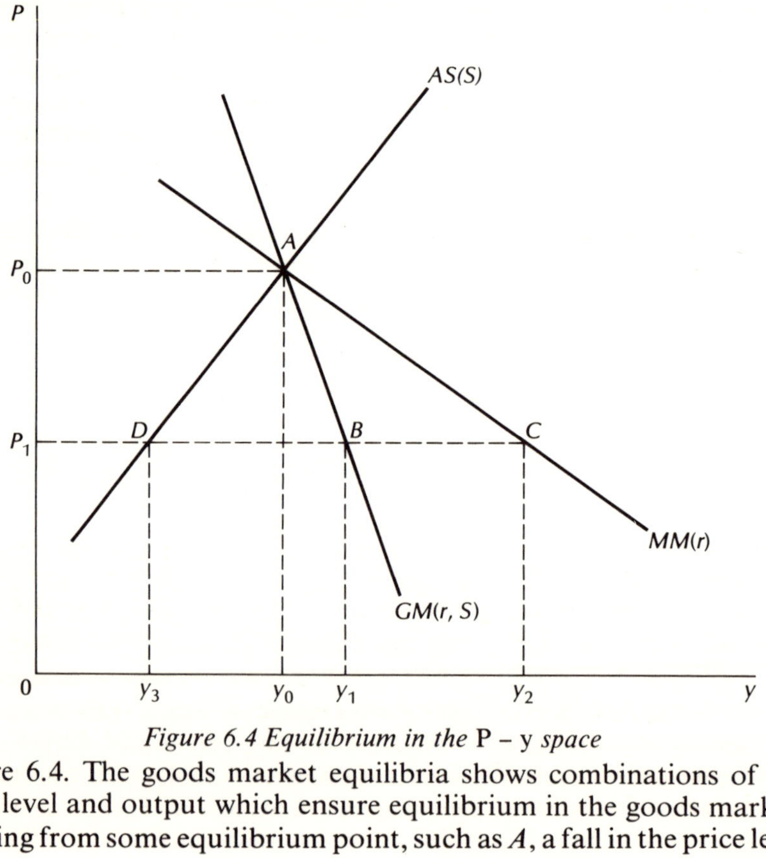

Figure 6.4 Equilibrium in the P – y *space*

Figure 6.4. The goods market equilibria shows combinations of the price level and output which ensure equilibrium in the goods market. Starting from some equilibrium point, such as *A*, a fall in the price level from P_0 to P_1 leads to an improvement in the trade sector and so to an excess demand in the goods market. To re-establish equilibrium, real income must rise (*A* to *B*). Similarly, a fall in the price level leads to an excess supply of real money balances which can be offset to establish equilibrium by a rise in real income, so raising the demand for real money balances (*A* to *C*).

When we come to aggregate supply, a fall in prices must be matched by a smaller output for equilibrium and hence by a smaller real income (*A* to *D*). One problem, which is clear from Figure 6.4, is whether *MM* is steeper than *GM*. It is also made clear in Figure 6.4 what is held constant. In the *IS-LM* diagram it is the price level and exchange rate which are held constant. In the *P-y* plane, however, it is the interest rate and the exchange rate which are held constant. In the case of the goods market the interest rate is held constant (which arises from the investment function and the capital account of the balance of payments) and the exchange rate is held constant (arising from the export and import functions). The money market equilibria, denoted by *MM*, hold the interest rate constant (which arises from the demand for money). Finally, aggregate supply involves the exchange rate since output depends on imported goods which in turn depend on the exchange rate. Any change in the interest rate will shift both the *MM* and *GM* schedules, while a change in the exchange rate will shift the *GM* and the *AS* schedules.

By means of this analysis, Artis and Currie investigate the three rules we set out above with respect to five sources of shocks:

(1) A shock arising in the goods market

(2) A disturbance in the demand for money

(3) An aggregate supply shock

(4) A shock arising in the foreign capital sector

(5) A foreign price level shock.

We shall here take just two to illustrate the points we have been making. Suppose there is a rise in expenditure, i.e., a rise in demand in the goods market. This shifts *GM* to the right, to GM^1 in Figure 6.5. Where the economy settles down depends upon which rule is being followed. In the case of Figure 6.5(a) we assume an exchange rate target. In this instance the exchange rate, *S*, is held constant and the money supply increases to prevent an appreciation of the exchange rate. Thus *MM* shifts to MM^1 to intersect *AS* at point *B*. The economy settles at *B* under an exchange rate target. What about a money supply target? This is shown in Figure 6.5(b). The shift in *GM* to GM^1 moves the economy to *B*. At *B* there is excess money supply, and since M_s is held constant, the exchange rate appreciates. This shifts AS to AS^1 and GM^1 to GM^2. The result under a money supply target is the economy moving to point C.[9]

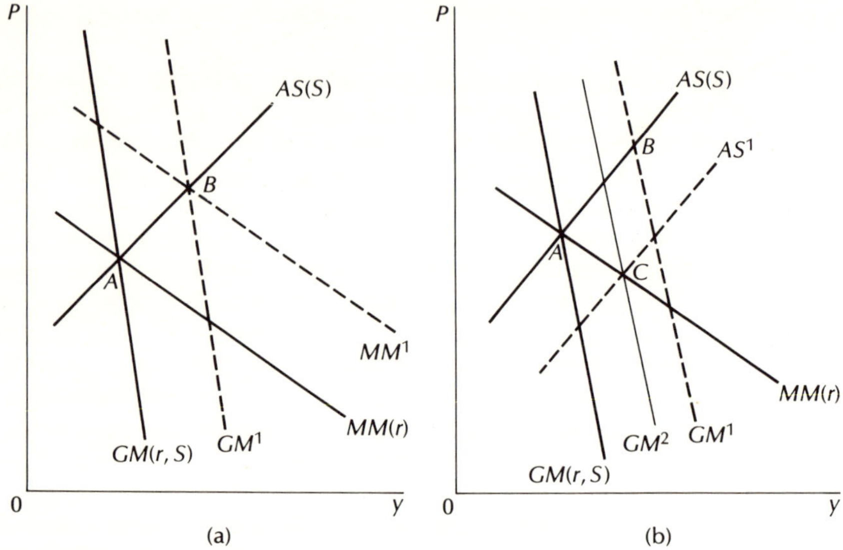

Figure 6.5 Domestic shock: (a) exchange rate target; (b) money supply target

The first observation is that the effect on the price level is opposite in relation to the rule followed – rising under an exchange rate rule and falling under a money rule. Does this suggest that a money supply rule is preferable?

Before answering this, consider the situation for a rise in foreign interest rates. This is shown in Figure 6.6, where again we consider the situation under the two rules. Under an exchange rate rule GM moves to GM^1 and the money supply is accommodating because the exchange rate is held fixed. Thus MM shifts to MM^1 and the economy moves to point B, as shown in Figure 6.6(a). In the case of a money supply rule, point B is associated with an excess demand for money which causes the exchange rate to depreciate. Thus AS shifts to AS^1 and GM^1 to GM^2, moving the economy finally to point C. Once again the price effect is opposite, but in this case a money supply rule increases the price level while it lowered it for a domestic shock.

These examples no more than illustrate the problem. They highlight to some extent that the effect depends on the movement in the schedules, the elasticities of the various schedules and also whether MM is more or less steep than GM. What is also shown is that we do not

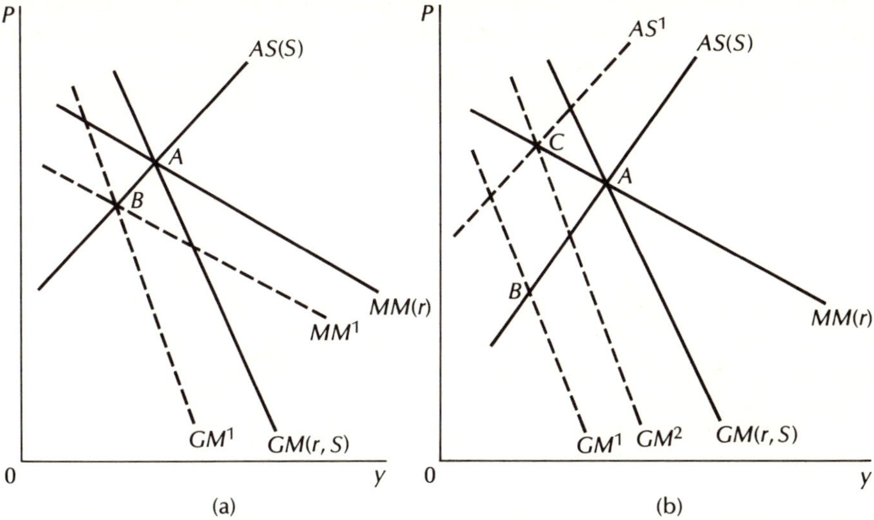

Figure 6.6 Foreign capital shock: (a) exchange rate target; (b) money supply target

obviously favour one target over another. Artis and Currie conclude:

> ...exchange rate targets will be superior to monetary targets in an open economy where cost-mark-up pricing predominates, unless the major source of disturbance to the economy is from shocks to the foreign price level. (p.192)

They further conclude that, since the two rules seem to have opposite effects on the price level, a *combined* rule could be more stabilising.

6.4 How Little We Know

This chapter has attempted to look at the issue of a monetary rule as against some other rule. It shows how little we know about the institutional framework and the transmission mechanisms that compose the main elements of economic theorising. The British government does have a monetary rule, so it is fitting that we investigate the rationale for it. The UK economy, however, is an open economy and the exchange rate plays a central role in any macroeconomic analysis that purports to give insight into policy questions. The neglect of the exchange rate and of how it links with other variables is a major failing of textbooks. In this chapter we have tried to redress this balance.

The conclusion that can be drawn from the above sections is that policy directed at the source of disturbances may be a very useful way of managing the economy. More work, however, is required on the source and effects of various disturbances before economists recommend such a form of management.

Questions

1. Is there any fundamental difference between an intermediate target and a primary target? If it was decided to target the exchange rate, is this a primary or intermediate targeting?
2. Can an exchange rate target be set independently of a money supply target? What implication does your answer have with respect to the government Budget constraint?
3. Compare and contrast setting instruments to achieve targets with instruments to minimise the effects of disturbances.
4. Why will it not generally be the case that an inflow of £*x* million will raise the domestic money supply by this amount?
5. Criticise the regressions in the text. What alternative regressions would you consider more appropriate?
6. 'The coefficient in the relationship between the change in £M3 and the PSBR is not significantly different from zero. There is, then, no relationship between the two, and so the government should not reduce the PSBR contingent on its cut in the growth of £M3.' Discuss.
7. 'Definitional equations can never give us insight into the causation which lies behind economic variables and precisely how changes in one variable get transmitted through the economy.' Discuss.
8. Are changes in the money supply a cause or a consequence of changes in output and prices?
9. What relevance has Walras' law to the transmission mechanism?
10. What role does the natural rate of interest play in the adjustment mechanism?
11. Compare and contrast the Keynesian and monetarist transmission mechanisms in the case of:
    (a) A closed economy
    (b) An open economy.
12. What is a conditionality rule? Argue for or against such a rule.

13. Why should the pricing behaviour of firms have any bearing on the issue of implementing rules?

14. In the text the *IS–LM* and aggregate supply is mapped into analysis in the *P–y* plane. Does this further our understanding of macroeconomic issues?

15. Do institutions matter in deciding on whether to follow rules, and if so the type of rules to follow?

Notes

1. See Tinbergen (1956) for a detailed treatment. A simple treatment can be found in Neal and Shone (1976, ch.6) and a useful discussion in the light of UK government policy is Graham (1977).
2. See Allin (1976) and Shone (1979, 1980) for a discussion of the balance of payments accounts in terms of above and below the line and how these are used by Keynesian and monetarist economists.
3. This supports the results found by Savage (1980) in contrast to those done earlier by Kaldor (1970).
4. A discussion of the controversy can be found in Coghlan (1980, ch.3).
5. Much has been written on the transmission mechanism but it has not always led to any greater clarity. Part of the reason lies in the fact that dynamic adjustments were not always explicitly set out. See Chick (1977).
6. For a simple discussion of Walras' law see Weintraub (1974).
7. Note that capital exports and imports refer to the movement of paper while the money flows in the other direction. Thus, a rise in interest rates at home attracts capital, leading to an increase in capital exports.
8. Interest parity can be considered by noting what happens if you wished to make a choice between investing in the UK or investing in the US. Let r^{uk} and r^{us} denote comparable interest rates (e.g., Treasury bill rates) and let S and F denote the spot and forward exchange rates. Now consider you have £x. If you invest it in the UK then you will recieve after, say, three months (£$x\ 1 + r^{uk}$). But there is the possibility of investing it in the US. First we note that £x becomes \$$x/S$. If this is now invested in the US then you would receive \$$x\ (1 + r^{us})/S$ after three months. But there is a problem. The exchange rate may change over this period. You could cover yourself, however, by buying forward sterling (selling forward dollars). This rate, denoted F, is known now and so all exchange rate uncertainty is eliminated. If you did this then you would have

$£x(1 + r^{us})\ (F/S)$ after three months. The choice is now clear. If

$$£x(1 + r^{uk}) > £x(1 + r^{us})\ (F/S)$$

then you would invest in the UK, while if the inequality were the other way then you would invest in the US. In the former case less capital would flow out (or capital would flow in) while in the latter case there would be a net capital outflow. If equality held there would be no incentive for capital to flow. Now we can think of the difference between F and S as the cost of covering yourself forward. This premium/discount is $\pi = (F - S)/S$, expressed as a percentage. By substituting and doing some re-arranging, while taking the product term $\pi r^{us} \simeq 0$, we have that you would invest in the UK if:

$$r^{uk} - r^{us} > \pi$$

i.e., if the interest differential exceeded the cost of covering yourself from exchange risk. It follows, then, that

$$K = K[(r^{uk} - r^{us}) - \pi]$$

and $K = 0$ only when

$$r^{uk} - r^{us} = \pi$$

i.e., when there is interest parity.

9. We have assumed no interest rate expectations so that the *MM* curve remains fixed. The treatment by Artis and Curris (1980) is more thorough and involves a number of expectations which lead to more complex shifts.

CHAPTER 7

Has monetarism failed?

In different parts of this book we have repeatedly made the point that the Conservative government under Margaret Thatcher's leadership took a distinctive change in direction with regard to macroeconomic policy. In this chapter the intention is to attempt some assessment of the strategy so far. It could be argued that it is a little premature to assess the policy at this point in time, but since no time period is usually specified by monetarists then no time is the 'right' time. Furthermore, one full period of office is now complete, and although the Conservatives claim that two periods are necessary in order to implement their policies, almost five years has elapsed and so some impact must have occurred.

In the first section we shall take a cursory look at the performance of the economy since the Conservatives took office in 1979. In section 7.2 we shall consider the fundamental postulates of monetarism and consider to what extent any government can follow them, and in particular whether the British government is adhering to them. In section 7.3 we discuss the rational expectations view of macroeconomics and the way in which this is broader than monetarism and underlies Mrs Thatcher's Conservatism. In section 7.4 we turn to the measurement of success/failure; and finally in section 7.5 we consider the extent to which the strategy can be adapted or even reversed if the need should arise. Although this last section appears somewhat negative, the intention is to consider to what extent a course of action, even if not agreed with initially, is still preferable to a complete reversal. (If you would like to go to Greece by plane but are forced to go by ship, then once the journey is underway it is not necessarily sensible, even if it does become possible, to return by ship to the starting point and then take a plane!)

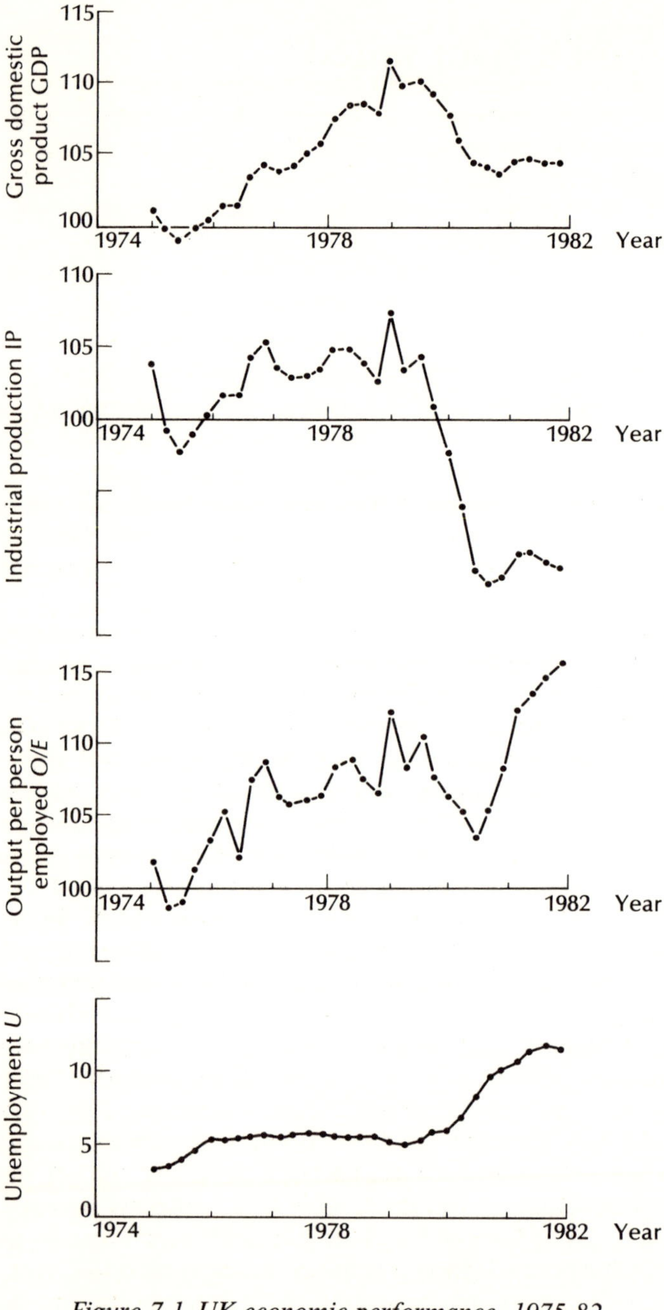

Figure 7.1 UK economic performance, 1975-82

7.1 The Evidence So Far

In Figure 7.1 we present some of the main economic trends over the period 1975-82 (second quarter). The very deep recession of 1980 comes out very clearly from these figures. The output measure of constant GDP decreased dramatically after the second quarter of 1979, falling by 4.8% in 1980. The same dramatic fall is also shown by industrial production of manufactures. With unemployment rising continuously from the second quarter of 1979, this gives rise to an upward trend in output per person employed. Whether we have reached the trough of the recession is difficult to ascertain from these figures, although industrial production does give some signs of levelling off.

All this is consistent with the policies being pursued by Margaret Thatcher. The cut in the rate of growth in the money supply to bring down inflation requires, as the next chapter makes clear, a consistent decrease in the growth of the PSBR. Both together imply a sharp fall in real income (output) and a rise in unemployment. As Figure 7.1 makes clear, there is little doubt that this feature of the policy is certainly taking place.

But what has been happening to prices, wages and earnings? In Table 7.1 we present quarterly figures of annual percentage changes in basic weekly wage rates, earnings and the retail price index for the period 1975 to the second quarter of 1982. The rate of weekly wage inflation reached its peak in the second and third quarters of 1980 and has thereafter showed a consistent decline. Earnings reached their peak in the third quarter of 1980 and have also shown a consistent decline thereafter. Price inflation, which peaked in the second quarter of 1980, although since then declining has been doing so only slowly. What these figures also indicate is that real weekly wage rates fell since the Conservatives took office (with the exception of the third and fourth quarters of 1980) but that real earnings generally rose, increasing by as much as 5.9% in the third quarter of 1980. The rise in real earnings is despite the growing rate of unemployment throughout the same period.

Although inflation is declining, as shown in Table 7.1, it does not seem to be declining as rapidly as industrial production and output has been doing, as shown in Figure 7.1. A major concern is whether this decline in industrial production and output is more a sign of the decline in UK competitiveness. There are a number of measures of competitiveness,[1] but in Figure 7.2 we have graphed the the index of the ratio of export prices, the index of normalised unit labour costs, the effective exchange rate index and the dollar/sterling exchange rate for the period 1975-82. Whether using the ratio of export prices or unit labour costs,

Table 7.1 Wage and price inflation, 1975-1982

Year and quarter	Basic weekly wage rates (1)	Average earnings whole economy (2)	Retail price index (3)	Real wage changes (1) – (3)	Real earnings changes (2) – (3)
1975 (I)	30.9		20.3	10.6	
(II)	33.1		24.3	8.8	
(III)	28.7		26.6	2.1	
(IV)	26.1		25.3	0.8	
1976 (I)	25.5		22.5	3.0	
(II)	20.7		15.9	4.8	
(III)	18.2		13.7	4.5	
(IV)	13.9		15.0	–1.1	
1977 (I)	9.4	10.6	16.5	–7.1	–5.9
(II)	6.8	8.9	17.4	–10.6	–8.5
(III)	5.0	7.9	16.5	–11.5	–8.6
(IV)	5.4	8.9	13.0	–7.6	–4.1
1978 (I)	6.5	10.1	9.4	–2.9	0.7
(II)	15.4	13.4	7.7	7.7	5.7
(III)	16.2	14.4	7.9	8.3	6.5
(IV)	18.1	13.8	8.1	10.0	5.7
1979 (I)	19.8	13.9	9.6	10.2	4.3
(II)	12.1	13.5	10.6	1.5	2.9
(III)	12.8	15.7	16.0	–3.2	–0.3
(IV)	15.5	18.5	17.2	–1.7	1.3
1980 (I)	17.6	19.7	19.1	–1.5	0.6
(II)	19.2	21.4	21.5	–2.3	–0.1
(III)	19.2	22.2	16.3	2.9	5.9
(IV)	16.3	19.5	15.3	1.0	4.2
1981 (I)	12.6	16.5	12.7	–0.1	3.8
(II)	10.7	13.0	11.7	–1.0	1.3
(III)	9.4	11.4	11.3	–1.9	0.1
(IV)	8.1	11.1	11.9	–3.8	–0.8
1982 (I)	7.1	11.1	11.1	–4.0	0.0
(II)	6.5	10.1	9.4	–2.9	0.7

Source: Economic Trends, Annual Supplement (1983 edition)

the decline in UK competitiveness is quite dramatic and coincides with the appreciation of sterling. Even the brief slowdown of lost competitiveness in 1981, coinciding with the appreciation of sterling, seems to be halted. The difficulty faced by the government is that, for its policy towards bringing down inflation, an appreciating pound can help in keeping down the general price level; but an appreciating pound, in so

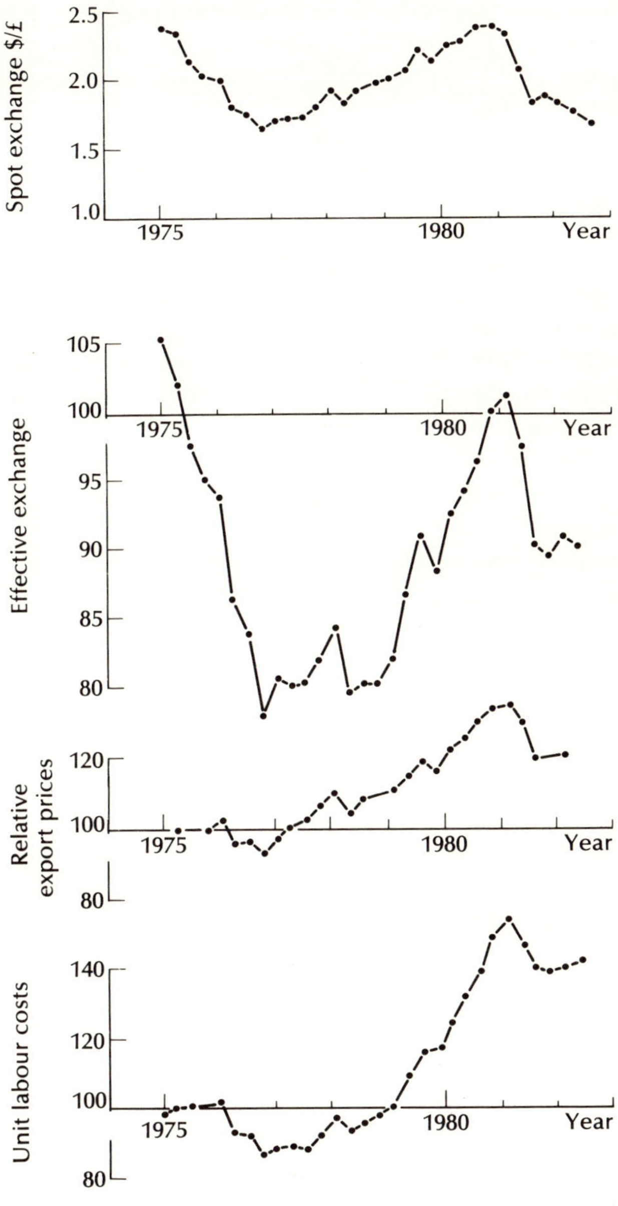

Figure 7.2 Measures of competitiveness, 1975-82 (1975=100)

far as it raises export prices, leads to a decline in UK competitiveness. From the beginning of 1979 oil production began to flow and oil prices began to rise; both had the effect of pushing up the sterling exchange rate. But simultaneously the Conservative strategy itself pushed up interest rates. This too leads to an appreciation of sterling. To what extent the appreciation was a result of North Sea oil or of the monetary policy of the Conservative government is difficult to disentangle.

One final set of observations can be made. The main instrument of the government's policy is a reduction in the money supply to bring down the rate of inflation. We have already noted in chapter 5 the difficulty the government faces in attempting such control. In Table 7.2 we show the growth in the money supply and the revision of monetary targets since 1976. These monetary targets have generally not been achieved, most especially since 1979. The obvious question to raise is, 'Is the decline in inflation shown in Table 7.1 not a result of monetary control, but rather a result of a stringent deflation of the economy carried out through monetary policy?'

Table 7.2 Monetary growth targets (% annual rate)

Year	Target range	Actual £M3	Achieved
1976/77	9-13	7.7	Yes
1977/78	9-13	16.0	No
1978/79	8-12	10.9	Yes
1978/79*	8-12	13.3	No
1979/80	7-11	10.3	Yes
1979/80*	7-11	17.8	No
1980/81	7-11	22.2	No
1981/82	6-10	14.5	No
1982/83	8-12†		
1983/84	7-11†		
1984/85	6-10†		

* November to October
† Planned targets to apply to the set of monetary aggregates M1, £M3 and PSL2

7.2 The Fundamental Postulates of Monetarism

If monetarism were well defined and monetarists themselves agreed on what it is, then it would be easy to state its fundamental postulates. Unfortunately, this is not the case. But we need to have some idea of what these postulates are, for how else can we decide on whether monetarism has succeeded or failed? Of course, it is possible to argue that what has succeeded or failed is purely the government's strategy, which bears no relationship to monetarism. Parkin and Bade (1982) argue that Margaret Thatcher's Conservatism is not an example of monetarism – at least not as they define monetarism. But there is a danger here of arguing that monetarism has never been implemented by any government and, therefore, has never been put to the test. However, before we can come to understand such a position we need to state, even if somewhat circumspectly, what appear to be agreed postulates of monetarism – realising that not all monetarists would necessarily agree with the list in total or in emphasis. The postulates are as follows.

(1) Growth in the money supply in excess of real income growth is the main, or only, cause of inflation.

(2) Changes in the money supply have a strong impact on nominal income.

(3) Output, employment and productivity growth are all determined by market forces independently of changes in the money supply – except for temporary disturbances.

(4) Governments should have policies towards just a few macroeconomic variables.

(5) Governments should follow fixed rules for the behaviour of the few macroeconomic variables chosen under (4).

(6) The monetary rule is a constant rate of growth of money supply at all times; the fiscal rule is a balanced Budget over four or five years.

(7) Fiscal policy is largely ineffective.

(8) Taxes should be reduced.

These postulates should be distinguished from the discussion surrounding the distinction between monetarists and Keynesians. Although they are relevant in this distinction, we are here concerned with highlighting what monetarism *is*, and not how it differs from Keynesian economics.

The two essential postulates of monetarism are that excessive growth in the money supply in excess of real income growth is the cause of inflation; and, second, that output, employment and productivity growth are determined by market forces independently of changes in the money supply – except for temporary disturbances. These two postulates together imply not only that fiscal policy is ineffective, but also that rules are preferable to fine tuning. This second set of implications we take up in detail in chapter 10. But what is not clear is why the rules should be *fixed,* and why for a growing economy the Budget should be balanced. As we point out in chapter 10, it is possible to accept the need for rules but not necessarily fixed ones. (An optimal monetary rule need not be a fixed simple rule.) This is important in attempting to answer the question posed for this chapter. If it is claimed, as Parkin and Bade do, that for a government to be monetarist then it must follow a simple fixed rule with respect to monetary growth, then Mrs Thatcher's government is not monetarist, since it has repeatedly revised its monetary growth targets (i.e., target *ranges*). But surely no government could follow such rigid policies with no deviation whatsoever? This implies that the real world should come into line with the theory! More to the point, it could be argued that, with the slightest deviation from such a rigid path, monetarism has not been 'truly' tested. If this is so, then monetarism will certainly never be 'truly' tested.

Postulate (2) states that changes in the money supply have a strong impact on nominal income. What it does not clearly indicate, however, is whether this impact falls largely on prices or largely on real income. The obvious implication of the first postulate is that a reduction in the money supply will reduce inflation and hence the major impact will fall on prices rather than output. But the evidence we considered in the first section would suggest that this may not be the case. Of course, monetarists could argue that this differential impact on prices and real income is only a short-term one, and that in the long run it will be prices that will be brought down. The reason for this, according to the list of postulates above, is because in the long run output, employment and productivity growth are determined by market forces. So long as the money supply follows a fixed rule and the Budget on average is balanced, then these market forces can establish equilibrium. Any shocks to the system will give rise to short-term movements, but so long as the rules are adhered to rational expectations will ensure that the long-run equilibrium is approached – unless another shock occurs.

Two difficulties arise in this line of reasoning. First, there is no clear idea how long the long run is. If no long run is specified, then it is always possible to state that the period is not long enough. Alternatively, the long run may never be allowed to be achieved because there are always shocks to the system. Second, there is a presumption that the long-run solution is totally independent of the time path of the economy over time. It is possible that the long-run solution, assuming that one exists, depends on the path the economy takes in its series of short periods. If, as a number of economists are arguing, it is important to minimise the effects of short-run shocks to the economic system, then it is possible to argue that there is no long run; that there is merely a series of short-run or medium-run positions each of which is disturbed by some future shock. It is in this sense that it is possible to interpret Keynes' adage that in the long run we are all dead!

7.3 A Rational Expectations View of the Government's Strategy

One justification for the government strategy, and one which is growing in terms of its adherents, is the rational expectations view put forward in Minford and Peel (1981) and Parkin and Bade (1982) and discussed in Professor Wickens' Inaugural Lecture (1981).

The rational expectations approach is based on 'the assumption that people use information efficiently in the pursuit of their interests' (Minford and Peel, 1981). This is interpreted to mean that consumers maximise their utility based on commodities and leisure and that this maximisation can be accomplished in the presence of perfect knowledge. In addition, people form 'rational expectations' in the sense that, given all publicly available information, individuals know the true probabilities to the different possible outcomes. This postulate of rational expectations is, however, combined with a second crucial postulate – namely, that markets always clear. In other words, transactions always take place at equilibrium. Both of these postulates are unrealistic ('unrealistic' in the same sense that physics assumes a vacuum for the law of falling bodies). Supporters of the new view argue that it is not the unrealism of the assumptions that matters: what matters is that the model incorporating these postulates performs better than any alternative model using different postulates. The importance of this approach is that it centres attention on the importance of information and the need to incorporate information in macroeconomic models.

The significance of these postulates is that consumers and producers engage in contracts in the light of all publicly available information at the time the contract is negotiated or agreed. In this sense all parties are maximising their own self-interest given the constraints imposed by law and Parliament. Outcomes are equilibrium outcomes and there is no slack in the system – unless created by government or arising temporarily from shocks to the system. In these terms all unemployment is voluntary and the business cycle occurs because of unanticipated random shocks which, because of lags in the system, lead to similar movements in output and unemployment. A further significant implication is with regard to stabilisation policy, which we take up in detail in chapter 10.

In one important respect the rational expectations view presents itself with a methodological dilemma. One rather technical result of the approach is that model predictions (using reduced-form equations) based on rational expectations cannot be distinguished from models incorporating, say, adaptive expectations. Furthermore, any policy changes which are pursued will make the models unstable, and consequently poor at predicting the outcome of any new policy. They would, therefore, caution against the uncritical use of econometric models. On the other hand, writers like Minford and Peel do in fact support their case using the 'Liverpool model'. The dilemma is that, if we take the new view at its face value, then we cannot use econometric models to compare it with other model specifications. In this extreme form, it becomes untestable. This means that justification for policy arises from the underlying theory rather than any econometric model.

What then would the new view advocate? Six points stand out.

(1) Governments should use only a limited number of macroeconomic policy instruments (intermediate targets).

(2) Monetary and fiscal policy rules should be followed.

(3) Governments should announce their intermediate targets.

(4) 'Immediacy' rather than 'gradualism' is preferable in bringing down inflation.

(5) Make short-run control of the money supply as independent as possible of short-run variations in the PSBR.

(6) Increase market efficiency:

Cut marginal tax rates
Cut the national insurance contribution
Increase privatisation
Increase competition in both the public and private sectors
Reduce monopoly power
Reduce trade union power
Reduce social security benefits
Reduce housing market distortions.

Although Parkin and Bade argue that Mrs Thatcher's government is not monetarist, it is clear that she is pursuing many, if not all, of the recommended policies just given. Not all at the same time, and not all in some absolute form – but realistically no government could do that. What can be argued is that the new view provides a theoretical justification for the policies being pursued. They are broader than monetarism – although the two clearly overlap.

7.4 Measuring Success or Failure

It is not only in this chapter that we have mentioned the difficulties of interpreting success or failure of a policy; we raised the same issue in section 3.4, when we discussed the costs of reducing inflation. The problem with Parkin and Bade's interpretation of Mrs Thatcher's government not following a monetary strategy because it has not adhered to a simple fixed rule for reducing the money supply is both theoretical and simply over-restrictive. It also confuses intermediate targets with final or primary objectives. The primary objective is a reduction in the rate of inflation. Whether a fixed monetary rule is followed or one which is less rigid, either will result in a time path of inflation. The question still remains as to which is the more successful. Of course, this does raise the counterfactual question, 'Had the government followed a fixed monetary rule, what would the path of inflation have been?' Since, as Parkin and Bade point out, it has not done this, we do not know what such a time path would be.

But if we turn to what the government has *actually* done, it is possible to make some observations. We can consider both its achievement of its monetary target range and the actual time path of inflation. The former we have done in Table 7.2, and it is clear that, not only has the government generally not succeeded in its monetary target, but this target has been revised fairly frequently.

But even when we turn to the actual inflation rate, how do we measure success or failure? In section 3.4 we hinted at one possible method. We can consider the sum of the squared deviations from the desired rates. Let $\hat{P}^*$ denote the desired inflation rate of the government and U_n the natural rate of unemployment. Then one such measure is:

$$W = (a/N)\,\Sigma\,(\hat{P} - \hat{P}^*)^2 + [(1 - a)/N]\,\Sigma\,(U - U_n)^2 \quad 0 \leqslant a \leqslant 1$$

where a denotes the weight the government attaches to inflation and $(1 - a)$ the weight it attaches to unemployment. Since W is in terms of the sum of the squared deviations, the aim is to reduce W to a *minimum*. The above formula divides each squared deviation by N, the period over which the sum is taken, so that we can compare two periods of different length. Thus, the formula can be thought of as the *average* of the squared deviations.

In the extreme case where the government is concerned only about inflation then $a = 1$. If the government is concerned only about unemployment then $a = 0$. Where the government takes account of both inflation and unemployment then $0 < a < 1$. But in this more likely case we do not know the actual value that the government places on a. Nor do we know what the present government's desired rate of inflation is;

i.e., we do not know $\hat{P}^*$, although a figure of 5% for the medium term has been suggested.

That is not all. We pointed out in chapter 2, when we discussed the rate of unemployment, that the natural rate of unemployment is a conceptual variable and that it is difficult to obtain an estimate of what it is – although it is not likely to be higher than 6%. All these unknowns would mean that it is not possible to say anything about success. We have one approach, however. Given the above formula, we can set different values for $\hat{P}^*$ and U_n and different values for the weight, *a*, and then compute the value of *W* for each possibility. This we have done in Table 7.3 for the two periods 1974(I)-1979(II) and 1979(III)-1982(II).

Table 7.3 Measuring government success

a	$\hat{P}^* = 2.5$, $U_n = 2$	$\hat{P}^* = 5$, $U_n = 3$	$\hat{P}^* = 7.5$, $U_n = 5$	$\hat{P}^* = 10$, $U_n = 6$	$\hat{P}^* = 5$, $U_n = 5$
			Period 1974 (I) – 1979 (II)		
0.0	9.0	4.6	1.6	3.1	1.6
0.1	8.6	4.6	3.2	7.1	1.9
0.2	8.2	4.7	4.8	11.1	2.3
0.3	7.8	4.7	6.4	15.1	2.6
0.4	7.4	4.7	8.1	19.0	3.0
0.5	6.9	4.8	9.7	23.0	3.3
0.6	6.5	4.8	11.3	27.0	3.7
0.7	6.1	4.9	12.9	31.0	4.0
0.8	5.7	4.9	14.3	35.0	4.3
0.9	5.3	5.0	16.1	39.0	4.7
1.0	4.8	5.0	17.7	42.9	5.0
			Period 1979 (III) – 1982(II)		
0.0	1.7	1.4	6.6	12.2	6.6
0.1	2.3	1.6	7.2	14.3	6.3
0.2	2.9	1.8	7.7	16.4	6.0
0.3	3.5	2.0	8.3	18.5	5.7
0.4	4.1	2.3	8.8	20.7	5.4
0.5	4.7	2.5	9.4	22.8	5.1
0.6	5.2	2.7	10.0	24.9	4.8
0.7	5.8	3.0	10.5	27.0	4.5
0.8	6.4	3.2	11.1	29.1	4.2
0.9	7.0	3.4	11.7	31.2	3.9
1.0	7.6	3.7	12.2	33.3	3.7

Note: Figures computed from: $W = (a/N)\ \Sigma\ (\hat{P} - P^*)^2. + [(1 - a)/N]\ \Sigma\ (U - U_n)^2$

Consider first the period 1974(I)-1979(II), when the Labour Party was in power. In the case of all the chosen values for $\hat{P}^*$ and U_n, the greater the weight attached to inflation, the smaller the value of W. In the second period the opposite is the case - with the exception of $\hat{P}^* =$ 5% and U_n = 5%. This should not be surprising. As we have already noted, inflation was greater in the first period and unemployment lower in comparison with the second period. The most interesting column in the second period is that where the desired rate of inflation and the natural rate of unemployment are both 5%, since both figures are fairly representative. Given these rates, the government objective will be more successful when $a = 1$; that is, where all effort is directed at reducing the rate of inflation. Of course, this depends not only on the measure here proposed, but it is based only on the rates of inflation and unemployment to date.

Although the present measure has many pitfalls, is does highlight the difficulty of interpreting 'success'. If the government does not announce $\hat{P}^*$, and if we have difficulty measuring U_n, as we do, then it is not surprising that we cannot come to any conclusion about the government's success or failure.[2]

7.5 Is the Strategy Reversible?

The present Conservative government in the UK has not only pursued a form of monetary strategy, but has also attempted some fundamental changes to the structure of the economy. Just as it is not possible to isolate a hypothesis in a model and test this in isolation from the model in which it is embedded, so too it is not possible to consider the success of Thatcher's monetarism independently of the other changes in the economy. The most obvious are a reduction of trade union power, a return to market forces and privatisation of a number of publicly owned corporations.

It has often been argued that the 'stop-go' policies of the late 1950s, 1960s and early 1970s led industry into a position of little or poor investment because any expansion was soon halted by the 'stop'. Uncertainty was so great that it hampered investment. An even greater uncertainty now presents itself. If a Labour government were returned to power, it is known that it would reverse all, or nearly all, of the policies pursued under the Thatcher administration, and it might go even further and nationalise the banks. Whatever the merits or otherwise of these intentions, such a complete switch can only lead to major adjustment problems. This may give rise to such anathema that pursuing the present course may seem preferable to a complete reversal!

To some extent we return to the question of the time period over which success or failure should be assessed. The Conservative government has repeatedly made the claim that it would require at least two parliaments to carry out its major changes and to achieve what it considers an acceptable rate of inflation. Let us suppose this is the case. In this instance, it would not be surprising to find that the situation halfway through would reflect the worst. But this cannot be counted as failure. What is necessary is to assess the whole period, and not just the terminal point. In order to reach the terminal point, however, the government must convince the voting public that the position at the end of the first five years is at the trough and that expansion will result thereafter.

The worry that some economists have, especially the neo-Keynesians, is that the policy being pursued will not in fact bring down the rate of inflation fast enough and that what will fall is real output. In other words, the eventual fall in inflation will be the result of a major deflation engineered by stringent monetary and fiscal policy. It is even possible for real output to decline before inflation reaches its desired target. The effect on British industry may then be catastrophic. The resulting loss of many firms' competitive position on world markets may be so great that they could be lost for ever! With markets functioning fairly freely, the decline could readily gather momentum. Furthermore, the outflow of capital, both short and long-term capital, could be very large. If these events were to come about (and it is possible to argue that they have been phrased in rather alarmist terms) then it would be most difficult to reverse the policies.

We arrive, then, at two extreme choices: either continue the monetarist strategy because reversing it will only lead to uncertainty and decline; or stop the monetarist policy, because otherwise the disaster to follow will not be capable of being averted: *reversal now as against the impossiblity of reversal in the future!*

Questions

1. What is the difference between monetarism and the rational expectations view?
2. Why should monetarists wish for only a few macroeconomic variables to be set as targets?
3. If the government sets a monetary target of 8-12% and the money supply grows at 13%, would you agree that this means that the government is not monetarist?
4. Does a long-run solution depend upon the *actual path* an economy follows?

5. Critically assess the measure of 'success' given in the text. Can you suggest any alternative?
6. Suppose the government has three objectives:

   (i) $U = U_n$

   (ii) $\hat{P} = \hat{P}*$

   (iii) $B = B*$ (a balance of payments surplus).

   How could you measure success? Would replacing $B*$ by $S*$ (the desired spot exchange rate) lead to any differences?
7. Let

$$\hat{P} = \hat{P}^e + f(U)$$

   represent a short-run Phillips curve. Using the measure in the text for welfare, how would you set up this problem in the form of an optimisation exercise?
8. List all the possible ways to assess government 'success' and compare them. Is it important to *measure* success?
9. Discuss the proposition that 'It is not possible to isolate a hypothesis in a model and test this in isolation from the model in which it is embedded.' What implications has this for assessing the government's approach to monetarism?
10. Does it matter if an economic policy is not reversible?

Notes

1. See Enoch (1978), Bank of England (1982a) and figures in *Economic Trends*.
2. For a test of monetarism, see Desai (1981).

PART IV

Fiscal Policy

CHAPTER 8

Should government expenditure be cut?

The 1970s saw a major change in fiscal emphasis in the UK. From the end of the Second World War until about 1970 there was a general belief that unemployment could be reduced by means of fiscal expansion. This fiscal expansion took the form of a rise in government spending. But the efficacy of this policy came into question, both from the point of view of practitioners and from the point of view of economic theory. The major theoretical change came from the realisation that the government Budget constraint (restraint?) must be taken into account; namely, in any year the government must pay for the government deficit, either from taxes, or from increases in the money supply, or from increases in bond sales (where for the moment we ignore the possibility of financing domestic expenditure from overseas sales of securities or overseas borrowing). In straightforward terms this means that *monetary and fiscal policy are not independent of each other.*

A second strand to the debate arose from the growing concern about the rise in the rate of inflation. As new theories of inflation stressed the importance of the growth of the money supply, so the immediate policy implication was to reduce this growth in order to reduce the rate of inflation. But because of the government Budget constraint, this in turn had implications for fiscal policy – namely, a reduction in the public sector borrowing requirement. The other issue here is whether the government deficit should be reduced; and if so whether this should be done through a reduction in government spending.

On the more political front there was also concern that the government sector was getting 'too large': that the size of the public sector ought to be reduced. Mixed with this was the belief some held that markets would work more efficiently without government interference. Although no government interference has the implication of a smaller government sector, the reasoning is not the same as that put forward for a reduced size of the public sector – which rests on arguments about its optimum size.

These introductory remarks indicate that, in answering the question, 'Should government expenditure be cut?' we must first be clear about its purpose. To highlight the differences, and the possible inter-relationships, let us list related questions:

(1) Should the absolute size of government expenditure *G* be reduced?

(2) Should the government deficit, $G - T$ (where *T* is taxes) be reduced? If so,
  (a) should this be done by reducing *G* alone?
  (b) should this be done by raising *T* alone?
  (c) should this be done by a combination of reducing *G* and raising *T*?

(3) Should the government Budget be balanced?

(4) Does it matter over which time period we are concerned with?

(5) What is the optimum size of the public sector?

What these questions highlight is the importance of distinguishing arguments concerning the Budget deficit (or the PSBR) from those concerned with the absolute size of government spending, i.e., the size of the public sector.

In the first section, therefore, we set out the developments which have taken place with regard to the Budget constraint, since this is central to many of the arguments which have been put forward. In the second section we consider the effect of reducing the Budget deficit, which in the light of the first section will depend on how the deficit is financed. In the third section we shall take up the issue of short-run and long-run considerations. It is clearly possible to argue for a rise in government spending in the short run and for an overall reduction in the long run. In section 8.4 we give some brief comments about market efficiency, which lays the foundation for the final section on the optimal size of the public sector. Although the final two sections draw on microeconomics, the size of the public sector clearly has macroeconomic implications when it means a change in government spending.

8.1 The Government Budget Constraint

In the 1950s and 1960s the textbook interpretation of monetary and fiscal policy was outlined in terms of the simple *IS* - *LM* model. This early treatment is shown in Figure 8.1. In Figure 8.1(a) we have a reduction in government spending, so shifting the *IS* curve from IS_0 to IS_1. In Figure 8.1(b) the situation is one where the money supply is reduced, so shifting the *LM* curve from LM_0 to LM_1. The first case shows a fiscal policy change while the second shows a monetary policy change. Both lead to a fall in income, but the former leads to a fall in interest

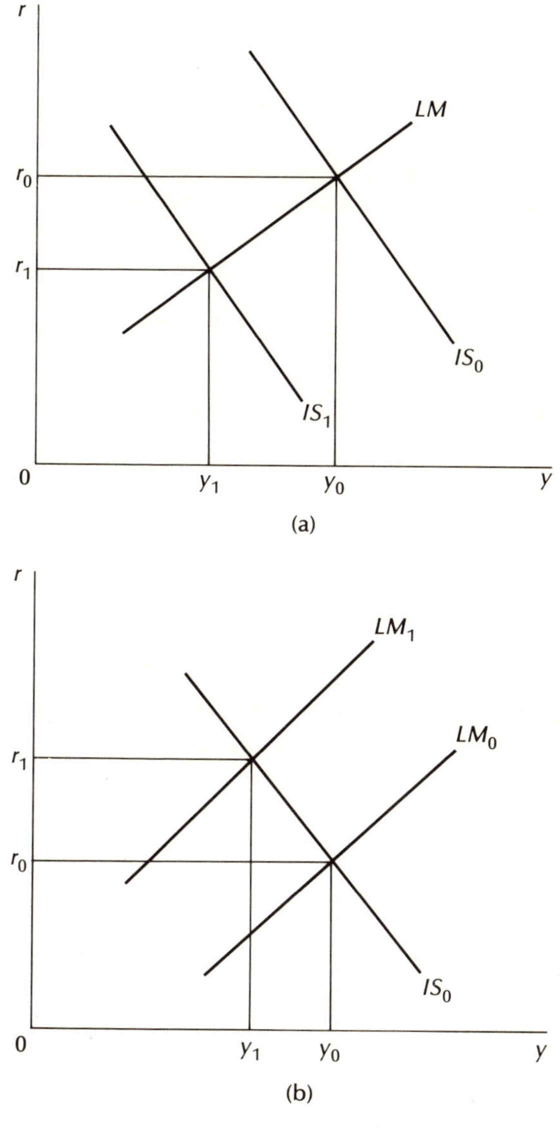

Figure 8.1 Pure fiscal and monetary policy

rates while the latter leads to a rise in interest rates.

This early literature was concerned with deriving the multipliers for each of these cases, showing the effect on income of some change in an exogenous variable: either government spending or the money supply. Depending on the various slopes of the *IS* curve and the *LM* curve, the comparative static results could be compared. It was clear that, in terms of this model, the relative importance of monetary or fiscal policy depended on the interest sensitivity of the money demand schedule and on the interest sensitivity of the investment schedule. For some time concern centred very much on obtaining measures of these various slopes.

Implicit in Figure 8.1(a) is that for fiscal policy there can be a change in government spending, holding other exogenous variables constant; and in Figure 8.1(b) that for monetary policy there can be a change in the money supply, holding other exogenous variables constant. This is why either the *IS* curve alone shifts or the *LM* curve alone shifts (what is sometimes referred to as 'pure fiscal policy', or 'pure monetary policy' respectively).

Let us assume that the situation is one of a government deficit. In the case of a bond-financed deficit the reduction in government spending means a reduction in the sale of bonds in this period as distinct from last period. It is now that we must be careful with regard to the type of model we are dealing with. The *IS* - *LM* model as portrayed in Figure 8.1 is a *stock-flow* model; that is to say, the *IS* curve denotes a flow equilibrium in the goods market and the *LM* curve denotes an equilibrium in the money market. In this early treatment the wealth position (which is a *stock* position) of the market participants was totally ignored. To see this, simply ask the question, 'Do market participants wish to hold their extra wealth in the form of bonds?' Let us suppose they do. Is it this reduced sale of bonds which leads to a fall in the interest rate, as shown in Figure 8.1(a)? The answer is, 'No'. The decrease in government spending leads to a fall in the level of income. But this fall in the level of income leads to a fall in the transactions demand for money. Since it is assumed that the supply of money is held fixed, then equilibrium in the money market can be established only if the rate of interest falls. We see from this analysis that the fall in interest rates from r_0 to r_1 in Figure 8.1(a) is a result of a fall in the transactions demand for money, and has nothing to do with the wealth position of market participants. Similarly, the increase in bond sales required to decrease the money supply by means of open market operations, shown in Figure 8.1(b), although it increases the bond holdings of the public, is assumed not to lead to any substitution of wealth from bonds into other assets. The rise in the interest rate occurs because the decrease in the money supply leads to a flow disequilibrium in the money market. Since this disequilibrium takes the form of excess demand, it can be eliminated only by means of a rise in the rate of interest. In other words, the change in the interest rate is due to the situation in the money market. In both cases the wealth position is not taken into consideration.

The analysis so far highlights two deficiencies:

(1) In a closed economy, the government can only raise money from taxes, from the sale of bonds or from printing more money; i.e.,

$$G - T = dM + dB/r$$

where $G - T$ denotes the Budget deficit/surplus, dM the change in the money supply, dB the change in the bond issue and $1/r$ the bond price (assuming, for simplicity, a perpetuity).

(2) Any changes in wealth will normally lead to stock adjustments which will affect the *IS* and/or the *LM* curve.

In the remainder of this section we shall concentrate on the Budget constraint; we shall take up the second aspect in the next section.

We can now see the meaning of a bond-financed increase in government spending. If the *LM* curve is to remain fixed then $dM = 0$ and the change in the Budget deficit is matched by the change in the bond issue; i.e., with $dM = 0$, then

$$G - T = dB/r$$

On the other hand, a pure monetary policy, which shifts the *LM* curve leaving the *IS* curve fixed, requires that $G - T = 0$ and

$$dM = dB/r$$

It is, however, possible to finance the Budget deficit/surplus by means of increases/decreases in the money supply; i.e., a money-financed Budget deficit requires $dB/r = 0$ and

$$G - T = dM$$

The situation is shown in Figure 8.2, where we begin with IS_0 and LM_0 and interest rate r_0 and real income at y_0. Government expenditure is now increased, so shifting the *IS* curve to IS_1. If, however, this is financed by means of printing more money, then the *LM* curve will shift to the right, to LM_1. Although the eventual outcome on the interest rate is uncertain, it is lower than a pure bond-financed deficit; income, on the other hand, unambiguously rises, and rises by more than a bond-financed Budget deficit. Of course, the reverse argument also holds true. If we begin at the position represented by IS_1 and LM_1 and reduce the Budget deficit and achieve this by reducing the money supply, then the eventual outcome is at the intersection of IS_0 and LM_0. Income is reduced, and reduced by even more than it would have been by a pure fiscal policy or a pure monetary policy.

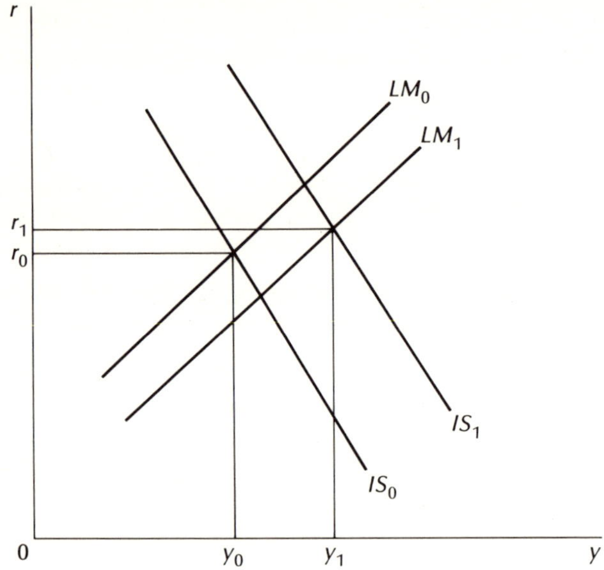

Figure 8.2 Money-financed Budget deficit

One further development requires mentioning. If the bond issue is B then the interest payment on this issue is £*B*, so that the government deficit/surplus is $G - T + B$. Hence, the correct form for the Budget constraint is:

$$G - T + B = dM + dB/r$$

We see from this equation that, even if the government balanced its Budget, in the sense of current expenditure equalling tax receipts ($G = T$), there would still be need of an increase in the money supply and/or an increase in the bond issue in order to cover the debt repayment.

The introduction of the government Budget constraint has a number of immediate implications. Here we shall concentrate on just one. Suppose, as seems to have been the case in the 1950s and 1960s, that the government Budget deficit was financed by increases in the money supply. If, as monetarists argue, it is excessive growth in the money supply which leads to persistent increases in the inflation rate, then this type of financing of larger and larger Budget deficits has been a major cause of Britain's inflation. To reverse this process, if true, the government requires to reduce the money supply growth. If it is not simultaneously going to increase the bond issue, then the implication of this is a fall in the Budget deficit, i.e., a fall in $G-T+B$ (in other words, a fall in the public sector borrowing requirement).

This is the very situation we described in Figure 8.2. If we take it that the initial position is represented by IS_1 and LM_1, the aim of Margaret Thatcher's government is to reduce the money supply to curb inflation, so shifting the *LM* curve to LM_0. But this is to be accomplished by reducing the PSBR, and so shifting the *IS* curve to IS_0. The reduction of real income (and hence employment) is far greater than with any other means of achieving the reduction in the money supply.

What should be appreciated in this argument is the following. Given that the main objective is full employment, this can be maintained by government spending; but then the money supply must be made consistent with this – even if this means a higher rate of inflation. If, on the other hand, the main objective is a low rate of inflation, then this means a reduction in the money supply and hence a concomitant reduction in the Budget deficit. It is this link through the government Budget constraint which has led to difficulties in achieving both a reduced rate of inflation and a fully employed economy. The Phillips curve trade-off simply ignored this constraint.

What comes out of this discussion is the relative importance that governments place on the main policy objective. So long as the main objective remains full, or near full, employment, this generally implies a passive monetary policy which tends over time to fuel inflation. If the main objective is a reduction in the rate of inflation, then it is fiscal policy which becomes passive and which must fall if the policy is to be consistent. With a bond issue that is unchanged, $dB/r = 0$, then it is simply not possible to reduce the money supply and simultaneously increase the government Budget deficit. This dilemma is at the heart of the monetarist/Keynesian debate. But whichever side is favoured, the Budget constraint cannot be violated since it is an accounting identity.

Whatever one's views about Mrs Thatcher's policies, they are consistent. In answer to the question, 'Should government expenditure be cut?' the answer in the present context is, 'Yes', if your major aim is to reduce inflation by reducing the money supply (and if simultaneously you want a reduction in the size of the government sector). If you are prepared to deal with inflation by some other means, such as a price and income policy, then the answer is, 'No'. The differing answers to the same question rest largely on what is believed to be 'the' major problem: inflation or the level of employment. But there remains the question of whether these are in conflict only in the short run but not in the long run. To this we shall return in the third section.

Two further points, which are also interrelated, need to be discussed. First, in Britain the rise in the Budget deficit has occurred largely from the increase in government transfers, such as unemployment benefits. If, therefore, we wish to separate these from government expenditure on goods and services, then G denotes this latter expenditure while TR denotes the nominal value of transfers. Hence, the Budget constraint now takes the form:

$$G + TR - T + B = dM + dB/r$$

The second point refers to the problem of nominal versus real changes. Even with real government expenditure constant there can be a rise in nominal government expenditure if there is a rise in the price level. Let $BD = G + TR - T + B$, that is the *nominal* Budget deficit, and $bd = g + tr - t + b$ denote the *real* value of the Budget deficit, so that $BD = Pbd$, where P is the general price level.

As unemployment rises, so too does the level of transfers, TR. We have already noted that a fall in the money supply, implemented as a means of reducing inflation, requires a concomitant fall in the Budget deficit if the bond issue is not to be increased. As Figure 8.2 makes clear, this results in a fall in income and hence a fall in the level of employment. The rise in unemployment, however, leads to a rise in transfer payments made by the government in the form of unemployment benefit. In addition, the fall in income will lead to a fall in the level of tax receipts. Both of these factors raise, rather than lower, the Budget deficit. In order, therefore, for the Budget deficit to actually decrease, consistent with the decrease in the money supply, government expenditure on goods and services must bear the brunt of the cut. In addition, this cut must compensate not only for the fall in the money supply, but also for the fall in tax receipts and for the increase in transfer earnings!

But this is not all. If the rate of inflation is high – even if the government policy is successful in reducing it over time – then the nominal value of government spending will rise for a *given* real government expenditure. For a given fall in the nominal money supply, therefore, the real fall in government expenditure is greater the higher the price level.

We see from this analysis that four factors impinge on the necessity (given the government's policy objective) to reduce real government spending on goods and services:

(1) A fall in the nominal money supply

(2) A fall in the level of tax receipts

(3) A rise in the level of transfer payments

(4) A higher price level.

To the extent that inflation is brought down by this policy, item (4) will lead to a smaller reduction required in real government expenditure. If, however, the rate of inflation increases (especially when the policy is first implemented) then an even greater decrease in real government expenditure on goods and services is required.

8.2 The Effects of a Cut in Government Expenditure

Let us first consider a reduction in government expenditure in terms of the effects on real income and interest rates. In doing this we must be clear on the forms of finance, which are three in number:

(1) A tax-financed cut in public expenditure

(2) A bond-financed cut in public expenditure

(3) A monetary-financed cut in public expenditure.

In terms of the Budget constraint

$$G - T + TR + B = dM + dB/r$$

(1) requires $dM = 0$, $dB/r = 0$ and $dG = d(T - TR - B)$

(2) requires $dM = 0$ and $G - T + TR + B = dB/r$

(3) requires $dB/r = 0$ and $G - T + TR + B = dM$

The situation is shown in Figure 8.3(a)-(c). We begin all situations with curves IS_0 and LM_0, which is also assumed to be a situation where the Budget is balanced at real income level y_0 and interest rate r_0. In Figure 8.3(a) we have a decrease in government expenditure which is matched by an equal fall in taxes; namely, a balanced Budget change. The initial fall in government spending is shown by the curve IS_1, and the simple multiplier, ignoring the financing aspect of the change, is shown by the income change $y_1 - y_0$ (which is negative, denoting the fact that income falls). Since the reduced expenditure is financed from taxes, the fall in the IS curve is not as great as indicated by IS_1 and is in fact shown by IS_2. There is still a fall in income and in the rate of interest because of the fall in taxes arising from the change in income. In other

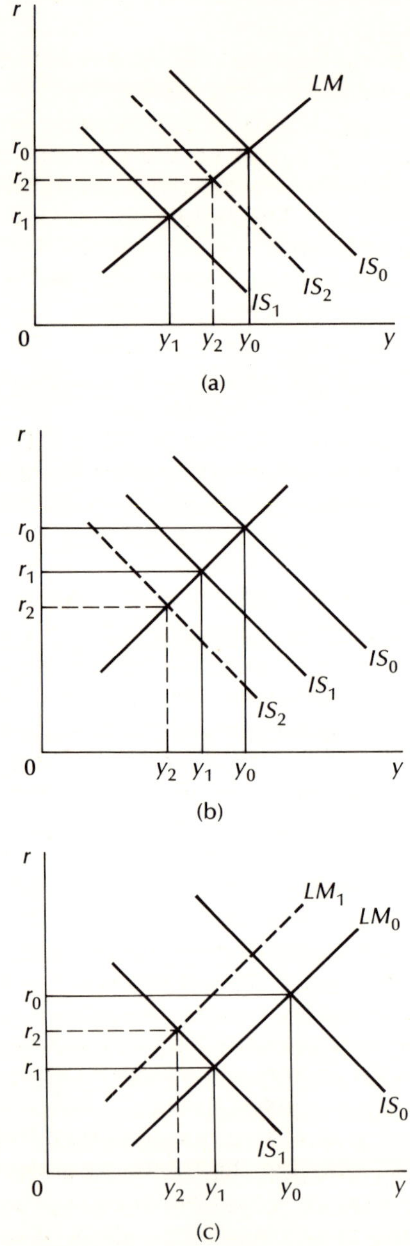

Figure 8.3 (a) Balanced Budget cut in G;
(b) Bond-financed cut in G;
(c) Money-financed cut in G.

words, income must fall for a decrease in government spending matched by an equal fall in taxes.

Next consider a bond-financed cut in government spending. The reduction in government spending means that the government does not have to sell as many bonds as it otherwise would. This in turn means that the interest payment on the national debt is less than it otherwise would be. This means a further fall in private income and a shift in the *IS* curve to IS_2. The result is an unambiguous fall in real income and the rate of interest.

In the case of a money-financed cut in government spending, the fall in government spending means that the money supply can be cut by the amount of the cut in government spending. Hence, the *LM* curve moves to LM_1. Although the result on the interest rate is uncertain, there is an unambiguous fall in real income.

It is clear from Figure 8.3(a)-(c) that both bond-financed and money-financed cuts in government spending have a greater impact on real income than a balanced Budget change in government spending. But how do the bond- and money-financed cuts compare? The bond-financed cut in government spending must have a greater impact on real income than the money-financed cut because the reduced interest payment on the debt requires a greater fall in income to balance the Budget than would a straight money-financed cut with the bond issue unchanged. The major difference between the bond-financed and money-financed cuts in government spending is with respect to the interest rate: in the bond-financed situation it unambiguously falls, whereas in the money-financed situation it may fall or rise, but will be higher than r_1, and hence higher than in the bond-financed situation. This could be an important consideration when an open economy is taken into account – which is clearly more relevant to the UK.

It is apparent from the foregoing analysis that the impact of a cut in government spending depends on how it is financed. The Conservative government under Margaret Thatcher chose to reduce the money supply in line with the requirement to bring down the rate of inflation. In this case the initial shift is not in the *IS* curve but rather in the *LM* curve. In terms of Figure 8.3(c) this means a cut in *G* in order to satisfy the government Budget constraint (or, strictly, an increase in the nominal amount of *G less* than in the past). Since the reduction in the money supply is determined by factors outside the goods and money market, the shift in *LM* can be greater than that indicated by LM_1 in Figure 8.3(c). If this is so, then the fall in government spending consistent with this is also greater than that indicated by IS_1. The final result of this is a reduction in income in excess of $y_o - y_2$ and hence a level of unemployment greater than that associated with income level y_2.

8.3 Wealth Effects

In the previous section we dealt with the interrelationships between the *IS* and *LM* curves arising purely from the Budget constraint. There is, however, one other reason why the two curves are interrelated. To appreciate this second interrelationship we must clearly define the private sector wealth position of the economy. In simple terms we can define private sector wealth (a stock) as the sum of the physical capital stock, K, the real value of money holdings, M/P, and the real value of bond holdings, $(B/r)/P = B/rP$; i.e.,

$$W = K + (M/P) + (B/rP)$$

In the case of a tax-financed Budget deficit, the wealth position of the private sector remains unchanged. In the case of a bond-financed deficit the bond issue is achieved by the public running down their money balances to pay for them; but then this money is put back into the economy by government spending. With constant prices, therefore, the real value of money holdings remains unchanged. There is, however, a rise in wealth as a result of the increased real value of bond holdings. This additional wealth will be distributed in some way between consumption goods, money holdings and bond holdings – unless in the unlikely situation where the private sector is willing to hold the whole of the increase in wealth in the form of bond holdings. Such an increase in consumption goods arising from increased wealth will lead to an outward shift in the *IS* curve (to the left for a fall in wealth). In addition, the increased wealth will in part lead to a demand for money balances. With a fixed supply of money balances, equilibrium in the money market can be restored only by a rise in the interest rate. In other words, the *LM* curve shifts to the left (to the right for a fall in wealth). The final result of the wealth effect is certainly to raise the interest rate (decrease it for a fall in wealth) but has an uncertain outcome with regard to the effect on real income. The result on real income depends on the elasticity of consumption with respect to wealth in comparison with the elasticity of the demand for money with respect to wealth. If the latter outstrips the former, the leftward shift in the *LM* curve will outweigh the rightward shift in the *IS* curve, with the result that real income will fall.

The wealth effects must be compared not with the initial position but with the position after the bond-financed increase in government spending. This is shown in Figure 8.4 for a bond-financed increase in government spending. The initial position is given by IS_0 and LM_0. A bond-financed government deficit shifts the *IS* curve to IS_1 – taking into account the government Budget constraint. But the wealth effect shifts the *IS* curve further to the right, to IS_2, and the *LM* curve to the left, to

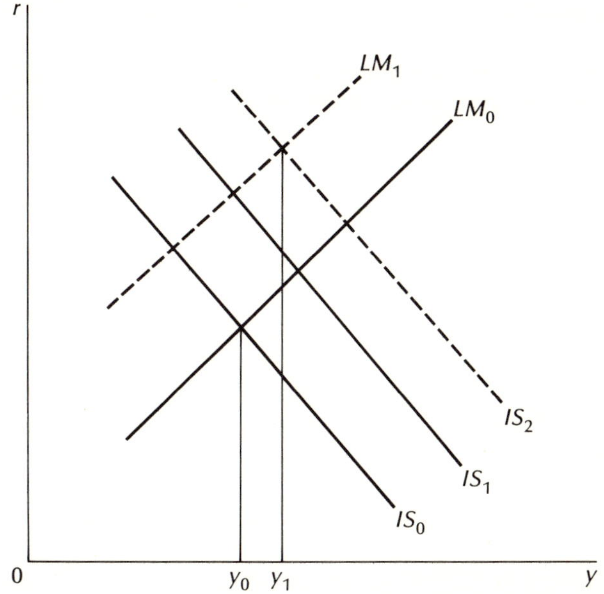

Figure 8.4 Wealth effects of a bond-financed Budget deficit

LM_1. It is possible for the final result to be the initial level of real income, y_0, or even a smaller real income! We shall take this issue up in more detail in the next chapter.

The issue being highlighted in the previous paragraphs is that the *IS* – *LM* framework is a stock-flow model. It does not indicate the stock position of the private sector. If we began at IS_0 and LM_0 in Figure 8.4 with the private sector in stock equilibrium as well as flow equilibrium, then the bond-financed Budget deficit must affect both the flow and the stock equilibrium positions. The situation where IS_1 intersects LM_0, although a flow equilibrium, cannot be maintained in the long run because there are still stock-adjustment flows taking place – in other words, flows which take place in order to re-establish a stock equilibrium. These are the very wealth effects we have just alluded to. The alteration in the wealth position of the private sector gives rise to changes in consumption (a stock-adjustment flow) and to changes in the demand for money (a stock-adjustment flow). The eventual equilibrium must be one of stock equilibrium, since this also implies a flow equilibrium.

One other issue which is not so obvious must be mentioned. In considering this let us take a money-financed Budget deficit. The situation is shown in Figure 8.5(a). The initial position, with curves IS_0 and LM_0, is one of stock and flow equilibrium and a balanced Budget. Government spending is now to be increased and financed from an increase in the money supply. Like a bond-financed Budget deficit, this

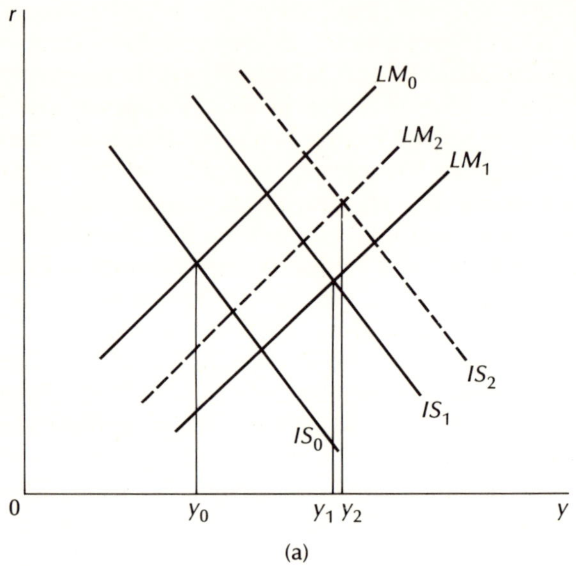

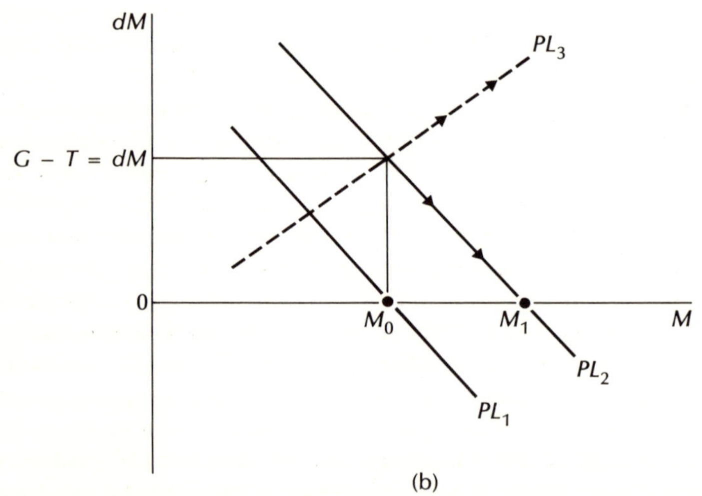

Figure 8.5 Price effect of a money-financed increase in G

also leads to a net increase in private sector wealth arising from an increase in real money balances, i.e., a rise in M/P. This will further shift the *IS* curve to the right and the *LM* curve to the left. The final outcome is shown by the curves IS_2 and LM_2.

There is a supposition in this analysis that the money supply will increase by a finite amount: that, given the situation where the Budget goes into deficit, an increase in the money supply to finance this deficit will not give rise to other factors which will further increase the deficit, and so require a further increase in the money supply. This can be appreciated with the help of Figure 8.5(b), which shows the relationship between the change in the money supply and the stock of money balances in the economy. At the initial position in terms of Figure 8.5(a), with the money supply denoted by M_o, the Budget is balanced and there is a position of stock equilibrium – shown in Figure 8.5(b) by the fact that the *phase line*[1] PL_1 intersects the horizontal axis at M_o. The increase in government spending shifts the phase line to PL_2. At the initial money stock there is now a Budget deficit which, if financed from an increase in the money supply, requires $G - T = dM$. The money stock will therefore rise from M_o to M_1. M_1 is a stock equilibrium and a flow equilibrium only in the absence of any wealth effects. With wealth effects coming into the picture, the phase line PL_2 shifts. The direction in which it moves depends on whether the shift in the *LM* curve outweighs the shift in the *IS* curve consequent on the wealth effects.

But even without the wealth effects, there is another complication. All the curves drawn in Figure 8.5 assume a *constant* price level (with the exception of the phase line PL_3). The effect of raising government expenditure financed from an increase in the money supply would result in a rightward shift in the aggregate demand schedule and hence in a rise in prices. The eventual rise in the money supply comes to a stop because, with constant prices, a rise in real income increases the real value of tax receipts and so lowers the real value of the Budget deficit (and hence the nominal value of the Budget deficit). Suppose, however, that the rise in prices leads to a larger *nominal* deficit even though real income is rising. This would occur if the greater impact of the change fell on prices rather than on real income. This would then call for an even bigger increase in the money supply. What is implied here is that the phase line is *positively* sloped, and the path is along the dotted phase line PL_3, indicating a time path of ever greater increases in the money supply, i.e., an unstable situation.

The issue of the impact of the wealth effect and the issue of whether a rise in prices leads to an unstable adjustment mechanism are both empirical issues. Although much of the discussion has surrounded the wealth effect (and in particular whether it is large or small), the issue over the price effect relative to the real income change has had less attention. But once again it is this issue which leads to differences of opinion between monetarists and Keynesians. The difference can be seen in terms of Figure 8.6. Monetarists assume that for any change in the money supply the impact on prices is more sensitive than the impact

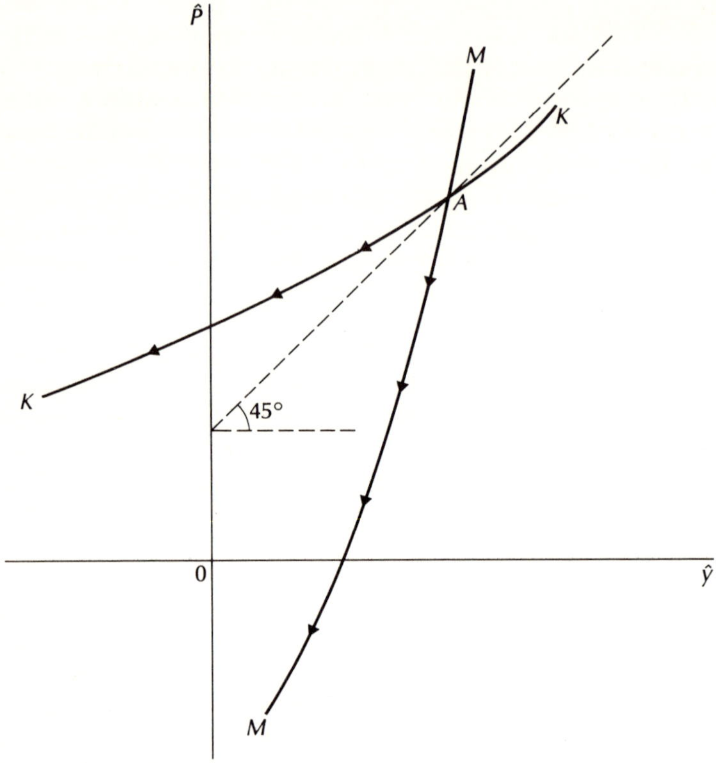

Figure 8.6 Consequences of reducing the growth of the money supply

on real income; Keynesians, on the other hand, believe the opposite is the case. Given an initial position *A,* the curve *MM* represents the monetarist belief, while *KK* represents the Keynesian belief. A rise in the money supply to finance a budget deficit would be unstable in the monetarist model but stable in the Keynesian model. Conversely, a policy of reducing the money supply to curb inflation has more impact on real income in the Keynesian model than it does in the monetarist model. Some Keynesians would go so far as to say that the policy could lead to an actual decline in the level of real GNP.

One final observation is worth making. The *IS – LM* framework was shown to be inadequate because it represented only a flow equilibrium. With the introduction of stock-adjustment equations a more complete model can be formulated. But as the previous analysis indicates, this too is inadequate. If prices are changing then the situation cannot be in long-run equilibrium. A 'full equilibrium' in the long run requires a constant inflation rate which is fully anticipated, i.e., where expected inflation is equal to actual inflation.

8.4 The Optimal Size of the Public Sector

One main reason for reducing government spending is the belief that the public sector is too large and that government spending is taking too large a proportion of GDP. There is little doubt that government spending had been growing up to 1975 no matter how this is measured,

Table 8.1 UK government spending, 1964-81

Year	GDP market prices	General government final consumption	PSBR	G/GDP (%)	PSBR/ GDP (%)
1964	33,135	5,466	989	16.5	3.0
1965	35,620	5,994	1,205	16.8	3.4
1966	38,009	6,520	963	17.2	2.5
1967	40,151	7,213	1,863	18.0	4.6
1968	43,519	7,662	1,291	17.6	3.0
1969	46,607	7,997	-449	17.2	-1.0
1970	51,107	8,991	-10	17.6	0.0
1971	57,339	10,250	1,364	17.9	2.4
1972	63,461	11,675	2,055	18.4	3.2
1973	73,025	13,380	4,200	18.3	5.8
1974	13,076	16,618	6,370	20.0	7.7
1975	104,760	22,950	10,505	21.9	10.0
1976	124,546	26,739	9,198	21.5	7.4
1977	143,775	29,244	5,997	20.3	4.2
1978	165,375	32,984	8,354	19.9	5.1
1979	193,368	38,324	12,608	19.8	6.5
1980	226,112	48,424	12,205	21.4	5.4
1981	248,398	55,151	10,629	22.2	4.3

Source: Economic Trends, Annual Supplement (1983 edition)

as is shown in Table 8.1. But while some would like to see the absolute size of government spending decreased, others would like to see greater government involvement. This issue is not as much related to the main objective of any government as some of the arguments we have already discussed, but it is related to a much broader political question of the role of government in a modern capitalist society.

There are basically two extreme views. One is that the least government involvement is the best, and the other is that more government involvement is required in order to protect the workers from the unfair power that society bestows on industry and the owners of capital. Of course, there are a number of views which come part way between these two extremes, but they do express fairly well commonly held views. Depending upon which category a person belongs to, it follows that the former will generally support a reduction in government spending while the latter will support a rise in public spending.

A reduced involvement of government in society is based on the belief that the market mechanism can do the job more efficiently; that markets which are unregulated can do the job which they are designed to do: namely, to allocate resources in an efficient manner. But a basic underlying economic assumption in this argument, which must be clearly spelled out, is that markets clear quickly. In other words, transactions take place at market-clearing prices and quantities. What if they do not? Does it mean that the assumption is incorrect? Here we face an immediate difficulty in the argument. Those who believe in the efficiency of markets will not simply accept that the assumption is false; on the contrary, they will argue that there are forces in society which are preventing the markets from clearing quickly. If these forces can be broken, reduced, or redirected in some way, then (it is argued) the market will work efficiently. The basic postulate, therefore, is that free unregulated markets work efficiently. It is not possible to prove this in the presence of regulated markets: it can only be asserted.

The counter-argument is that markets do not work efficiently; and even if they did, they deal only with effective demand. It is important to recall that demand means not only willingness to pay but also ability to pay. The ability to pay is related to many factors – not least to past savings and wealth accumulation (including bequests). Society's production of goods and services will, so this argument goes, be greatly influenced by the demands of wealth owners. The point made here, and in any microeconomics text, is that efficiency does not imply a desired distribution of either income or wealth.

In the case of goods which have a great deal of 'publicness' about them, e.g., defence and law and order, they are considered to be obvious candidates to be supplied by the government. But the literature on public goods is very confused at the present time. Not only is the idea of a 'public good' vague, but some would argue that public goods should be provided by the government. There is a danger here of assuming (wrongly) that if something can be provided by the government then it must be a public good. This involves a circular definition of a public good. Every known good and service can be, and has been, supplied privately. The issue here is the *degree* of public involvement in the supply of the good or service. When we consider such services as education and health, for example, there is only a *degree* of 'publicness', and these are not obvious candidates to be *wholly* supplied by the government. But even if true, the obvious question is, 'Then what amount should be provided by the government?'

No one would seriously advocate no government involvement in any society. At the other extreme is total government involvement. But not even a socialist model as presently pursued in the USSR would advocate government involvement in all decision-making. It is a question of degree. Accepting this, we can approach the issue in two different ways:

(1) What is the optimal size of the government?

(2) Given that we are presently at the position where *x*% of GDP is government expenditure, should this be cut, left unchanged or raised?

Although (1) is the more theoretical, the answer to (2) is in part based on some idea of the answer to (1) for a given economy at some point in time. Even more difficult is the idea that 'optimal' has also built into it the notion of maximum welfare for society.

Setting up a model to analyse the optimal size of the government is very difficult, and we have not got space here to cover it. But one model is fairly indicative of the type of model which is being used. This is the Niskanen model, which combines vote-maximising behaviour and utility-maximising behaviour – on the lines of Downs' theory of democracy.[2] By incorporating the assumption that bureaus are utility-maximising bodies it is possible to deal not only with allocative inefficiency but also with *x*-inefficiency. The concentration is then on seeing how to reduce government spending in order to reduce the inefficiency – especially the *x*-inefficiency.

This type of argument is quite different from the optimal size itself. What it does indicate is that government spending is high because of inefficiencies. Government spending can, therefore, be cut by eliminating such inefficiencies. The model consequently directs attention to where the inefficiencies occur and how to eliminate them. One way to deal with the inefficiency is to privatise some of the services. The implicit argument here is that there is less inefficiency (of the *x*-inefficiency type) in the private sector than in the public sector.[3] But this is very difficult to prove.

This section has dealt with two features:

(1) The degree of government involvement in society

(2) The inefficiency of government bureaucracies.

The first is very entrenched in political views and cannot be answered within the confines of economics. The second would suggest, however, that, to the extent that there are inefficiencies in the public sector, then there is always some room for a reduction in government spending if some of this inefficiency could be eliminated. Exactly how it can be eliminated is, however, a moot point!

8.5 Conclusion

There has been no attempt to answer the question posed as the title to this chapter. Rather, the aim has been to lay out the alternative views and hypotheses involved in coming to some answer. It is possible, however, to come to a number of conclusions.

(1) The desire to reduce government spending is related to the main objective of the government; if this aim is full employment then there is less pressure to reduce government spending than if the main objective is to reduce the rate of inflation by reducing the money supply.

(2) The government Budget constraint relates monetary and fiscal policy. Without an independent policy instrument to deal with inflation, then monetary policy, fiscal policy and inflation policy are all interconnected through the government Budget constraint.

(3) The cut in government spending could be counter-productive if it raises the level of unemployment benefits arising from the increased total of unemployed.

(4) If the level of transfers rises as a result of the cut in government spending, then the other components of government spending will have to bear a greater burden of the adjustment.

(5) A failure to cut government spending will almost inevitably lead to an increase in the money supply. To the extent that this is inflationary, this disbenefit must be weighed against the effect of cutting government spending.

(6) The result of a cut in government spending has two effects: first, on the flows of goods and services and money demanded and supplied; second, a stock effect in that it will influence the wealth position of the private sector.

(7) The reduction in the money supply consistent with a cut in government spending can influence real output and/or prices. This will determine whether the nominal value of the Budget deficit increases or decreases with a decrease in the money supply.

(8) The absolute size of the government sector depends on a political standpoint. The decision to reduce government spending, therefore, depends fundamentally on the role of government. It also

depends on the belief in the efficiency of markets and how quickly they clear.

(9) The theory of public goods has not progressed far enough at the present time to give enough guide to governments on the degree of their involvement in services which have differing degrees of 'publicness'.

(10) To the extent that government bureaucracies are inefficient, government spending can be cut if these can be identified and eliminated. This may or may not involve privatisation. If undertaken, it is likely to be a one-off reduction in government spending.

Questions

1. Explain fully why government monetary and fiscal policies are not independent of one another.
2. In what way, if at all, does causation enter the government Budget constraint?
3. Explain what is meant by:
   (a) A *pure* fiscal policy
   (b) A *pure* monetary policy.
4. In what way does wealth enter the *IS* curve and the *LM* curve? How does the presence of wealth influence the concept of equilibrium in macroeconomics?
5. Excluding wealth changes, compare the different impacts on real income of a rise in government spending of £100m financed by means of:
   (a) An equal rise in taxes
   (b) An equal rise in the money supply
   (c) An equal rise in bond sales.
6. If a cut in the money supply leads to higher unemployment, how are the increased unemployment benefits to be financed?
7. Analyse a *persistent* bond-financed increase in government spending. In particular, what happens to the national debt and how is the debt to be financed?
8. Explain fully how an increase in the money supply to finance an increase in the nominal Budget deficit can lead to yet further increases in the money supply.
9. Of the three ways of financing an increase in the Budget deficit (from taxes, from increases in the money supply and by borrowing from the public), which have the effect of increasing wealth? Can this wealth effect swamp the initial impact of the increase in the Budget deficit?

10. What is a phase line? In what way can phase lines clarify the meaning of stock and flow equilibria?
11. Analyse in detail the results in Table 8.1.
12. Would you advocate:
    (a) More government involvement in the economy?
    (b) Less government involvement in the economy?
    (c) No change in the level of government involvement in the economy?

Notes

1. An elementary treatment of phase diagrams can be found in Neal and Shone (1976) and Chiang (1967); for a more advanced discussion, with applications, see Takayama (1974).
2. See Downs (1957), Niskanen (1973) and Jackson (1982).
3. See Rowley (1977).

CHAPTER 9

How important is crowding out?

Crowding out is one of those issues which theoreticians discuss in some detail and politicians talk about with emotion. In its simplest and crudest form, it says that if government spending is increased by £100m then private investment will fall by £100m: that is, government spending crowds out private investment. It is from this simplistic view that the importance of the concept stems. If it is true, then it means that fiscal policy in the long run has no impact on the economy and merely changes the composition of national income.

In the previous chapter we discussed the issue of the size of the public sector and the decision of whether to cut government spending. One reason for such a decision is to reverse the crowding out. Put differently, if crowding out is real, then cutting government spending by £100m will expand private investment by £100m. But even if crowding out does in fact occur, it does not follow that it is a symmetrical relationship. The point at issue is the long and old one of 'whether fiscal policy matters'. As we have just mentioned, if crowding out occurs then fiscal policy has no real impact on the economy except to change its composition. In this extreme form, fiscal policy does not matter. This view was held by classical economists and is to a large extent held by modern monetarists – albeit for different reasons. Keynesians do not accept complete crowding out and have always maintained that fiscal policy matters. It is clear, therefore, that one reason why the issue is important is because it has tremendous policy implications.

In the first section we shall provide a taxonomy of crowding out. Although we have stated above what it is, the concept is not at all a clear one. Given that the policy implications are so tremendous and important, the concept does require full elucidation. In section 9.2 we shall consider the evidence that is available on the degree of crowding out. In the third and final section we shall take up the issues raised by the Bacon-Eltis thesis. This particular debate is dependent on the assumption that crowding out is very large – if not complete. Unlike the monetarists' arguments, which are an update of classical ideas, the Bacon-Eltis thesis is a return to Physiocratic ideas.

9.1 Taxonomy of Crowding Out

The basic taxonomy is given in Figure 9.1, which first distinguishes between physical and financial crowding out. Physical crowding out

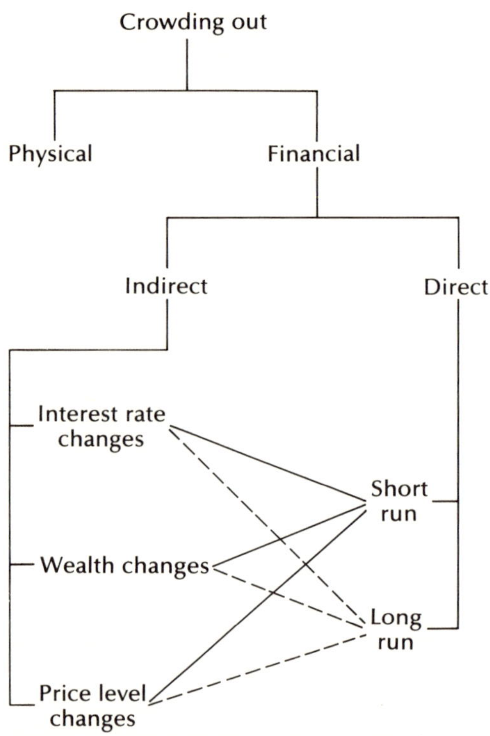

Figure 9.1 Taxonomy of crowding out

refers just to specific projects where, because of the government entering the market place as a buyer, the price of the project is pushed up over what it would have been had the government not increased its spending. This is, however, very like the direct crowding out, as analysed by Buiter (1977). It rests on the degree to which the public sector can be subsumed under the private sector. In other words, the government is merely another 'person' in the market place: if I buy a loaf of bread then you cannot buy *that* loaf of bread; if the government buys steel then the private sector cannot buy *that* steel. In this instance there is a direct crowding out of private purchases by government purchases. In terms of the static *IS–LM* model, it means that the *IS* curve remains fixed.

Indirect crowding out has had the most attention in the literature. In terms of Figure 9.1, this is divided into three categories: crowding out due to: (1) a change in the interest rate, (2) a change in wealth, and/or (3) a change in the price level. We shall take each of these in turn.

Figure 9.2 shows a typical bond-financed increase in government spending (where for the moment we shall assume that there are no wealth effects). The *IS* curve moves from IS_0 to IS_1. The resultant change on income and the interest rate depends on the slope of the *LM*

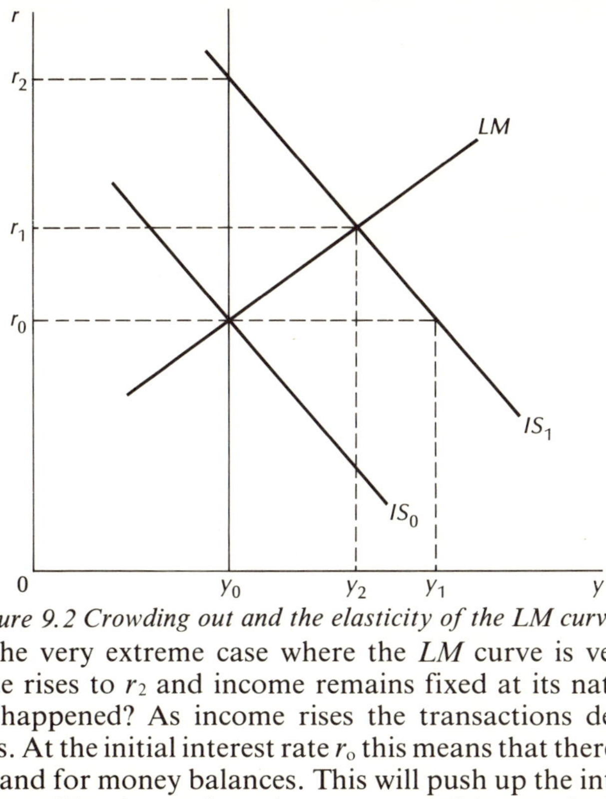

Figure 9.2 Crowding out and the elasticity of the LM curve

curve. In the very extreme case where the *LM* curve is vertical, the interest rate rises to r_2 and income remains fixed at its natural level. What has happened? As income rises the transactions demand for money rises. At the initial interest rate r_0 this means that there is now an excess demand for money balances. This will push up the interest rate, which in turn will reduce private investment. With a vertical *LM* curve private investment will eventually be reduced by exactly the amount of the increase in government spending. With a positively sloped *LM* curve the result is a rise in the interest rate to r_1 ($<r_2$) and a rise in the level of income to y_2. In this second case the rise in the interest rate cuts back private investment but not as much as the increase in government

spending. With a vertical *LM* curve the income multiplier with respect to an exogenous change in government spending is zero. In the situation where the *LM* curve is upward-sloping the multiplier is positive. In both cases the multipliers are less than the simple Keynesian multiplier (with constant interest rate) which is indicated by the change in income from y_0 to y_1.

It is worth noting how the argument goes for a fall in government spending. This will move the *IS* curve to the left, to IS_1 in Figure 9.3. Income falls to y_1 and the interest rate falls to r_1. Private investment rises, relative to the initial equilibrium, as the interest rate falls. Is the argument symmetrical? If we assume that investment is a function only of the interest rate, then the answer is, 'Yes'. If, however, we assume that investment is also a function of real income, then symmetry may not be true. Not only that, but the crowding out that occurs from a rise in interest rate will be offset to the extent that private investment is raised as a result of income rising. In the case of a fall in government spending, the increase in private investment will be offset by the fall in real income brought about by the reduction in government spending. This analysis is very important for discussions of reduced government spending which are advocated by the Thatcher government. The stimulus to private investment which the government is hoping for may be thwarted by the fall in private investment which is occurring as a result of the fall in real income.

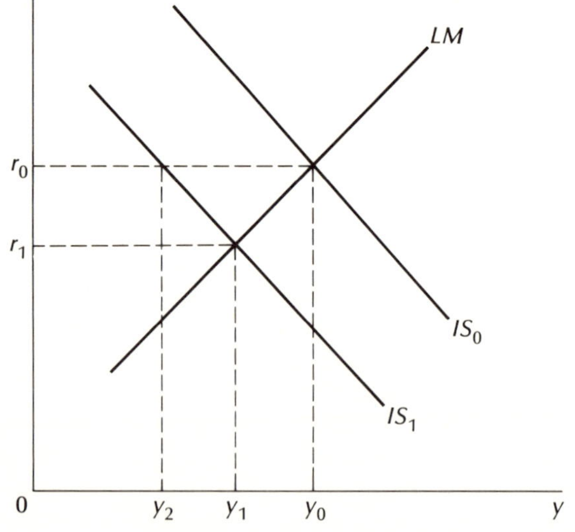

Figure 9.3 Crowding in

This early discussion of crowding out, like so many of the early discussions between the Keynesians and the monetarists, was concerned with the slope of the *LM* curve – and this in turn depended on the interest elasticity of the demand for money function. A totally interest-inelastic demand for money schedule, i.e., a demand for money schedule which is basically a function only of income, results in a vertical *LM* curve. This led to a number of empirical investigations which are summarised in Laidler (1969). It is now accepted that the *LM* curve has *some* positive slope. Does this mean that monetarists have conceded that complete crowding out does not occur? Not at all. They have switched their argument to the impact of the changes in wealth.

We dealt with the impact of wealth changes from a bond-financed increase in government spending in the previous chapter, and the result is summarised in Figure 9.4. The crowding out from the change in the interest rate is not complete, and income rises from y_o to y_1. Wealth, however, affects both the *IS* curve and the *LM* curve, shifting *IS* to IS_2 and the *LM* curve to LM_1. This results in a level of income of y_2, which is less than y_1. If crowding out is complete then the resulting level of income, y_2, coincides with the original level, y_o. It may even result in a negative multiplier, with the final level of income falling below y_o.

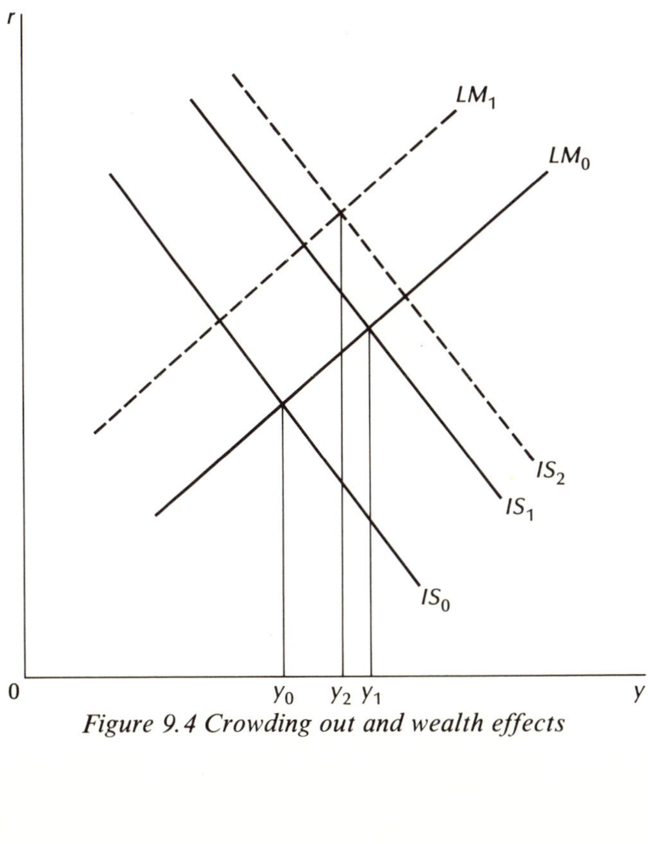

Figure 9.4 Crowding out and wealth effects

It is this wealth effect on the final level of income which monetarists argue is the reason for crowding out. Like the previous discussion in terms of the slope of the *LM* curve, the wealth impact is also an empirical question. The wealth impact, whether in the short run or the long run, can only be ascertained from looking at the workings of the economy. Without such empirical observation we are reduced to belief, and the beliefs about the wealth effects in a macro-economy have always been seen differently by monetarists and Keynesians (see, for example, Dow and Earl, 1982).

So far we have said nothing about the price level. Nor have we made it clear whether real income can in fact rise. When income is at the full employment level then it cannot, in the long run, rise above this level. Any change in aggregate demand must, under these conditions, result in changes in the price level. With an economy at full employment, indicated by a vertical section of the aggregate supply curve, any increase in aggregate demand must eventually result in a rise in the price level and a crowding out of private spending.

Notice in this case that it is a crowding out of private *spending* and not simply of private investment. This is an important point. Monetarists generally argue in terms of long-run models where income is at the natural level. Any level of income above this level, created for instance from a bond-financed Budget deficit, must inevitably result in higher prices. The higher prices will simply reduce real private spending to compensate for the increase in government spending. What this indicates, therefore, is the level of income relative to the natural level. Once again, the issue is critical when considered for a reduction in government spending. Will this result in a fall in prices, and hence a rise in private spending, or a fall in income, and hence a fall in private spending? Given that real income cannot in the long run exceed the full employment level of income, it would appear that there must be an asymmetry in the impact of a rise in a bond-financed government deficit to a fall in a bond-financed government deficit. But at the moment we have too little knowledge on the differential impact on income as opposed to prices.

One final point is worth making. The impact of any of these changes will take time to have an impact on the economy. Some will have more immediate impact than others. One of the issues that has occurred in the literature is that of long-run versus short-run impacts. What matters to policy-makers, however, is a time period of about two or three years. However many years are of interest, we need a model to carry out simulations in order to arrive at some quantitative estimate of what the likely impacts will be. To this we now turn.

9.2 Empirical Evidence on Crowding Out

The empirical evidence on crowding out has usually involved employing large simulation models. It will help, therefore, if we first say something about a simulation model. In doing this the simplest model will be used, namely a single dynamic equation model which takes the form:

$$Y(t) = a + bY(t - 1) + G(t)$$

Model builders go about their work basically in three stages. First they attempt to obtain an equation that has a basis in economic theory. This may or may not have some bearing on the functional form, and on the dynamic properties of the model. The equation above we shall take to be such an equation. The next stage is to obtain estimates of the parameters of the model: here, the parameters are a and b. When it is difficult or impossible to obtain estimates of the parameters by statistical means, guess estimates can be imposed. Let us take it that $a = 2$ and $b = 0.5$, whether obtained statistically or imposed.

Table 9.1 Simulation of $Y(t) = a + bY(t - 1) + G(t)$
$a = 2, b = 0.5, Y(0) = 100$

Period	Y1	Y2	Y3
1	2	12	12
2	3	8	18
3	3.5	6	21
4	3.75	5	22.5
5	3.875	4.5	23.25
6	3.9375	4.25	23.625
7	3.96875	4.125	23.8125
8	3.98438	4.0625	23.9063
9	3.99219	4.03125	23.9531
10	3.99609	4.01563	23.9766
11	3.99805	4.00781	23.9883
12	3.99902	4.00391	23.9941
13	3.99951	4.00195	23.9971
14	3.99976	4.00098	23.9985
15	3.99988	4.00049	23.9993
16	3.99994	4.00024	23.9996
17	3.99997	4.00012	23.9998
18	3.99998	4.00006	23.9999
19	3.99999	4.00003	24
20	4	4.00002	24

Notes: Y1: for all $G(1) = 0$
Y2: for $G(1) = 10$ and all remaining $G(I) = 0$
Y3: for all $G(I) = 10$

Given that we have only one simple dynamic equation, we could in fact solve this difference equation. In a large dynamic model, however, this will be most unlikely. It is at this third stage that a simulation can be undertaken. We know the values of the parameters, and we know the value of $Y(t-1)$ if we intend to consider $Y(t)$ from the present period t. We can calculate the time path of $Y(t)$ for different assumptions about $G(t)$ (which you can think of as a change in government spending). For instance, in Table 9.1 we have three simulations of the model under various assumptions. The first simulation, Y1, assumes $G(t) = 0$ for all periods; i.e., there is no change. Y2 assumes that an injection of 10 is undertaken in the first period only; i.e., $G(I) = 10$ and thereafter $G(I) = 0$. Finally, Y3 assumes that an injection of 10 is undertaken and maintained thereafter; i.e., $G(I) = 10$ for all periods.

Although the simulations in Table 9.1 are purely hypothetical, they do illustrate a typical feature of dynamic simulations in economics. In particular, notice that simulation 2 has a temporary boost to the variable $Y(t)$, but that by the twentieth period it is the same value as in the base comparison (where Y1 is the base). Y3 on the other hand also settles down by the twentieth period, but at a higher value than either Y1 or Y2. This should not be surprising. Y2 is a one-off injection while Y3 denotes a continuous injection. One value of simulation models, therefore, is seeing how sensitive the system is to changes in assumptions. It can also be used for investigating the sensitivity of the results to changes in the parameter values. Will, for instance, a small change in the value of b in the above equation have a large or small impact on the time path of $Y(t)$? This is especially important when values for some of the parameters are imposed.[1]

Let us now turn to the empirical simulations. There are two approaches to estimating the possibility of crowding out. One is to estimate a series of multipliers for each set of assumptions. In doing this a base is necessary which comes as close as possible to an expansion in government spending with a constant interest rate. If crowding out occurs, then the series of multipliers for other situations, where interest rates and other variables are allowed to alter, should be smaller. No crowding out will give rise to a zero multiplier and negative crowding out will give rise to a negative multiplier. The results will clearly depend on both the model and the set of assumptions being made. An alternative measure of crowding out is to subtract the multiplier for the variable case from the base multiplier and take this as a ratio of the base multiplier. Thus, if we suppose that $k(r_o)$ is the base multiplier with constant interest rate, and $k(r)$ is the multiplier with variable interest rate, then a measure of crowding out is:

$$c = 100 \quad [k(r_o) - k(r)] / k(r_o)$$

where the resulting measure is given as a percentage. It must be realised that for a given model there is no necessity for c to lie between zero and 100%. Clearly, if $k(r) = k(r_o)$ then there is no crowding out, and $c = 0\%$. If there is complete crowding out, then $c = 100\%$; while if c is negative, there is a situation of 'crowding in'. In the situation where c exceeds 100%, the multiplier expansion in that period is in fact negative. As can be seen in the results presented in Tables 9.2 and 9.3, all these possibilities occur.

Table 9.2 NIESR model (crowding out, c%)

Year	1	2	3	4	6
(2)	36.3	49.2	38.1	31.8	385.7
(3)	65.9	58.5	35.1	12.1	204.8
(4)	40.7	90.7	105.2	125.8	295.2

Notes: see Table 9.3

Table 9.3 Treasury model (crowding out, c%)

Year	1	2	3	4	6
(2)	-3.2	0.0	-10.0	17.3	19.2
(3)	72.4	55.0	6.9	-18.4	-38.4
(4)	22.8	44.0	158.8	137.8	160.6

Notes

(i) The base for comparison involves an increase of public authority consumption by £100m per quarter, 1970 prices; interest rates, earnings and exchange rate fixed. (2) involves the same as the base, except that earnings are endogenous and the exchange rate is floating. (3) involves a reduction in income tax by £100m per quarter, 1970 prices; interest rates fixed, earnings endogenous and the exchange rate floating. (4) denotes a balanced Budget increase in public spending of £100m per quarter, 1970 prices; interest rates fixed and earnings and the exchange rate endogenous.

(ii) The figures are computed by taking the multiplier for each of the situations and subtracting it from the base muliplier for the base run and taking this as a percentage of the base run multiplier.

Tables 9.2 and 9.3 present a measure of crowding out, using the formula for c as given above, for two UK models – the National Institute (NIESR) model and the Treasury model – where all figures have been computed from results given in the simulations undertaken by Lewis and Ormerod (1979). The first observation is the great differences between the computations for the two models. This is a common feature of all comparisons using large econometric models. The differences in the results reflect the different assumptions on which the models were constructed. For most of the years (although not all) the NIESR model gives higher values for c than the Treasury model. This is to some extent a reflection of the fact that the updated version of the Treasury model which is used in these simulations incorporates wealth effects – of the type we outlined in the previous section. In terms of these computations, only the Treasury model reveals any negative crowding out. By the sixth year the NIESR model reflects a very strong element of crowding out, but this is not reflected in the Treasury model, except for the fourth set of assumptions. In fact, for the third set of assumptions the Treasury model reflects growing negative crowding out.

The results are by no means conclusive. If anything, the simulations reflect the underlying assumptions of the respective models rather than any clear indication of the extent of crowding out. There is no doubt that we shall have to wait for further research into the quantitative estimates of crowding out in the UK before any clear conclusion can be arrived at.

9.3 The Bacon-Eltis Thesis

The Bacon-Eltis thesis, now outlined in full in their book, *Too Few Producers* (Bacon and Eltis, 1976), is a form of crowding out argument with a quite different conceptual basis from that so far outlined. They divide the economy into two groups: the 'marketable' sector and the 'non-marketable' sector. The former produces goods and services which can be bought and sold in the market place; while the non-market sector involves those activities for which there is no market and so they cannot be bought and sold – especially in the international market. In this sense it is very like the Scandinavian model which divides goods into tradable and non-tradable (see for instance Corden, 1977).

The development of their argument is rather slippery because they introduce a very special idea of wealth. They argue that the market sector provides the productive base of the economy and provides the goods and (some of the) services from which consumption, investment and exports must be financed. The non-market sector, on the other hand, is a claim on the wealth of the community but does not (so they argue) provide any wealth itself. What they of course mean is that it provides no *direct* wealth. What they fail to see, or ignore, is the fact that the public services (which comprise most of the non-market sector) contribute *indirectly* to the wealth of the community. Take the health service, for instance. Whether publicly or privately supplied, in terms of the Bacon-Eltis thesis this provides no wealth and is parasitic on the productive base of the economy. But without such a service it is highly likely that the productive level of the marketable sector would not be as great as it would be in the presence of such a service. In this case the health service provides wealth *indirectly* through the marketable sector which it helps to keep functioning efficiently. The same argument applies to most of the public services that comprise the public sector. Even if one were to argue that the public services contain a great deal of inefficiency, this does not detract from the point being made that they still provide wealth indirectly. Where there is inefficiency this level of indirect wealth is not as great as it might have been; but this is an argument about inefficiency, and not about the provision of wealth as such.

The Bacon-Eltis argument develops in terms of the growth of employment in the non-marketable sector relative to the marketable sector, the former growing at a much greater rate than the latter in the UK. It is now that the idea of crowding out occurs. The increase in employment in the non-marketable sector places a constraint on the growth of the marketable sector and so takes resources away from the productive base of the economy.

It should be noted here how close this is in conception to the monetarist argument when the economy is at the natural level of employment. If the economy is at the level of full employment then it is true that any expansion of the non-marketable sector must place pressure on the marketable sector. But this implies two conditions which may not in fact be true. First, it implies that the economy is at full employment. Second, it implies that over the period this level of full employment remains fixed. Both of these together imply that any expansion of the non-marketable sector must be at the expense of the marketable sector. If, however, neither of these assumptions holds true, then it is possible for expansion of the non-marketable sector to occur at no expense to the marketable sector. Basically, the argument holds only if, over the same interval of time, there could be growth in the marketable sector which is prevented because of the claim on resources arising from the growth of the non-marketable sector.

It is of course possible that the growth in employment in the non-marketable sector has led to an increase in inflation, to the extent that in the short run there is a greater demand for goods and services which is not matched by an increase in the level of output (at least during the same time period). This form of crowding out is exactly that which we discussed in the previous section, which arises from a rise in the general price level. But it becomes more likely if over the same period the natural level of employment has been declining, i.e., if the natural rate of unemployment has been increasing, as some believe to be the case for the UK. As the natural rate of unemployment rises, there is greater impetus on the government to decrease the level of unemployment by increasing the employment in government services. This, so the argument runs, will simply lead to inflationary pressure, as the level of employment is maintained above its natural level. But like the Bacon-Eltis thesis, this seems to be arguing that only non-government employment is to be counted in the concept of full employment! The reason seems to be that 'real' goods and services can be produced only by employment in the non-government sector (synonymous with the marketable sector?), while over-all aggregate demand for goods and services arises from the level of total employment. This fuzziness does seem to be arising from the fuzziness of the meaning of the 'natural rate of unemployment'.

The difficult item to disentangle in the argument is cause and effect. Is the rising employment and growth of the non-marketable sector a cause of the declining marketable sector? Or, alternatively, is the rising employment and growth of the non-marketable sector merely a reflection (the effect) of a declining marketable sector? If it is the latter, then reasons must be sought elsewhere for the decline in output and productivity. This form of crowding out has not really been proved. On the other hand, the decline in the industrial base of the economy has definitely taken place, de-industrialisation has undoubtedly occurred. The reason for de-industrialisation must be explained, but the explanation is unlikely to be the rise in the non-marketable sector.

Questions

1. What is the distinction between direct and indirect crowding out? Is this distinction important?
2. Why, when considering crowding out arising from interest rate changes, may the result be asymmetrical for a rise as against a fall in government spending?
3. What difference is there between crowding out arising from interest rate and wealth changes as distinct from price changes?
4. 'The more interest-elastic the *LM* curve, the greater the crowding out.' Discuss.
5. What is a simulation model? Why do economists use such models?
6. Critically assess the formula:

$$C = 100\,[k(r_o) - k(r)]/k(r_o)$$

as a measure of crowding out. Why should different models give

different figures for the same period?
7. Do you agree with the Bacon-Eltis thesis?
8. 'The crowding out argument is not true when savings change as a result of government borrowing.' Discuss.
9. 'The effect of government spending on aggregate demand may actually "crowd-in" aggregate investment through the accelerator mechanism.' Discuss. (See Kaldor and Trevithick, 1981.)

Notes

1. On simulations of UK economy models, see Posner (1978), Arestis and Hadjimatheou (1982) and Holden, Peel and Thompson (1982).

CHAPTER 10

Has fine tuning failed?

Government stabilisation of the economy has always led to difficulties, and has at various times in history required justification. Even when there has been agreement that some form of intervention is required, there have still been disputes over the precise form the intervention should take. What separates stabilisation from other forms of intervention is the fact that stabilisation is concerned largely with the overall performance of the economy while intervention is usually concerned with specific markets. This distinction in itself is very revealing. Macroeconomics, as we now understand it, arose largely out of Keynes' *General Theory of Employment, Interest and Money*. It was this book which supplied a macroeconomic justification for government intervention. Prior to this publication, and to a large extent today, the reasons given for government involvement in the economy have been on microeconomic grounds, namely:

(1) Market failure

(2) Externalities

(3) Public goods.

But it should be noted that these three reasons for government involvement are concerned with economic *efficiency* and not with macroeconomic objectives. They lay behind the idea of *laissez-faire,* and any intervention required strong justification. In addition, ever since Adam Smith's *Wealth of Nations*, there has always been a strong belief in the efficacy of the 'invisible hand'. In other words, the best way to allocate resources in society is by leaving the market mechanism alone and letting it do the job of allocation. Implicit, if not explicit, is the belief that the market mechanism can do the job of resource allocation better than any government, and that any interference from the government will simply lead to incorrect signals, and hence to a misallocation of resources.

The invisible hand, however, operates only where markets exist. For example, there is no market for pensioner payments, for future generations (which means that the market is biased towards presently existing consumer preferences), etc. Market failure, externalities and public goods are a means of patching up certain weaknesses in the workings of the invisible hand, but that is all. Furthermore, markets are about demand and supply, which in turn refer to the ability to pay and the ability to supply, and not merely on wishes. Demand patterns are therefore dependent upon income distribution, while supply is dependent upon the present structure, conduct and performance of industry – most particularly its power base (*à la* Galbraith).

One other general observation is worth making. We talk of the economic *system,* for it is a system. But two views about the economic system run through the debate of stabilisation policy:

(1) The economic system is *stable.*

(2) The economic system is *unstable.*

It is difficult to prove either of these opposing views about the economic system, but it is important to realise that classical economists, and the present-day new classicists, believe that the economic system is stable – but subject to random shocks. Hence, what matters in their view is how the system copes with such random shocks. Other economists believe that the economic system is inherently unstable, and so requires constant control by the government. This latter view is partly, although not wholly, related to the idea that government policy is a means of achieving macroeconomic objectives. The point is straight forward, but often is not noticed for this reason. If the economy is stable and suffers no random shocks, then it will (or may), when left alone, settle down at an equilibrium. This equilibrium, however, may not be a desired position. If it is not a desired position, then either the government must accept that the equilibrium is not a desired position or it must set things in motion to move the economy to a position which is desired. More than that, once at the desired position (assumed different from the equilibrium position), the government must now implement other policies to *keep* the economy at such a desired position. If, however, the economy is unstable, this simply means that the policies necessary to attain a desired position and remain there are different. The issue, therefore, is not simply about stable and unstable systems, but also about equilibrium versus desired positions. By stating it in this way we immediately notice the explicit values:

A free market supporter *is stating a belief that he prefers the*

> *market equilibrium to any other (a policy of 'do nothing').*
>
> *An* interventionist *states his desired objectives and the policies necessary to achieve and maintain them (a policy of 'do something')*

The free market supporters argue that the market mechanism is efficient, that market-clearing occurs quickly, and that the economy will, if not suffering a random shock, settle down at an equilibrium. The equilibrium is stable and can be maintained, therefore, without government intervention. The only unknown is that of random shocks. Any attempt at intervention by the government will simply lead to a greater variation of economic variables and to even greater uncertainty. Implicit, rather than explicit, is the belief that any government intervention will result in a lower economic welfare than no intervention. Interventionists point to the failure of the market mechanism, and the presence of externalities and public goods; but they also openly state (usually) what they would set as targets for macroeconomic variables. Interventionists would argue, therefore, that the welfare of society consistent with the target economic variables is greater than the level of these variables when the economy is left to its own devices. (In the international trade literature this distinction was well recognised in the form of internal and external equilibrium versus internal and external balance. The failure to distinguish equilibrium from desired positions led to much confusion and to what Machlup (1958) called 'disguised politics'. The same is true of the present debate, which is over internal equilibrium as distinct from internal balance.)

It should be noted that these debates are about systems and how systems move over time. It has been argued that the basic distinction between monetarists and neo-Keynesians is not about the slopes of curves, but rather about the speed of adjustment and the lag structure inherent in the dynamics of the economic system. The *IS–LM* analysis is static and of no use in discussing the movement of the economy from one equilibrium to the next. This does not mean that the analysis is useless; it merely means that it was never devised for answering questions about dynamics. But it is the time paths and the lag structures which matter to the government. Gordon crystallises it as follows:

> Monetarists believe that the private economy is basically stable and that fixed policy rules are necessary to protect the economy against ill-conceived and poorly timed government actions that in the past have caused economic instability. In contrast, the nonmonetarists pinpoint private spending decisions as the main source of instability and generally support an activist government countercyclical

policy (both monetary and fiscal) to achieve economic stability. (Gordon, 1981, p.363)

It is clear from these introductory remarks that the dynamic path of macroeconomic variables is important, as is the lag structure of these variables. We shall take up these points in the next section. In section 10.2 we turn to the traditional arguments which have been put forward for rules and against fine tuning. In the third section we consider a more technical argument against fine tuning which has arisen from the rational expectations literature. Although the early debate simply argued for 'rules', it was rarely made clear precisely what rules were called for. The rule put forward by Friedman was a simple fixed rule, but it does not follow that, even if rules are called for, they will be either simple or fixed. In the final section we shall make an attempt to sum up the debate so far.

10.1 Stabilisation: Its Meaning

Stabilisation policy, fine tuning or counter-cyclical policy are all terms to mean short-term intervention by the government, either to counter-balance some trend in an economic variable or to speed up (slow down) its natural time path. (Demand management is not another term for stabilisation but rather a *method* for achieving it. As the term indicates, stabilisation is carried out through changing aggregate demand.)

The first thing we note about stabilisation is that it is concerned with economic variables which *cycle*. But which variables? The two most obvious are national income and unemployment. The second feature is that intervention is meant to be in the 'short run'. In practical terms this can be thought of as policies which can be implemented within one year – the two most obvious being monetary and fiscal policy. We shall deal with this more fully in a moment when we discuss inside and outside lags.

For the present let us consider in more detail the meaning we give to stabilisation, and in particular to the meanings of stable and unstable counter-cyclical policies. To carry out this clarification we must distinguish a number of possible time paths that a variable can take. For the sake of illustration let us suppose we are dealing with GDP. Three time paths must be distinguished:

$y^e(t) =$ the equilibrium time path of income without government intervention and with market-clearing

$y^a(t) =$ the actual time path of income without any government intervention

$x(t) =$ the path of income in the presence of government intervention.

In theory we are concerned with two deviations: first, the deviation of the actual time path, $y^a(t)$, from the expected time path, $y^e(t)$; i.e., $y^a(t) - y^e(t)$. This is referred to as the *pure cycle deviation*, and denotes how far an unregulated economy is from its equilibrium path. The second deviation is the time path of income in the presence of intervention, $x(t)$, from the expected time path, $y^e(t)$; i.e., $x(t) - y^e(t)$. We shall refer to this second deviation as the *government-induced cycle deviation,* and it denotes how far a regulated economy is from its equilibrium path. The debate for and against fine tuning, therefore, is concerned with a comparison between the pure cycle deviation, $y^a(t) - y^e(t)$, and the government-induced cycle deviation, $x(t) - y^e(t)$. If the latter shows less variation than the former then government policy is stabilising, while if it shows greater variation then government policy is destabilising.

Having established that the main comparison is between the pure cycle deviation and the government-induced cycle deviation, let us concentrate on what the government must do to bring about perfect stabilisation. First we note that the time path of income in the presence of government intervention, $x(t)$, must equal the time path of income without intervention, $y^a(t)$, plus an adjustment (positive or negative) for government policy, $a(t)$; i.e.,

$$x(t) = y^a(t) + a(t).$$

For perfect stabilisation, then, the time path of income in the presence of government intervention must be the same as the time path of equilibrium income; i.e., $x(t) = y^e(t)$. If this is to be the case then we must have:

$$y^e(t) = y^a(t) + a(t)$$

or

$$a(t) = -\,[y^a(t) - y^e(t)]$$

In other words, for perfect stabilisation the policy-induced change must be exactly equal to the pure cycle deviation with the opposite sign. The situation is shown in Figure 10.1. The pure cycle deviation is given by $y^a(t) - y^e(t)$, while the government is pursuing a policy the complete reverse of this, namely $a(t) = -\,[y^a(t) - y^e(t)]$. The result is that the economy follows a path $x(t) = y^e(t)$. In other words, if the government achieves perfect stabilisation then the economy will move along its equilibrium path. (Notice that the path $z(t)$ when added to the path $y^a(t)$ gives the path $y^e(t) = x(t)$. Any misjudgement on the government's part will show up in path $z(t)$).

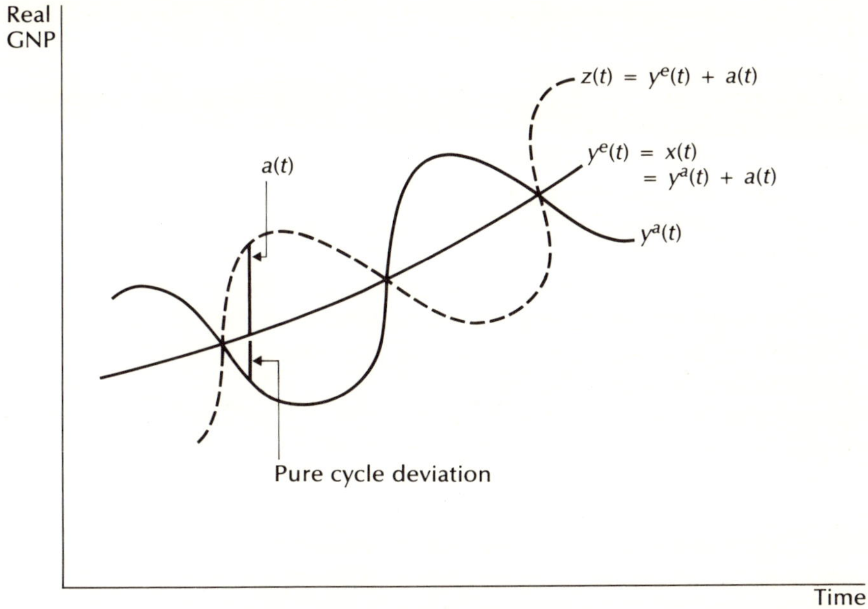

Figure 10.1 Cycle deviations

With perfect stabilisation we have:

$$x(t) - y^e(t) = 0$$

which is preferable to the pure cycle deviation,

$$y^a(t) - y^e(t) \neq 0$$

But what if government stabilisation is not perfect? The adjustment, $a(t)$, undertaken by the government may be too large (small) or mistimed. In Figure 10.2 we illustrate a case of mistiming. For simplicity we have that $y^e(t)$ is a horizontal straight line. The path $z(t)$ is the mirror image of path $y^a(t)$ – except that it is displaced to the right. When $z(t)$ is now added to $y^e(t)$ then the resulting path of the economy, $x(t)$, shows an even more marked cycle pattern than $y^a(t)$. In other words, government policy is destabilising. It is not difficult to see why this is so. The adjustment by the government is in the *same direction* as the pure cyclic deviation, and so the induced policy change *reinforces* the cycle rather than countering it.

The discussion highlights two difficulties that the government can encounter when undertaking stabilisation:

(1) The *timing* of intervention

(2) The *amount* of intervention.

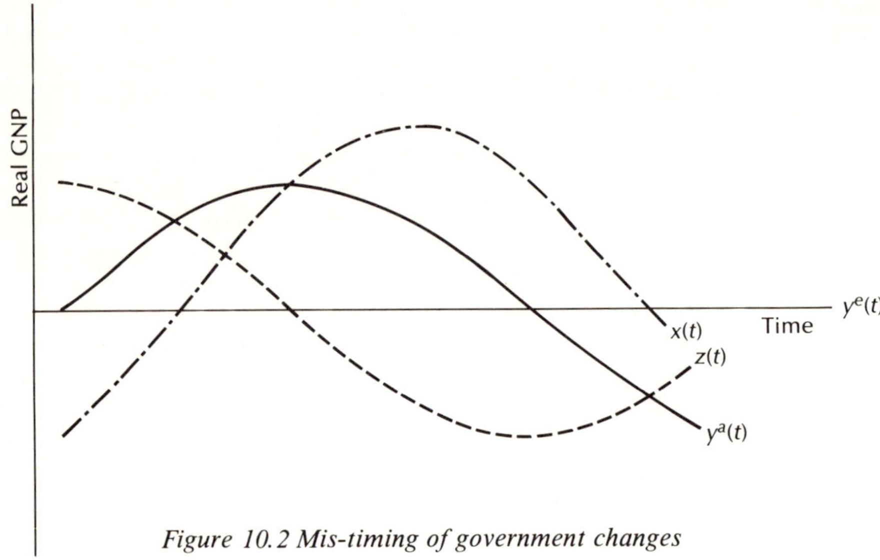

Figure 10.2 Mis-timing of government changes

We shall take each of these in turn. Why is the timing of economic policy such a problem? Consider the situation where a shock happens to the economy. The first difficulty is to decide whether the shock is a one-off event (i.e., is transitory) or is going to persist some time into the future. Stabilisation policy is largely directed at shocks which lead to persistent changes. But the government at some point must decide whether it is or is not persistent. Having decided it is persistent, then it must make a decision about what to do. These two lags, the *recognition* lag and the *decision lag,* both make up what is referred to as the *inside lag.* Once action has been taken, there will be a first-round effect on the economy; that is to say, the immediate impact of the policy. Suppose, for example, the government lowers taxes in order to stimulate the economy and increase the level of employment. As the (dynamic) multiplier takes effect, there will be second-round effects which will be distributed over time. The time period taken for the target variable to be affected (both first- and second-round effects) by the policy instrument is referred to as the *outside lag.* The inside lag refers to the period of time taken for decisions to be made by the bureaucratic machinery, while the outside lag refers to the time the policy takes to influence the actual economy.

The recognition lag is more important than it first appears. In some cases the recognition is straightforward – such as the requirement for extra liquidity at Christmas time (this is a negative lag in the sense that it is known before the event itself takes place). More usually the lag is positive and arises from taking time to recognise that something must be done, e.g., that a devaluation is necessary. The difficulty here is that market participants may themselves recognise that the government must do something even sooner than the government itself! This means that, by the time the government recognises that something must be done, the time path of the variable concerned has already begun to change as the expectations of market participants begin to take effect. The decision lag depends on which particular policy instrument is being used (e.g., a monetary, fiscal or employment instrument) and the particular institutional set-up. Suppose, for instance, that the government recognises the need for a tax change in November. Does it wait until the Budget of April the following year or does it have a mini-Budget in November? (Interesting observations on the decision lag, especially in the case of the Treasury, will be found in S. Brittan's *Steering the Economy* (1971) and W. Keegan and R. Pennant-Rea's *Who Runs The Economy?* (1979).)

Difficulties with outside lags in large part reflect our ignorance of the precise workings of the economy. Take for example a policy to deal with unemployment. Unemployment is seen to rise. There is the inside lag involving the recognition of a problem and a decision to do something about it. Suppose a policy such as the Youth Opportunities Programme is decided upon. How long is it before YOP has any appreciable effect on the level of unemployment? Let us suppose the inside lag is six months. Further, let us suppose the outside lag is 18 months (which is not unreasonable). Then the total lag is two years! By the time the programme begins to have its full impact the economy could readily have changed direction. This may be true. It does not imply that the policy should not be undertaken, however; it merely indicates that the question of timing is a very complex issue. (It almost suggests that when the economy is booming an *expansionary* policy should be pursued, because by the time it begins to take effect the economy is likely to be in the downswing of the business cycle!)

Even if the timing is correct, there is still the amount (and hence direction) of the change required to be considered. This in turn implies agreement on the type of policy required – for example, whether it should be monetary or fiscal policy. Suppose a fiscal expansion is agreed on. What amount of fiscal expansion is required? If too much it could be inflationary. If too little it will not solve the problem. In this case it is not simply that it could be extended if too little, since the inside and outside lags may mean that the two attempts together could sum to four or more years! Furthermore, the amount depends very much on the assessment of the problem. This assessment in turn rests on the various macroeconomic models in existence. The Treasury model, the London Business School model and the National Institute model (not to mention the few other large models around the country) all assess the economic climate differently. Which one does the government choose – if any?

It must be recognised that there will always be uncertainty about the economic system. Given this uncertainty, the issue is: What is the best way of managing the economy (where we include in the term 'management', doing nothing)?

10.2 The Traditional Argument for Rules

Before we begin discussing rules versus fine tuning it is important to realise that the discussion about rules has two quite distinct elements (which are often taken as one, and so lead to confusion). They are:

(1) Arguments in favour of rules (or against them)

(2) Arguments about the choice of rule to follow.

The confusion arises from the fact that the original discussion in favour of rules posed the argument in terms of simple fixed rules. It is possible to be in favour of rules only where the rules are of a particular form, where the form may or may not be a simple fixed rule. In this and the next section we shall deal only with point (1), leaving point (2) to section 10.4.

In the previous section we pointed out that one of the arguments against fine tuning was the fact that, if the policy was mis-timed or involved too much or too little adjustment, it was possible for the policy to be destabilising. The previous section basically demonstrated that uncertainty is increased because of an unknown lag structure (both inside and outside lags). When we consider more explicitly monetary policy – within which most of the debate has taken place – we find that two characteristics are agreed upon:

(1) Behaviour of the money stock is important for real income and money income.

(2) Money influences the economy with:
  (a) a *long* lag
  (b) a *variable* lag.

If these two points are accepted, and notice that they are both *empirical* observations, then monetarists argue that fine tuning should not be undertaken. Any fine tuning could very well destabilise the economy. But is this claim justified?

We noticed in the previous section that this claim rests on comparing the pure cycle deviation, $y^a(t) - y^e(t)$, with the government-induced cycle deviation, $x(t) - y^e(t)$. Monetarists are claiming that fine tuning leads to greater variation in the government-induced cycle deviation than in the pure cycle deviation. But both deviations are *unobservable* because the equilibrium time path of income (or any other equilibrium variable) is unobservable. Short of setting up a full dynamic macro-economic model which will supply the equilibrium time path of the endogenous variables, the only operational equivalent in the present case for $y^{e}(t)$, is the deviation of income from a (logarithmic) trend. The (logarithmic) trend of income, $y^{T}(t)$, is acting as a proxy for the equilibrium time path of income. But even doing this allows us only to compute $x(t) - y^{T}(t)$, since the government does step in. The actual time path of income without any intervention is not known because the government did not choose to remain passive. The *proximate* pure cycle deviation, $y^{a}(t) - y^{T}(t)$, is accordingly unknown. It is possible to construct a second proxy, this time for $y^{a}(t)$, by using a simulation model and assuming that the economy moves along a path governed by the situation at some base period and assuming that the government no longer intervenes (at least not in the money market).

It should be apparent that things are now getting complicated, and that we seem to be moving very much away from the initial comparison. It is not clear any longer what, in fact, we are testing. This arises not only from the inherent uncertainty in the economic system, but also from the fact that the questions being posed involve counter-factual information (i.e., what would the state of the economy be if the government did not do what it is doing but did something else?).

Notwithstanding these practical difficulties, there is also a conceptual difference of opinion. An essential feature of fine tuning is that there is constant monitoring of the economy, and, in the light of this information, further adjustment is made. In other words, fine tuning involves closed loops, or what elsewhere is referred to as a feedback mechanism. Given the difficulties discussed above, monetarists argue that it is this constant adjustment which destabilises, because by the time the policy becomes effective the situation has changed. Monetarists have therefore advocated the use of rules. The point about rules, at least the simple fixed variety, is that they do not take account of any temporary reaction on the economy; in other words, they involve no feedback mechanism. No matter what is happening to the economy, the rule is followed.

Notice the implicit importance of the assumption about the stability of the economy in this argument. Assuming the economy is stable, a fixed rule will not disturb this stability, while fine tuning can (and according to monetarists does). Consequently, the debate of rules versus discretion is not just about lags and uncertainty, but also about whether you believe that the economic system is stable or unstable. Even more, it rests on the *degree* of belief you have in the stability or otherwise of the economic system. The point is that both monetarists and non-monetarists agree that there are long lags and uncertainty in the economic system. Non-monetarists, however, argue that if the economy is left to its own devices the adjustment will be painfully slow in reaching a solution. Fine tuning is then applied not so much to reach some desired position, but to speed up the workings of the economic system. In other words, fine tuning is used to *reinforce* the workings of the market mechanism and not to replace it.

This discussion highlights two totally different reasons for fine tuning:

(1) As a means of reaching some desired goal, which may or may not be the equilibrium solution

(2) As a means of reinforcing the workings of the market mechanism.

The argument in favour of rules is largely (although not totally) as a counter to (2). The argument for rules to achieve (1) is more ambiguous.

Those in favour of rules tend to argue their case by appealing to the facts. 'Look at the evidence, does it not show that fine tuning has failed!' Let us take it that fine tuning has not succeeded in achieving what it set out to achieve. This does not, however, suggest that rules are the solution. Consistent with this 'evidence' is that a 'better' approach to fine tuning is necessary. (Suppose your leg is infected by a virus and you are taking some medication which is not helping the matter: does this mean that you should amputate, or try a 'better' medication?)

The conclusion we draw from the traditional arguments for rules is that they are weak. They are difficult to support because they involve unobservable variables and pose counter-factual questions. In addition, they rest on the assumption that the economic system is stable – which can only be a matter of belief.

There has, however, been a growing interest in rules arising from work being undertaken by new classical economists. To this we now turn.

10.3 New Classical Arguments for Rules

Rational expectations theorists have also argued against fine tuning – but for totally different reasons than those traditionally put forward. Their basic contention is that any attempt at fine tuning will already be embedded in rational expectations behaviour. What this means is that, in a world of rational expectations, the model is known (or people behave as if the model were known), and consequently the parameters of the system will already incorporate any response on the part of the government. Put another way, fine tuning is based on the assumption that the structural model will remain the same both before and after the policy change; i.e., the structural parameters will remain the same. Because of this there will be a resultant change in the endogenous variables of the model. Rational expectations theorists, on the other hand, argue that the structural parameters will not remain the same, that they will change as account is taken of the government policy. This will mean no change in the equilibrium values of the endogenous variables. Any feedback policy will, therefore, fail.

Thus any attempt by the monetary authorities to affect the level of income will be unsuccessful. In the same way, systematic fiscal policy is fully anticipated by market participants and, according to rational expectations, cannot bring about any divergence between actual and expected price level changes. Since aggregate supply is dependent on the expected price level, no change in the aggregate supply curve will result and hence no change in output – in the long run. All such fine tuning, therefore, is ineffective.

Of course, the conclusion rests on the confidence you place in the rational expectations model. The problem is that this model assumes not only that expectations are rationally formed, but (more significantly) that markets clear quickly. The conclusions of rational expectations depend more on the assumption of quick market-clearing than they do on how expectations are actually formed. (The point is that, in a given model, the same long-run solution will occur with either rationally formed expectations or with adaptive expectations – only the actual time path of the endogenous variables will be different.) But the assumption of quick market-clearing is just another aspect of the assumption that the economic system is basically stable. The difficulty with the new classical reasoning is in trying to separate off arguments which involve only an assumption about the formation of expectations from the (often implicit) assumption that markets clear quickly. The former is an issue in model construction, while the latter is an empirical question.

10.4 What Type of Rules?

We have talked a lot about rules, but have so far not specified any. It is now time to be somewhat more specific about what type of rules are being advocated. (It is like debating for or against punishment without specifying the type of punishment that is being advocated.) The early rules were monetary rules and had the characteristics of being *fixed* and *simple*.

Consider the simple Cambridge version of the quantity equation:

$$M_d = kPy$$

Assuming quick market-clearing so that $M_d = M_s$, then with k assumed constant, the price level change, $\hat{P}$, is given by:

$$\hat{P} = \hat{M}_s - \hat{y}$$

It is now clear from this result that, if the money supply growth is set equal to the growth of real income, inflation will be zero. The *monetary rule* is then to set the rate of growth of money supply equal to the rate of growth of real income. (An extreme form is a stationary economy in which there is no growth of real income and hence no change in the money supply; i.e., $\hat{M}_s = 0$.) This is the simple fixed monetary rule advocated by Friedman.

Does there exist any simple fixed fiscal rule? This is less straightforward. Let us approach this by first considering a very extreme case of a long-run stationary economy. In such an economy, income is at its natural level and so is the rate of interest. With no shocks to the system these will continue at the same levels. With income at its natural level then $\hat{y} = 0$, which, according to the monetary rule just discussed, implies that $\hat{M}_s = 0$ (or $dM = 0$). Furthermore, if the interest rate is to remain at its natural level, then the bond issue must remain unchanged. This implies $dB/r = 0$. From the government Budget constraint (discussed fully in chapter 8) we have, therefore:

$$G - T = dM + dB/r = 0$$

The *simple fixed fiscal rule* advocated, therefore, is one of a balanced Budget. Whether this is the rule to be followed for a situation where real income is growing is not made clear.

The monetary and fiscal rules just outlined are both simple and fixed. They are based on typical monetarist analysis with its emphasis on the long-run stationary state. Two questions naturally arise:

(1) Is the 'best' rule necessarily a simple rule?

(2) Is the 'best' rule necessarily a fixed rule?

These two questions are not in fact independent of each other. To see this consider the difference between a fixed and flexible monetary rule. Consider being at some point in time t. The information at time t will suggest some growth of real income at time $t + 1$. Based on this information, the money supply under a fixed monetary rule will be allowed to grow at the same rate as real income. Regardless of what actually happens to real income at time $t + 1$, the growth of money supply remains at its fixed rate determined by the information at time t. A flexible monetary rule, on the other hand, recognises that the situation at time $t + 1$ is uncertain and may take a variety of forms, contingent states of the world – which we shall label S1, S2, S3, etc. Continuing with our present example, income growth in each of these states is assumed to be different. For each state the same fixed policy rule is advocated; namely, money supply growth must equal the growth of real income. The only difference now is that different contingent growths of real income are taken into consideration. As further information becomes available to determine which state of the world applies, only then is the growth in money supply determined. In other words, further information is taken into account in a flexible policy rule.

The difficulty with the flexible policy rule is that there is an infinite number of future possible states of the world. It is difficult enough to carry out a single forecast of real income growth without having to do so for all possible contingencies. This could suggest that a simple policy rule may be the most suitable in such an uncertain situation.

The discussion so far has been carried out in an apolitical world. It has been argued that political parties in a democracy are often required to state in their manifestos what they would do if they took office. Since rules can be stated fairly clearly, certainly in comparison with the vagueness of demand management, then political considerations also give a leaning towards rules. Even more, the rules are likely to be simple ones that the voting population can understand.

10.5 A Summing Up

The basic question of this section is whether one should advise the government to abandon any attempt at fine tuning the economy and instead follow a set of simple rules. Like so many issues in this book, the answer to this question partly depends on one's economic leaning.

Non-monetarists are not totally persuaded by the monetarists' arguments against fine tuning. In the first place, the fact that fine tuning has not succeeded at stabilising the economy has only highlighted how complex the economic system really is. Keynesian demand management, as a means of stabilisation, certainly does have its drawbacks. One of the reasons for this is inherent in Keynesian economic analysis. The analysis was geared to an unemployment economy with little or no inflation. In the post-war period inflation was certainly at a low level and Keynesian demand management was successful. But its very success is probably one of the reasons why inflation became a major problem in the 1970s and 1980s. Whether this is true or not, inflation in most Western countries began to rise after 1970. In addition, unemployment began to grow. The situation was one of unemployment and inflation – what became known as *stagflation*. Keynesian analysis was not designed for such a situation.

There was, to use Hicks' phrase, 'a crisis in Keynesian economics'. Part of this crisis was the lack of success at fine tuning. Like many crises, the question arises as to whether the existing economic analysis requires improving, or whether a totally new economic analysis is called for, which can deal with the issues – and deal with them better than any *ad hoc* change in the existing theory.

One thing is clear from a number of issues discussed in this book. Any improvement at fine tuning must incorporate policies on both the demand and the supply side. The old form of demand management is one-sided. Furthermore, fine tuning on the supply side is likely to be microeconomic in nature and not macroeconomic, as we shall demonstrate in the next chapter. But there is one major difficulty here. Microeconomic adjustments on the supply side are likely to lead to long-term adjustments rather than short-term adjustments. If this is so, it may mean that such adjustment can hardly be part of stabilisation. But whatever we call it, the purpose remains to reduce the government-induced cycle deviation.

If the crisis requires a totally new thinking about economic analysis, then there is justification for suggesting the use of policy rules. But before any rules are implemented they should be spelled out more explicitly and fully embedded in an institutional framework. If the institutional framework is ignored, there is no guarantee that a rule will eliminate some of the uncertainty about inside lags – with the possible exception of a fixed simple rule. Furthermore, there must be some discussion under what conditions a rule will be abandoned. Some shocks to the economic system will be more disturbing than others. Is it proposed that, regardless of the shock, a rule will be blindly followed? If it is accepted that a rule can be changed or abandoned then there must be discussion about what can be put in its place. This will require a more thorough analysis of economic shocks than has hitherto taken place. Although in its infancy, research has shown that it is important to distinguish domestic from foreign shocks. The point about this analysis is that a rule may be good, say, for a domestic shock but not so good if the shock is from a foreign source. We discussed this point in some detail in section 6.4.

The discussion surrounding rules has largely been in terms of monetary rules. It must be realised that in the United States, where most of this debate has taken place, monetary policy has always been more important than fiscal policy. The opposite has been the case in the

United Kingdom. Part of the reason for this difference in emphasis is because of the difference in the institutions of the two countries (something often overlooked by monetarists). Fine tuning has involved not only the money supply (or the interest rate) but also budgetary policy and exchange rate policy. For the UK the balance of payments is quite important, and if rules are the main form of policy then it is essential that an exchange rate rule is also established.

One further issue that immediately arises, which is not very often considered, is: given that an economy will require a number of rules – at the very least three (a monetary rule, a fiscal rule and an exchange rate rule), are these rules compatible? Incompatible rules may be more damaging to an economy than fine tuning which is not fully successful. One reason why fine tuning has not been so successful is the presence of the government Budget constraint. But this constraint will also impose limitations on a set of rules.

The conclusion that I draw from this issue is that the time is not suitable for abandoning fine tuning. Certainly, fine tuning must be improved. But any attempt at abandoning it in favour of rules would first require a more thorough analysis of the type of rules, how they would work in a given institutional arrangement, and whether they are compatible given the government Budget constraint. In addition, analysis is required on how rules would operate for domestic as well as foreign shocks; and, if they were to be abandoned, under what conditions this would occur and what they would be replaced with.

Questions

1. Justify government involvement in the economy from both the microeconomic and macroeconomic perspective.
2. What does it mean to say that an economic system is stable? Can an economic system be statically stable but dynamically unstable?
3. How does 'disguised politics' enter many arguments about economic equilibrium?
4. 'If there were no economic cycles there would be no need for demand management.' Do you agree?
5. Explain the meaning of:
   (a) Pure cycle deviation
   (b) Government-induced cycle deviation.
   How are these used to explain
   (a) Perfect stabilisation?
   (b) Destabilising government intervention?
6. Why is it important to have a full knowledge of all the lags in implementing government policy? Given uncertainty about such

lags, would this be sufficient for you to advocate no fine tuning?

7. Why would the recognition of a particular economic problem depend upon the actual macroeconomic model one used to manage the economy?
8. Analyse fully the distinction between:
   (a) Arguments in favour of rules
   (b) The choice of rule to follow.
9. Why do monetarists advocate:
   (a) Rules?
   (b) *Simple, fixed* rules?
10. How would you test the monetarist claim that fine tuning is destabilising?
11. Analyse fully the two reasons for fine tuning:
    (a) As a means of reaching a desired goal
    (b) As a means of reinforcing the workings of the market mechanism.

    Can these be in conflict?
12. Critically assess the new classical arguments in favour of rules.
13. Argue for or against a monetary rule which allows the money supply to grow at the same rate as real output.
14. Argue for or against a fiscal rule, stating clearly the type of rule you would advocate.
15. Would you advise the British government to follow a flexible monetary rule?
16. 'Fine tuning has failed only because it has not involved any tuning of supply.' Do you agree?
17. Can a monetary rule be set without any rule attached to the exchange rate?
18. Are the following rules compatible?

    (a) $\hat{M}_s = \hat{y}$ (monetary rule)
    (b) $\Delta G = \Delta T$ (balanced Budget change)
    (c) $\hat{S} = \hat{P}^{uk} - \hat{P}^{w}$ (relative PPP rule)

    where the first says that money supply is to grow at the same rate as real income; the second advocates a balanced Budget increase/decrease in government spending; and the third, a purchasing power parity rule for exchange rate changes.

PART V
Management

CHAPTER 11

Will supply management be superior to demand management?

Up until a few years ago there was little if any mention in the economics literature about supply-side economics, or what we shall also call 'supply management'. Certainly much had been written on 'demand management', but interest began to turn to reasons why demand management was not succeeding. To a large extent, the success of demand management in the 1950s and 1960s could be a major reason for its failure in the 1970s and 1980s. Keynesian economics was largely a macroeconomics to deal with unemployment and little or no inflation. This was exactly how it was used in the early post-war period – not only in Britain but in Europe and the United States. Many important economic relationships were fairly stable, and as such various multipliers could be calculated and used for policy prescriptions. But by the late 1960s, and certainly in the 1970s, inflation began to take off in many countries. Furthermore, a number of shocks from the supply side arose in the 1970s, such as OPEC price rises, commodity price rises and a depreciating pound. These led to many of the main economic relationships either breaking down or becoming very unstable. The Keynesian conventional wisdom accordingly came under scrutiny.

At the same time, it was realised by a number of economists that many of the problems faced by countries in the 1970s and 1980s were dominated by the supply side of the market, as we indicated in chapter 1. In one extreme form the issue can be put in the following way. If the aggregate supply curve is vertical at the natural level of income, then any increase in the level of aggregate demand will only have a temporary effect on income, and will inevitably lead to an increase in the price level. Furthermore, any supply shock which shifts the aggregate supply to the left will not only raise prices but also lead to a fall in real income. What is required, then, is policies to raise the natural level of real income; i.e., policies to shift the aggregate supply curve to the right.

But is this what economists and others mean when they talk of supply-side economics? We shall take up this point in section 11.1 and attempt to come to some understanding of what is meant by the term 'supply-side economics'. In section 11.2 we shall try to see whether demand management has failed, and if so, in what way. In the third section we shall turn to a brief discussion of some of the policies which have been carried out in the UK which could be classified as supply management. One difference between supply-side economics in the USA and that in the UK is the interest in, and relevance of, the Laffer curve. We shall take up this issue of relevance in section 11.4. In the final section we shall turn to management of the British economy in the future and the form that it is likely to take.

11.1 What is Meant by Supply-side Economics?

In formal, and to some extent simplistic, terms, supply-side economics is to do with the aggregate supply curve: its position, its slope, why it shifts, and the policies which can be implemented to counteract any unfavourable shifts. For any given aggregate demand, a supply shock which shifts the supply curve to the left, as shown in Figure 11.1, will result in a rise in prices and a fall in real income. This result is

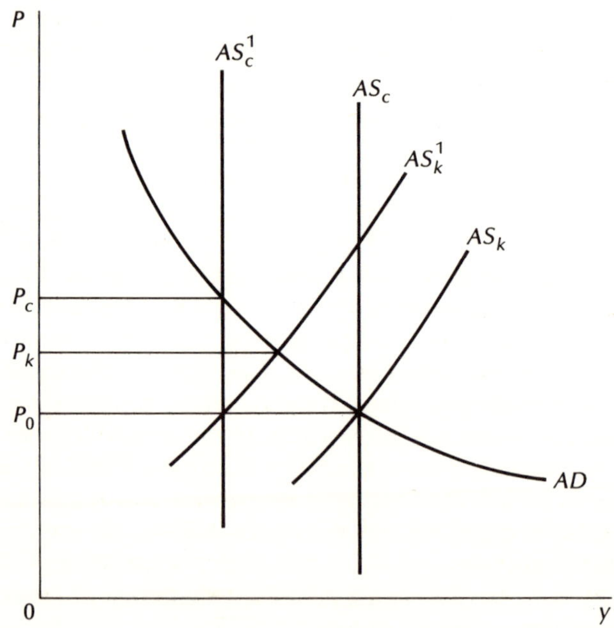

Figure 11.1 Supply shocks

independent of whether the supply curve is vertical (as in the classical and neo-classical systems) or upward-sloping (as in the Keynesian and neo-Keynesian systems). What the different systems do give rise to is the differential impact on prices as against real income.

But to discuss supply management in these terms requires an acceptance of the existence of an aggregate supply curve. Does such a thing exist? This is a methodological question. An aggregate supply curve exists in a macroeconomic model where appropriate assumptions are made – most particularly the existence of an aggregate production function. With the capital stock held constant, and so dealing with the short run, output (and hence real income) is related to labour input. Once labour employed has been determined then real income follows immediately from the aggregate production function. As we outlined in chapter 2, the labour market is independent of other sectors of the economy in the classical model but not in the Keynesian model. In the latter case employment, output (real income), prices and the interest rate are simultaneously determined – along with other variables, such as consumption and investment. Both systems give rise to an aggregate supply curve: the classical aggregate supply is vertical while the Keynesian aggregate supply is upward-sloping – becoming vertical at some level of prices.

There is no doubt that aggregate supply has had far less attention than aggregate demand. But an obvious question to ask is, 'Why have governments chosen almost exclusively to pursue demand management?' Is it because:

(1) Aggregate supply does not exist and so there can be no supply management?

(2) Aggregate supply has a poor underlying rationale and it is difficult for governments to pursue supply-side policies?

The first is simply a question of model construction, and we shall take it that some form of aggregate supply does exist. This would suggest that the answer is the second. We shall pursue this throughout this chapter.

It must be pointed out, however, that not all discussion of supply management has been in terms of movements in, or policies to shift, the aggregate supply curve. A far less precise discussion has surrounded the concepts of incentives and markets (Lomax, 1982). It is, however, possible to demonstrate that both incentives and markets refer to the underlying building blocks of the aggregate supply curve. In order to demonstrate this point it will be useful to present a brief discussion of the construction of the aggregate supply curve. A more thorough treatment can be found in Branson (1979).

The demand curve for labour is derived from firms' profit-maximising behaviour. An individual firm equates the marginal cost of hiring labour with the marginal revenue product of that labour. If we assume this also holds in the aggregate, then:

$$W[1 + (1/\theta)] = P[1 + (1/\eta)]\ MPP_L$$

where the left-hand side represents the marginal cost of hiring labour and θ the elasticity of labour supply, and the right-hand side represents the marginal revenue product of labour and η is the elasticity of demand for the economy's product. (Notice, in the case of perfect competition in the labour market and perfect competition in the product market, that both elasticities are infinite and the expression simply reduces to the real wage (W/P) equalling the marginal physical product of labour (MPP_L).)

Now assume that there exists an aggregate production function:

$$y = F(L,K)$$

where we note that $y \equiv Y/P$. If K is constant at $K = K_o$, then:

$$MPP_L = \partial y/\partial L$$

If we let:

$$\mu = [1 + (1/\theta)] / [1 + (1/\eta)]$$

and treat W as the average money wage for the whole economy and P the general price level, then the real wage ($w = W/P$) is:

$$w = W/P = \mu(\partial y/\partial L) = f(L)$$

which represents the *demand curve for labour*.

The supply curve of labour is derived by considering the income-leisure choice which an individual undertakes. The individual is assumed to derive utility from both income and leisure: $u = u(y, l)$. The maximisation of this utility is constrained, however, because the person's income is limited to unearned income, $\bar{y}$, plus earned income, $w(\bar{l} - l)$, where $\bar{l}$ is total hours available. In the more realistic case, where the individual is taxed (an important point in the discussion by supply-side economists) and works either a standard working week or longer, constraint takes the more involved form:

$$y = (1 - t)\bar{y} + ty_a + (1 - t)\ w\ (1 - \alpha)h_s + (1 - t)\ \alpha\ wh$$

where y_a is the person's income not subject to tax, t the marginal rate of tax, h_s the standard hours and α the overtime premium.[1]

From this constrained maximisation comes a supply curve of labour *for the individual* of the form:

$$h = h(w, t, h_s, \alpha)$$

If we now assume that a similar relationship holds for the economy as a whole, and we write it in the inverse form (i.e., the real wage as a function of labour employed), then we have *at the aggregate level*:

$$w = H(L, t, h_s, \alpha) = g(L)$$

which denotes the *the aggregate supply curve of labour*.

We have, then, three important aggregate relationships:

(1) The short-run aggregate production function:

$$y = F(L, K_o)$$

(2) The aggregate demand for labour:

$$w = \mu(\partial y/\partial L) = f(L)$$

(3) The aggregate supply of labour:

$$w = H(L, t, h_s, \alpha) = g(L)$$

If we make the classical assumption that wages and prices are completely flexible; or if, alternatively, we make the assumption that the labour market always clears (i.e., always establishes an equilibrium price and quantity), then the demand and supply curves of labour together determine the equilibrium real wage and labour employed – *totally independent of other markets in the economy.* Given this equilibrium labour employed, real income is determined from the short-run production function, $y = F(L, K_o)$. Regardless of the price level, the equilibrium labour employed will always be the same; and so the relationship between the price level and the level of real income is a vertical aggregate supply curve. How then do we arrive at an upward-sloping supply curve as drawn in Figure 11.1?

It depends on the assumptions made. Here we shall just consider one possibility so that we can incorporate expectations into the argument. So far in this discussion we have assumed that prices are fully expected, i.e., that expected prices and actual prices are the same. In the present climate of uncertainty this is not a very sensible assumption. Let us make the following assumptions (there are, of course, others that could be made):

(1) Employers know the wage charged and can predict prices accurately – so that for demanders of labour we have:

$$w = f(L) \text{ or } W = Pf(L)$$

(2) Workers are unclear about price levels and have an expected price level, P^e, which governs their supply based on an expected real wage, $w^e = W/P^e$, i.e., $w^e = g(L)$. Thus the aggregate supply of labour is:

$$w = (P^e/P)\,g(L) \quad \text{or} \quad W = P^e g(L)$$

Notice that in this version of the model the classical theory requires that expectations are fulfilled, i.e., that $P = P^e$. But we now need to make a further assumption about how expected prices are determined.

We shall not go into this here. Simply consider Figure 11.2. Here we have assumed that expected prices are based on actual prices (precisely

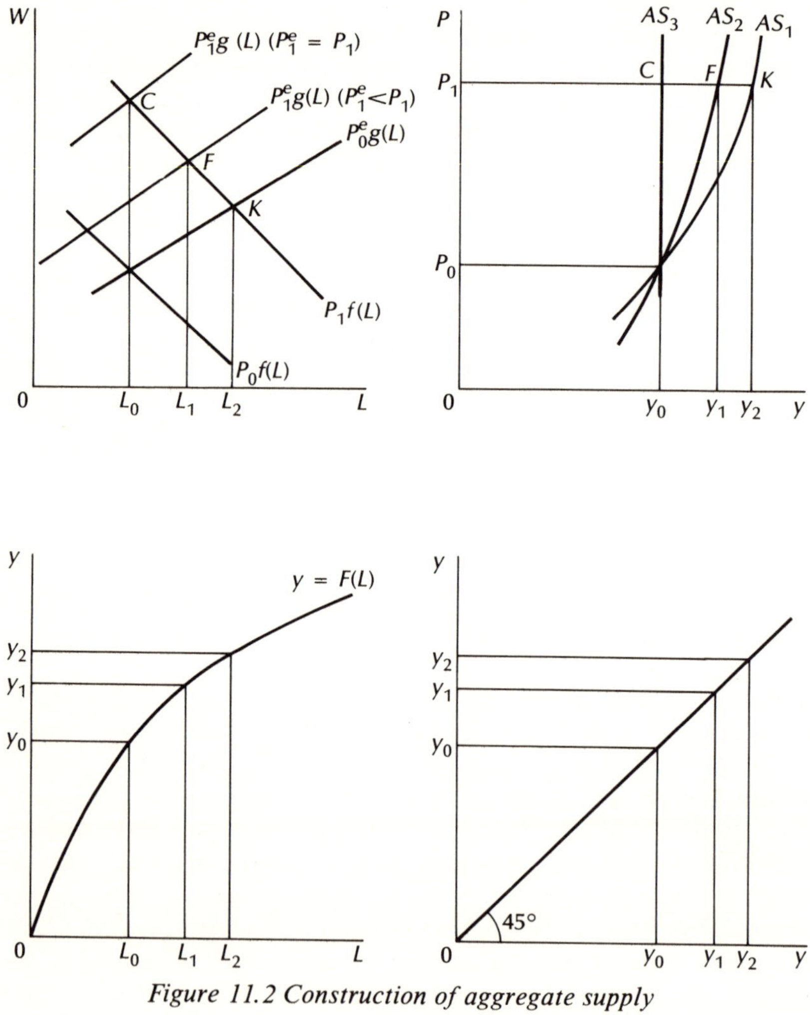

Figure 11.2 Construction of aggregate supply

how is not specified). Suppose actual prices rise from P_o to P_1; then under the two assumptions made above, the demand curve for labour moves to $P_1 f(L)$. Where the supply curve of labour moves to depends on the assumption about expectations. If labour does not revise its expectations at all (an extreme Keynesian assumption) then $P^e_o\, g(L)$ remains the relevant supply curve of labour and the labour market moves to point *K*. If we assume some change in expectations, but not perfect foresight, then the relevant supply curve of labour becomes $P^e_1\, g(L)$, and the labour market moves to point *F*. In this case the labour employed is L_1 and income is y_1. Hence, the aggregate supply curve is upward-sloping. (Note that the classical position is point *C* at income level y_o regardless of the price level.)

One important conclusion we draw from this discussion is that the aggregate supply curve for the economy is a function of the expected price level. If expectations lead to a revision upwards in the expected price level then the aggregate supply curve shifts upwards (i.e., to the left). It can be further shown[2] that the aggregate supply curve is also a function of the full employment level of real income, y_f, the exchange rate, *S*, and the foreign price level, P_f. Bringing all this information together, we have that the aggregate supply curve is:

$$y^s = y^s(P, P^e, t, h_s, \alpha, y_f, S, P_f)$$

The basic reason for going into this detail about aggregate supply is because it is usually given very little discussion and so the suggested policies of supply-side economists cannot be seen in any formal model. Although our discussion is not complete it will provide a basis on which to analyse supply management.

11.2 Has Demand Management Failed?

The underlying construction of the aggregate demand curve has been investigated more thoroughly elsewhere, so we shall be very brief in our discussion of its derivation. The aggregate demand curve is based on the combined equilibrium in the goods market and the money market for different price levels. The basics are shown in Figure 11.3. Equilibrium in the goods market is given by the *IS* curve, and here we assume it is independent of the price level.[3] The *LM* curve denotes equilibrium in the money market and this curve is a function of the price level - where a rise in the price level reduces real money balances and so shifts the *LM* curve to the left (to the right for a fall in prices). For all-round equilibrium in both the goods market and the money market, real income must fall to y_1 if the price level rises to P_1. Hence there is an inverse relationship on the aggregate demand side between the price level and the level of real income.

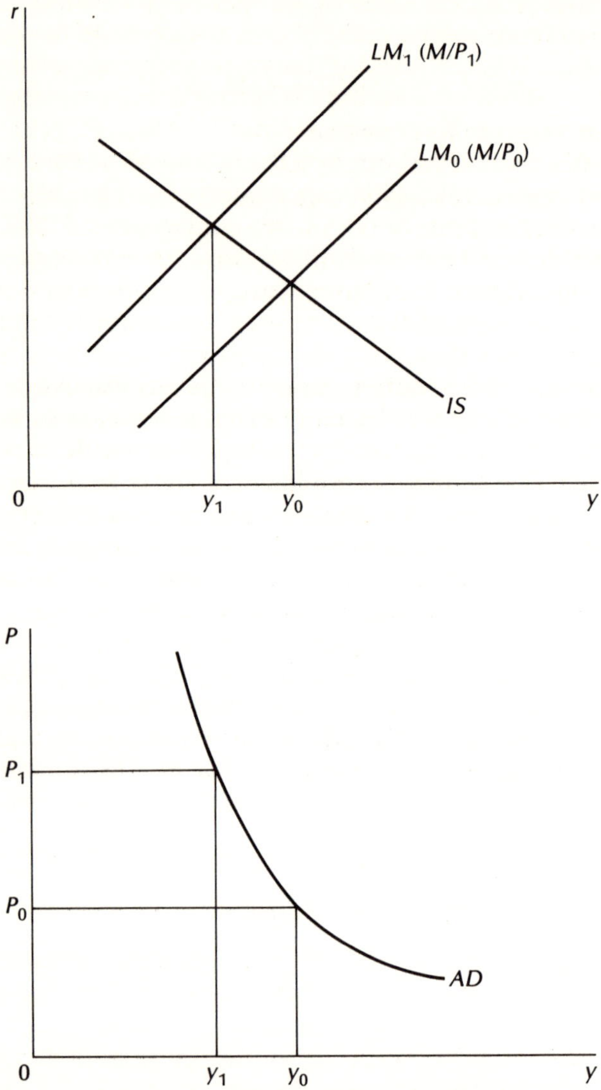

Figure 11.3 Construction of aggregate demand

It follows from the foregoing analysis that lying behind the aggregate demand curve are the *IS - LM* curves; or that aggregate demand involves both fiscal policy and monetary policy. Of course, this analysis can be made more complex by considering a more complex model. But rather than set out such a complex model, let us simply state that aggregate demand will depend on the level of government spending, *G*, the marginal rate of tax, *t*, the money supply (or the money base), the exchange rate, *S* and a number of autonomous elements (such as autonomous investment); i.e.,

$$y^d = y^d\ (P,\ G,\ t,\ M_s,\ S,\ A)$$

where *A* denotes autonomous items.

One significant observation can be made immediately. Both aggregate demand and aggregate supply have a number of variables in common; namely, the marginal rate of tax and the exchange rate. This means that the aggregate demand curve is not independent of the aggregate supply curve. One significant interdependence, so often overlooked, is that arising from the exchange rate. If the exchange rate is highly variable then this will mean that both the aggregate demand curve and the aggregate supply curve could themselves be quite unstable.

The *initial* significance of demand management can be seen in terms of Figure 11.4. In an economy with high unemployment and stable prices, the aggregate supply curve can be taken to be horizontal. In this instance, a stimulation of demand either by means of fiscal expansion or by means of monetary expansion will shift the aggregate demand curve to the right, to AD_1, and raise income and employment. More significant from our present discussion is the fact that the government had control of major variables in the aggregate demand function – such as the marginal rate of tax, government spending and high-powered money. During the Bretton Woods era it also had control over the exchange rate. It therefore had at its disposal not only instruments under its direct control, but instruments which had significant effects on the aggregate demand curve.

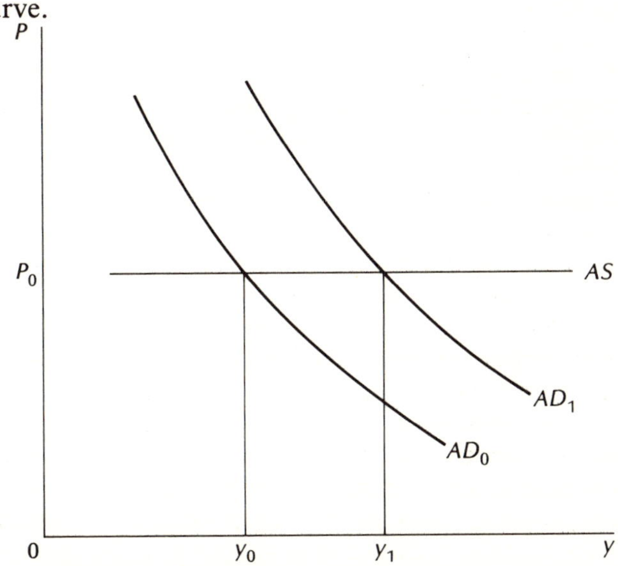

Figure 11.4 Importance of demand management

So long as prices were relatively stable, then, demand management seemed to serve its purpose. When employment was declining it could be stimulated and a return to full or nearly full employment could be achieved. However, a horizontal aggregate supply curve makes sense only for an underemployed economy. The very success of Keynesian demand management led in the 1950s and 1960s to a fairly low level of unemployment. Although there exist few estimates of the level of the 'natural rate of unemployment', it is possible to argue that during this period the actual level of unemployment was below the natural level. The result was a rising rate of inflation. As inflation began to take off this led to a revision upwards in price expectations. This in turn moved the (now upward-sloping) supply curve to the left, which led to a decline in the level of real income and a rise in the level of unemployment. This in turn meant even larger increases in fiscal expansion. But, as chapter 8 makes clear, the increase in government spending was largely financed by means of increases in the money supply; which in turn provided fuel for yet further inflationary pressure.

There was further inflationary pressure arising from the exchange rate. After sterling was floated in June 1972 the pound depreciated. In terms of aggregate demand and supply, this leads to a rightward shift in the aggregate demand schedule and a leftward shift in the aggregate supply schedule. Although the resulting effect on the level of income is uncertain, the effect on the price level is unambiguous – it is raised!

What this discussion indicates is that, during the 1970s, a growing proportion of the impact of demand management was going into price rises rather than rises in real income. It is in this sense that demand management was failing. The Keynesian conventional wisdom at the time could not, of course, deal with the situation of both rising unemployment and rising inflation. The point is that the models that had been constructed did not adequately take account of inflation. Once inflation took off, the analysis became less relevant – not wrong, simply not applicable. The turn to price and income policies, which we discussed in chapter 4, was an artificial means of attempting to hold prices constant so that the traditional policies could be adhered to. In so far as price and income policies were unsuccessful in holding back inflation, the success of demand management became less obvious.

In the light of these remarks, it seems not unreasonable to turn to the supply side. But before we return to supply management it is important to raise a not unrelated question: 'Was the failure of demand management because it was based on a too restrictive a model which assumed constant prices?' If the answer is, 'Yes' then the only failure is not in demand management *per se*, but rather in applying too simplistic a model.

One final question remains: 'If demand management was failing, why did governments not immediately turn to supply management?' This can best be answered by simply looking at the aggregate supply curve we derived above; i.e.,

$$y^s = y^s\,(P,\ P^e,\ t,\ h_s,\ \alpha,\ y_f,\ S,\ P_f)$$

The only variable directly under the control of the government was the marginal rate of tax, *t*, and the exchange rate during the Bretton Woods period. Once the exchange rate was floated this left only the marginal rate of tax! This is a very crucial observation in the present debate between demand and supply management. At the aggregate level, the government has far more variables under its direct control that it can use to influence aggregate demand than it has to influence aggregate supply. Does this suggest that aggregate supply requires microeconomic policies rather than macroeconomic ones? To this we now turn in the light of the British experience.

11.3 The British Approach to Supply Management

When the Conservatives took office in 1979 they had made a pledge to bring down the rate of inflation as their major economic policy objective. In attempting to do this they also made it clear that they had little faith in pursuing policies of the demand management type. Instead, they talked of raising incentives, of creating a climate for industry to thrive and grow; to curb (as they saw it) the growing power of the unions and to decrease the overall size of the government sector – in other words, supply-side economics. Supply 'management' is not quite appropriate, because one major theme of the present government's approach is a return to market forces and ensuring that they work unhindered; 'management' implies more direct involvement on the side of the government than appears to be the case with the Conservative strategy.

There are, therefore, three strands to the present strategy:

(1) A stimulus to incentives

(2) A reduction in trade union power

(3) A series of policies to ensure the workings of the free market system.

In this section we shall largely concentrate on the first and third strands.

By far the most common suggestion of supply-side economists is the reduction in the tax on wages in order to raise the incentive to workers. We noted in section 11.1 how the tax rate enters the Budget constraint on an individual's decision between work and leisure. The presumption involved by those who suggest a reduction in the tax rate is that this will raise the level of employment and hence will raise the level of output (real income). In diagrammatic terms, a reduction in the tax rate, *t,* will shift the aggregate supply curve to the right. As virtually every intermediate microeconomics textbook shows, at the individual level a reduction in the rate of tax will raise hours worked if the substitution effect outweighs the income effect (and assuming there are no complications arising from the standard working week). But there is no clear evidence that this is true at the individual level. There is even less evidence that it is true in the aggregate. The evidence that is available for the UK would, if anything, suggest that at the aggregate level the income and substitution effects cancel each other out. If this is indeed the case, then the aggregate supply curve is independent of the change in the tax rate.

This has far-reaching consequences for supply-side economists. We made the point in the last section that the only variable in the aggregate supply schedule which is directly under the control of the government is the tax rate. We now find that a change in this probably has no effect on the aggregate supply curve!

Such an empirical doubt about the effect of a tax change on labour is not the only reservation. Suppose we abstract from this difficulty by assuming that, even at the aggregate level, the substitution effect outweighs the income effect. All we can conclude, however, is that the supply curve of labour moves to the right. But will the level of employment rise? It will rise only if firms simultaneously demand more labour. This in turn will be dependent on whether firms can sell what this extra labour produces. If the labour market clears, then a movement to the right of the supply curve of labour will raise the amount of labour employed (and lower the real wage). But is this a sensible assumption with respect to the labour market? Policy-makers may of course argue that it is not a question of whether it is a sensible assumption; what is required is a series of policies to ensure that the labour market clears – that is, change the world to fit the theory! The fact that limited demand in the goods market can create a quantity rationing in the labour market, and that a constraint in the labour market can create a quantity rationing in the goods market, has only just begun to be investigated by economists.[4] Limited as the work is, it does not suggest that there will be an unambiguous rise in the level of employment if the tax rate is decreased.

Another similar suggestion has been to reduce the tax on capital. If this is done, this not only will increase the use of capital but also will lead to a demand for more labour. The argument here is that the marginal product of labour, $\partial y/\partial L$, is also a function of the level of capital. If the tax on capital is reduced, this will increase the marginal product of labour and so lead to a rise in the demand for labour. Since it is the demand for labour which tends to be realised (i.e., becomes the level of employment), this is likely to be more successful in shifting the aggregate supply curve to the right. But this too is fraught with difficulties. It depends very much on the type of capital utilised by firms. It is possible that the demand for labour rises but not the level of employment – the impact may fall on an increase in vacancies!

An alternative procedure is to reduce the tax on profits. If this leads to greater undistributed profits, then firms can raise the level of investment from this source. Moves in this direction, however, have largely been in the form of changes in taxes to adjust for the rate of inflation. The dilemma the government faces is whether the reduction in tax revenue can be recouped from the stimulus to real income. But we shall take up this point in the next section.

The move to curb trade union power can be seen not only as a change in the power base but also as a means of making the labour market work more efficiently. The government has also reduced the power of monopolies, both private and public, for exactly the same reason. The increase in privatisation is based, in part, on the belief in the free workings of the private market. The government is basically pursuing a policy of withdrawal from markets to the limit which it can. What appears to many as a non-policy towards industry is a belief in the market mechanism and that, once this is allowed to work properly, it will shift the aggregate supply curve to the right. Such a policy, however, is inevitably *long-run*. Furthermore, it is possible that such a policy can easily be swamped by exchange rate changes which arise from such policies. Nor is it clear that they will succeed in a world where other countries are not following similar policies.

The conclusion that is drawn here is that the supply policies being pursued by the British government are essentially microeconomic, that they are solutions for the long run, and that there is no clear supportive evidence (theoretical or empirical) for their success.[5] They are based on belief. Whether this belief is justified only time will tell.

11.4 Is the Laffer Curve Relevant?

The Laffer curve (named after Arthur Laffer, an economic adviser to President Reagan) has become prominent in the discussions of supply-side economists, most especially in the United States. It arises from the obvious observation that if the tax rate is zero the government will receive no tax revenue because it chooses not to collect any; while if the tax rate is 100% there is no incentive at all for people to work and earn, and so the tax base is zero and so will be the tax revenue. Since tax revenue is either zero or positive, these observations imply that there is some tax rate for which tax revenue is a maximum. The Laffer curve denotes the relationship between tax revenue, R, and the tax rate, t; i.e., $R = R(t)$. (Strictly, Laffer considered only three points: when $t = 0$ then $R = 0$; when $t = 1$ then $R = 0$; and there exists some t_m for which R is a maximum, which we shall denote R_m). Since its suggestion, a number of economists have become attracted by the idea and have slipped in further assumptions about the shape of $R(t)$ – usually that it is smooth and takes the form shown in Figure 11.5.

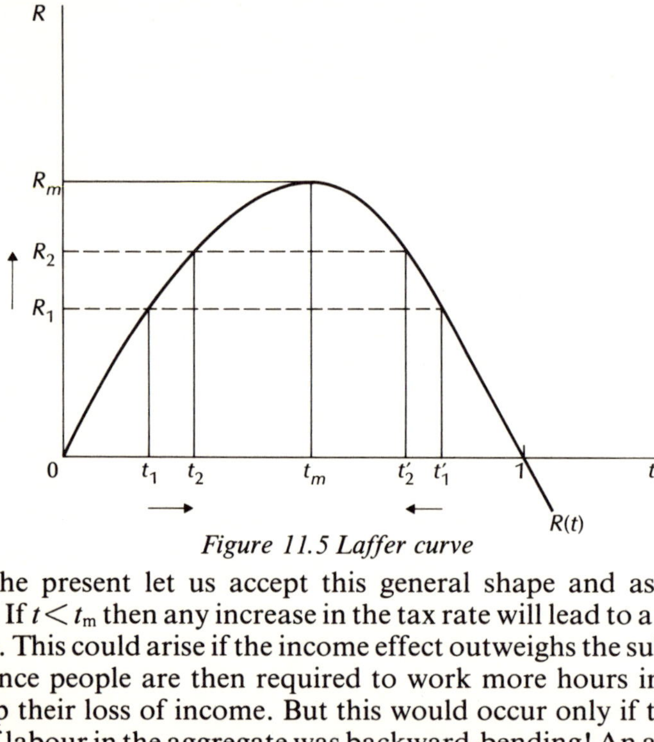

Figure 11.5 Laffer curve

For the present let us accept this general shape and ask what it implies. If $t < t_m$ then any increase in the tax rate will lead to a rise in tax revenue. This could arise if the income effect outweighs the substitution effect since people are then required to work more hours in order to make up their loss of income. But this would occur only if the supply curve of labour in the aggregate was backward-bending! An alternative explanation is that, with the substitution effect dominating the income effect, then, so long as the marginal reduction in the tax base (from working fewer hours) is less than the marginal percentage increase in the tax rate, revenue will rise. Notice that, if in the aggregate the income and substitution effects cancel out, it will follow that a rise in tax rates will lead to a rise in tax revenue for tax rates below the maximum, t_m. To the right of t_m the opposite is the case.

The reasoning given so far has been based on the microeconomic analysis of the leisure-income choice. It can also be approached from the macroeconomic point of view. A rise in the tax rate will shift the aggregate supply curve to the left (or possibly leave it unchanged). If revenue does rise with a rise in the tax rate, the aggregate demand curve will shift to the right. Income will rise if the aggregate demand shift outweighs the aggregate supply shift. As Figure 11.6(a) makes clear, however, whatever the relative shifts, a rise in the tax rate (for $t < t_m$) will lead to higher prices. If an economy is to the right of the maximum, then

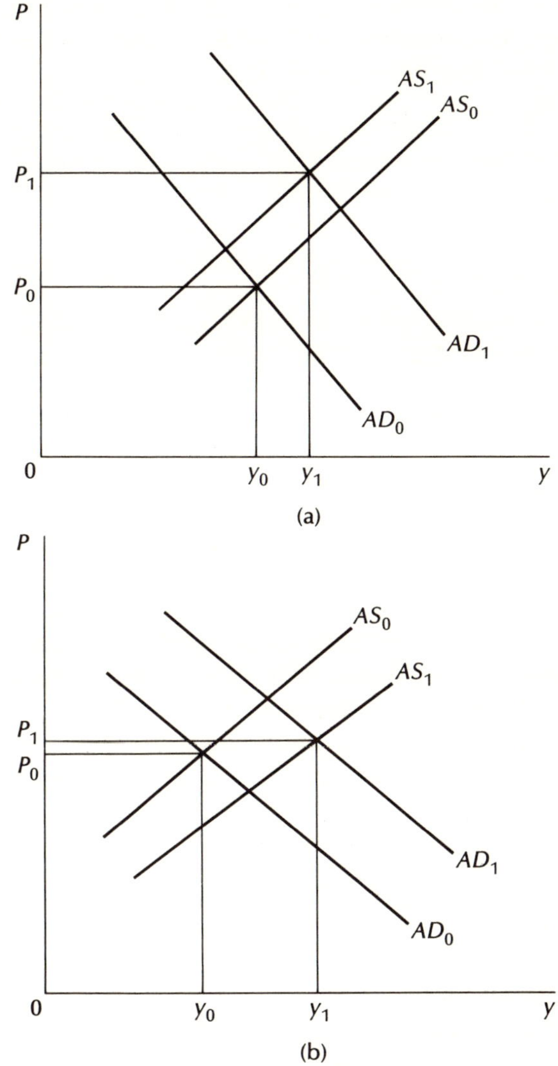

Figure 11.6 Aggregate results of a tax change

it is possible to reduce the tax rate and so shift the aggregate supply to the right and simultaneously shift the aggregate demand to the right because of the increased revenue obtained. The result, shown in Figure 11.6(b), indicates that income will rise unambiguously and there could be little impact on the price level, and possibly even a reduction!

It should be observed that the arguments presented so far are based on the existence and known shape of the Laffer curve. The observations by Laffer only point out that a maximum exists: there could of course be more than one maximum and the curve could take a very irregular shape. The point is that the Laffer curve is an *ex post* statement about tax rates and tax revenue and, so far at least, is not based on any economic analysis. Any such relationship between tax rates and tax revenue will depend on the tax structure, the tax base and the progressivity of the tax system. The claim by Beenstock (1979) to have obtained a 'Laffer curve' for the UK seems quite unjustified. What he obtains is a time series plot of tax rates against tax revenue. It is hardly surprising that some positive relationship will be obtained, but it can hardly be a Laffer curve.

The danger in this type of approach is in accepting without reservation statistical relationships which have no grounding in economic theory. To state unequivocally that the maximum tax rate is 60% for the UK while the present average tax rate is about 40% can only mislead. On the other hand, the study by Hemming and Kay (1980) does attempt some underlying economic basis for the Laffer curve. They conclude:

> ... the evidence runs strongly against the argument that tax rates in Britain, or any other country, are at levels such that the maximum available tax revenue is close to being obtained... [A]ny view that cuts in taxation might ultimately prove self-financing through the beneficial effects of taxation on incentives is chimerical. (pp. 86-7)

The conclusion we draw from this section is that the Laffer curve has a simplistic attraction which can be misleading in arguments about tax disincentives. There appears no evidence to date that a reduction in the tax rate will lead to a rightward shift in the aggregate supply curve. It would appear, then, that the main prop of supply-side economics is on rather weak ground.

11.5 Management in the Future

The above sections would suggest that demand management has a tendency to be inflationary while supply management, although not inflationary, is very difficult for governments to implement. The present government is hoping that its policies towards industry, a possible reduction in the tax rate and the reduction of controls so that markets can work more efficiently will be sufficient to shift the aggregate supply curve to the right. But it is a *passive* policy and a *long-run* policy.

Notwithstanding a number of the reservations given above, this has one major weakness. The economy will be very prone to major shifts arising from changes in the exchange rate. If markets are allowed to work efficiently, then frequent (although not necessarily large) changes will be necessary. If the exchange rate changes frequently and in large amounts, this will affect both aggregate demand and aggregate supply. A floating exchange rate does not, then, isolate the economy from outside influences. It may insulate the domestic economy from world inflation (from price changes) but this must be at the expense of real trade flows, i.e., the flows of goods and services at constant prices. If British industry is to survive in such a climate then it has to learn to adapt. The question is whether it can.

The Conservative strategy is based on the belief in the market: that a free market equilibrium is the only long-run solution for the British economy. There is no doubt that it is *a* solution. But it is only one. There is no reason why the free market equilibrium is at all a desirable one. This, of course, is a value judgement. But there is no getting away from it. Supply-side economics is not just a strategy of the Conservative Party. Looked at analytically, it has merit. A shift in the aggregate supply curve to the right will not only reduce prices but also raise national income, and hence employment. But the exchange rate can be a problem. It is therefore necessary to have *three* strands to management in the future:

(1) Demand management

(2) Supply management

(3) Trade and exchange rate management.

These are not independent and so must be made consistent with one another. The belief in free markets is one method of achieving consistency.

If a more positive interventionist approach is taken, it is essential that this does not simply lead to a rightward shift in the aggregate demand curve, which was largely the case in the past. We have noted that there is very little in the aggregate supply curve directly in the control of the government. This would suggest that government can only stimulate supply through indirect means. On the tax incentive side, what matters is raising the *demand* for labour rather than the supply of labour, for only this will raise the level of employment and hence output. The reduction in the employment surcharge is an obvious case in point. More attention could be given to investment incentives and to what extent the government could guarantee a market for early years.

We have said very little about trade unions, but it is clear that they play a major role in the aggregate supply relationship. The power of a union will, for example, influence whether employment is related to the demand for labour or the supply of labour, or is independent of them both. To a large extent this will determine how adaptive industry will be to changing patterns of demand for products. In brief, trade unions can influence both the slope and shift in the aggregate supply curve. If supply management, in any form, is going to lower prices and raise output, then some form of co-operation with the unions is necessary. Only if the power of the unions is dramatically eroded will they be unimportant in supply management. But if their power is eroded, then greater onus is on the government to be more positive in shifting aggregate supply to the right – and we have just seen how limited that can be.

Questions

1. 'Supply-side policies must inevitably favour the rich.' Do you agree?
2. Discuss under what conditions a successful tax cut which affects aggregate supply can also lead to a concomitant fall in aggregate demand.
3. Consider any tax cut that has been mentioned to shift the aggregate supply curve to the right. Discuss in detail all the uncertainties surrounding the outcome. Why has aggregate supply more uncertainty attached to it than aggregate demand?
4. 'While supply-side economics has a role to play in bringing down inflation, it cannot be expected to be the cornerstone of such a policy.' Do you agree?
5. What is the effects of North Sea oil on:
   (a) Aggregate demand?
   (b) Aggregate supply?

   Hence, what is its impact (short-run and long-run) on prices and output?
6. What result does a rise in OPEC prices have on aggregate supply? Is such a one-off rise inflationary? Will the 1983 cut in OPEC oil prices reverse the effects of the oil price rises of the 1970s (assuming the over-all size of the price change is the same)?
7. Would those who advocate supply-side economics support a

programme of greater expenditure on research and development?

8. What role does resource utilisation play in the shape of the aggregate supply curve?
9. 'Stagflation is the typical result of adverse supply shifts.' How must this proposition be modified (or clarified) to reflect stagflation and not simply a once-and-for-all rise in prices and fall in output? Does this modification give any insight into the possible causes of stagflation?
10. For tax cuts not to raise aggregate demand they must be accompanied ('financed') by a reduction in government spending. Why is this the case? Is it possible for the demand side to be effective but the supply side ineffective? If this were true, what would be the result?
11. Suppose you have just two alternative tax reductions you could choose:
    (a) A reduction of taxes on investment
    (b) A reduction of the standard rate of tax.

    If your objective were to raise the level of output with the least inflationary impact, which would you choose and why?
12. 'Without a knowledge of the impact of tax cuts on work effort, productivity, and investment, we cannot know their impact on aggregate supply. Supply-side economics is, therefore, a matter of belief'. Do you agree?
13. Mrs Thatcher has to a large extent pursued supply-side policies. Why, then, has she not reduced the standard rate of tax to the level of about 25%?
14. What is the Laffer curve? Do you consider that this curve contributes anything to our understanding of the economic system?
15. Analyse the role of trade unions in the success of any supply management of the British economy.
16. Is supply management more difficult or less difficult under a floating exchange rate system than under a fixed exchange rate system?
17. Will a rise in the black economy limit the effectiveness of supply-side policies?
18. Why would supply-side economists tend to support such policies as:

    (a) A reduction in unemployment benefits?
    (b) Privatisation?
    (c) Abolition of the employment surcharge?
    (d) A curb on secondary picketing?

Do you consider such a view economically justified?

Notes

1. A more detailed discussion of this decision problem faced by the individual can be found in Shone (1981).
2. This not easy to show simply. One approach is given in Dornbusch and Fischer (1981), which indicates that material prices are related to the general price level and also to the relative gap between income and full employment income. If we abstract from this second consideration, one simple way to model the problem, for illustrative purpose, is as follows.

   We suppose wage changes, $\hat{W}$, are related to unemployment by means of a simple reaction function:

$$\hat{W} = -aU \qquad 0 < a < 1$$

   which leads to the simple relationship

$$W = W_{-1}(1 - aU)$$

   Further we suppose that the general price level is indicated by a mark-up over costs. Let C_m represent material costs, and π the profit margin; then

$$P = (1 + \pi)(W + C_m)$$

   Finally, we make the simple assumption that material goods costs are proportional to the price of imported goods; i.e., $C_m = \beta SP_f$. Substituting, we get:

$$P = P_{-1}(1 - aU) + \beta(1 + \pi)\,\triangle\,(SP_f)$$

   Using Okun's law, given by

$$U = h[1 - (y/y_f)] \qquad h > 0$$

   we arrive finally at the aggregate supply curve relating P with y, given by:

$$P = P_{-1}[1 - ah(y/y_f)] + \beta(1 + \pi)\,\triangle\,(SP_f)$$

3. If consumption is related to real money balances or real wealth, then the *IS* curve will also be related to the price level, a rise (fall) in prices shifting *IS* to the left (right).
4. See Clower (1965), Muelbauer and Portes (1978), Malinvaud (1977) and Backhouse (1980).
5. For an argument against their likely success, see Midland Bank (1982).

Bibliography

Addison, J.T and Siebert, W.S (1980) *The Market for Labor: An Analytical Treatment.* Goodyear Publishing Co.

Akerlof, G.A (1979) "The Case Against Conservative Macroeconomics: An Inaugural Lecture" *Economica,* Vol.46, No.183, August 1979.

Allin, P (1976) "Drawing the Line in the Balance of Payments Accounts" *CSO Statistical News,* No.36.

Arestis, M.J and Hadjimatheou, G (1982) *Introductory Macroeconomic Modelling.* Macmillan.

Artis, M.J and Currie, D.A (1980) "Monetary Targets and the Exchange Rate: A Case for Conditional Targets." *Oxford Economic Papers,* Vol. 33, July (Supplement).

Artis, M.J and Lewis, M.K (1981) *Monetary Control in the United Kingdom.* Philip Allan.

Backhouse, R (1980) "Fix-Price versus Flex-Price Models of Macroeconomic Equilibrium with Rationing" *Oxford Economic Papers,* Vol.32, No.2, July 1980.

Bacon, R and Eltis, W (1976) (2nd ed. 1978) *Britain's Economic Problem: Too Few Producers.* Macmillan.

Bank of England (1982a) "Measures of Competitiveness" *Bank of England Quarterly Bulletin,* Vol.22, No.3, September 1982.

Bank of England (1982b) "Venture Capital" *Bank of England Quarterly Bulletin,* Vol.22, No.4, December 1982.

Batchelor, R, Bendle, E and Griffiths, B (1980) *The Future of Pay Bargaining.* Heinemann.

Beenstock, M (1979) "Taxation and Incentives in the UK" *Lloyds Bank Review,* No.134, October 1979.

Begg, D.K.H (1982) *The Rational Expectations Revolution in Macroeconomics.* Philip Allan.

Bhagwati, J and Ramaswami, V.K (1963) "Domestic Distortions, Tariffs and the Theory of Optimum Subsidy" *Journal of Political Economy,* Vol.71, February 1963.

Blackaby, F.T (ed.) (1978) *British Economic Policy 1960-74.* Cambridge University Press.

Bond, M.E and Knobl, A (1982) "Some Implications of North Sea Oil for the UK Economy" *IMF Staff Papers,* Vol.29, No.3, September 1982.

Branson, W.H (1972) (2nd ed. 1979) *Macroeconomic Theory and Policy.* Harper & Row.

Brittan, S (1971) *Steering the Economy.* Penguin.

Brown, W.A (1980) "The Structure of Pay Bargaining in Britain" In F. Blackaby (ed.) *The Future of Pay Bargaining.* Heinemann.

Buiter, W.H (1977) "'Crowding Out' and the Effectiveness of Fiscal Policy" *Journal of Public Economics,* Vol.7, No.3, June 1977.

Chiang, A.C (1967) (2nd ed. 1974) *Fundamental Methods of Mathematical Economics.* McGraw-Hill.

Chick, V (1977) *Theory of Monetary Policy* (rev. ed.). Basil Blackwell.

Chiplin, B and Wright, M (1980) "Divestment and Structural Change in UK Industry" *National Westminster Bank Quarterly Review,* February 1980.

Chrystal, K.A (1979) *Controversies in British Macroeconomics.* Philip Allan.

Clower, R.W (1965) "The Keynesian Counter-revolution: a theoretical appraisal" In F.H Hahn and F Brechling, (eds) *The Theory of Interest Rates.* Macmillan.

Cobham, D (1981) "Definitions of Domestic Credit Expansion for the United Kingdom" *Journal of Economic Studies,* Vol. 8, No. 3, 1981.

Coghlan, R (1980) *The Theory of Money and Finance.* Macmillan.

Colander, D.C and Guthrie, R.S (1980-81) "Great Expectations: What the Dickens Do 'Rational Expectations' Mean?" *Journal of Post Keynesian Economics,* Winter 1980-81.

Connell, D (1980) The UK's Performance in Export Markets – Some Evidence from International Trade Data. *National Economic Development Office,* Discussion Paper 6.

Corden, W.M (1977) (2nd ed. 1981) *Inflation, Exchange Rates and the World Economy.* Oxford University Press.

Cuthbertson, K (1979) *Macroeconomic Policy.* Macmillan.

Dahrendorf, R (1982) *On Britain.* BBC Publications.

Dawkins, D.J (1980) "Incomes Policy" In P. Maunder (ed.) *The*

British Economy in the 1970s. Heinemann.

Desai, M (1981) *Testing Monetarism.* Frances Pinter (Publishers) Ltd.

Donaldson, P (1982) *10x Economics.* Penguin.

Dornbusch, R and Fischer, S (1981) *Macroeconomics.* McGraw-Hill.

Dow, S.C (1982) "Recent Developments in UK Monetary Policy" *Stirling Economics Teaching Papers,* No.8.

Dow, S.C and Earl, P.E (1982) *Money Matters.* Martin Robertson.

Downs, A (1957) *An Economic Theory of Democracy.* Harper & Row.

Enoch, C.A (1978) "Measures of Competitiveness" *Bank of England Quarterly Bulletin,* Vol.22, No.3, September 1982.

Flemming, J (1976) *Inflation.* Oxford University Press.

Foot, M.D.W *et al.* (1979) "Monetary Base Control" *Bank of England Quarterly Bulletin,* Vol.19, No.2, June 1979.

Friedman, M and Meiselman, D (1963) "The Relative Stability of Monetary Velocity and the Investment Multiplier in the United States, 1897-1958" In *Research Study Two in Stabilization Policies,* prepared by E.C. Brown *et al.* for the Commission on Money and Credit. Prentice-Hall.

Goodhart, C.A.E (1975) *Money, Information and Uncertainty.* Macmillan.

Gordon, R.J (1978) (2nd ed. 1981) *Macroeconomics.* Little Brown and Company.

Gordon, R.J (1981) "Output Fluctuations and Gradual Price Adjustment" *Journal of Economic Literature,* Vol.19, No.2, June 1981.

Gowland, D (1978) *Monetary Policy and Credit Control.* Croom Helm.

Graham, A.W.M (1977) (2nd ed. 1979) "Objectives and Instruments" in D. Morris (ed.) *The Economic System in the UK.* Oxford University Press.

Griffiths, B and Wood, G.E (eds) (1981) *Monetary Targets.* Macmillan.

Hahn, F (1982) "Reflections on the Invisible Hand" *Lloyds Bank Review,* No.144, April 1982.

Hawkins, K (1979) *Unemployment.* Penguin.

Hemming, R and Kay, J.A (1980) "The Laffer Curve" *Fiscal Studies,* Vol.1, No.2, March 1980.

Hicks, J (1976) "The Little that is Right with Monetarism" *Lloyds Bank Review,* July 1976.

HM Treasury (1980) *Monetary Control,* Green Paper, Cmnd 7858

Holden, K, Peel, P.A and Thompson, J.L (1982) *Modelling the UK Economy.* Martin Robertson.

Jackson, P.M (1982) *The Political Economy of Bureaurcracy.* Martin Robertson.

Kaldor, N (1970) "The New Monetarism" *Lloyds Bank Review,* No.97, July 1970.

Kaldor, N and Trevithick, J (1981) "A Keynesian Perspective on Money" *Lloyds Bank Review,* No.139, January 1981.

Kantor, B (1979) "Rational Expectations and Economic Thought" *Journal of Economic Literature,* Vol.17, No.4, December 1979.

Keegan, W and Pennant-Rea, R (1979) *Who Runs the Economy?* Maurice Temple Smith.

Keynes, J.M (1936) *The General Theory of Employment, Interest and Money.* Macmillan.

Laidler, D (1969) *The Demand for Money: Theories and Evidence.* International Textbook Company.

Levacic, R and Rebmann, A (1982) (2nd ed.) *Macroeconomics.* Macmillan.

Lewis, G. R and Ormerod, P.A (1979) "Policy Simulations and Model Characteristics" In S.T. Cook, and P.M. Jackson (eds) *Current Issues in Fiscal Policy.* Martin Robertson.

Lomax, D.F (1982) "Supply-side Economics: The British Experience" *National Westminster Bank Quarterly Review,* August 1982.

Lucas, R.E Jr and Prescott, E.C (1974) "Equilibrium Search and Unemployment" *Journal of Economic Theory,* Vol.7, 1974.

Machlup, F (1958) "Equilibrium and Disequilibrium: Misplaced Concreteness and Disguised Politics" *Economic Journal,* Vol. 68, 1958.

Maddock, R and Carter, M (1982) "A Child's Guide to Rational Expectations" *Journal of Economic Literature,* Vol.20, No.1, March 1982.

Malinvaud, E (1977) *The Theory of Unemployment Reconsidered.* Basil Blackwell.

Meade, J (1978) "The Meaning of 'Internal Balance'" *Economic Journal,* Vol.88, No.351, September 1978.

Midland Bank (1977) "The British Economy: Problems and Policies in the Late 1970's" *Midland Bank Review,* February 1977.

Midland Bank (1982) "Problems of Industrial Recovery" *Midland Bank Review,* Spring 1982.

Miller, R and Wood, J.B (1982) *What Price Unemployment?* Institute of Economic Affairs, Hobart Paper No. 92.

Minford, P and Peel, D (1981) "Is the Government's Strategy on Course?" *Lloyds Bank Review,* No.140, April 1981.

Muelbauer, J and Portes, R (1978) "Macroeconomic Models with Quantity Rationing" *Economic Journal,* Vol.88, No.352, December 1978.

National Institute Economic Review (1982) Special Issue on "Britain's

Comparative Productivity". *National Institute Economic Review,* No.101, August 1982.

Neal, F and Shone, R (1976) *Economic Model Building.* Macmillan.

Niskanen, W.A (1973) *Bureaucracy: Servant or Master?* Institute of Economic Affairs, Hobart Paper No.5.

OECD Economic Surveys (1980) *United Kingdom.* OECD, February 1980.

Oliver, A (1980) "Skill Shortages" *Economic Trends,* September 1980.

Panic, U (1975) "Why the United Kindom's Propensity to Import is High" *Lloyds Bank Review,* No.115, January 1975.

Parkin, M and Bade, R (1982) *Modern Macroeconomics.* Philip Allan.

Posner, M (ed.) (1978) *Demand Management.* Heinemann.

Pratten, C.F (1977) "The Efficiency of British Industry" *Lloyds Bank Review,* January 1977.

Rowley, C (1977) "Efficiency in the Public Sector" In C. Bowley (ed.) *Industrial Efficiency and the Role of Government.* HMSO.

Sargent, S.R (1979) "Productivity and Profits in UK Manufacturing" *Midland Bank Review,* Autumn 1979.

Sargent, T.J (1973) "Rational Expectations, the Real Rate of Interest and the Natural Rate of Unemployment" *Brookings Papers on Economic Activity,* No.2, 1973.

Savage, D (1980) "Some Issues of Monetary Policy" *National Institute Economic Review,* No.91, February 1980.

Schiltknecht, K (1981) "Targeting the Base – the Swiss Experience" In B Griffiths, and G.E. Wood (eds) *Monetary Targets.* Macmillan.

Sen, A (1983) "The Profit Motive" *Lloyds Bank Review,* January 1983.

Shone, R (1979) "Internal and External Balance: Problems of Interpretation" *Journal of Economic Studies,* Vol.6, No.2, November 1979.

Shone, R (1980) "The Monetary Approach to the Balance of Payments: Stock-Flow Equilibria" *Oxford Economic Papers,* Vol.32, No.2, June 1980.

Shone, R (1981) *Applications in Intermediate Microeconomics.* Martin Robertson.

Solow, R.M (1980) "On Theories of Unemployment" *American Economic Review,* Vol.70, No.1, March 1980.

Stigler, G.J (1962) "Information in the Labour Market" *Journal of Political Economy,* Vol.70 (Supplement), October 1962.

Takayama, A (1974) *Mathematical Economics.* Dryden Press.

Taylor, C.T (1978) "Why is Britain in a Recession?" *Bank of England Quarterly Bulletin,* Vol.18, No.1, March 1978.

Tew, B (1981) "The Implementation of Monetary Policy in Post-war Britain" *Midland Bank Review,* Spring 1981.

Theil, H (1966) *Applied Economic Forecasting.* North-Holland Publishing Company.

Thirlwall, A.P (1978) "The UK's Economic Problem: A Balance of-Payments Constraint?" *National Westminster Bank Quarterly Review,* February 1978.

Tinbergen, J (1956) *Economic Policy: Principles and Design.* North-Holland Publishing Company.

Tobin, J (1980) *Asset Accumulation and Economic Activity.* Basil Blackwell.

Weintraub, E.R (1974) *General Equilibrium Theory.* Macmillan.

Wickens, M.R (1981) "The New Conservative Macroeconomics" Inaugual Lecture, delivered 5 February 1981.

Author Index

Subject Index